Lecture Notes in Computer Science   13887

The series Lecture Notes in Computer Science (LNCS), including its subseries Lecture Notes in Artificial Intelligence (LNAI) and Lecture Notes in Bioinformatics (LNBI), has established itself as a medium for the publication of new developments in computer science and information technology research, teaching, and education.

LNCS enjoys close cooperation with the computer science R & D community, the series counts many renowned academics among its volume editors and paper authors, and collaborates with prestigious societies. Its mission is to serve this international community by providing an invaluable service, mainly focused on the publication of conference and workshop proceedings and postproceedings. LNCS commenced publication in 1973.

Xiaofeng Meng · Xiang Li · Jianqiu Xu ·
Xueying Zhang · Yuming Fang · Bolong Zheng ·
Yafei Li
Editors

Spatial Data and Intelligence

4th International Conference, SpatialDI 2023
Nanchang, China, April 13–15, 2023
Proceedings

Editors
Xiaofeng Meng
Renmin University of China
Beijing, China

Jianqiu Xu
Nanjing University of Aeronautics
and Astronautics
Nanjing, China

Yuming Fang
Jiangxi University of Finance and Economics
Nanchang, China

Yafei Li
Zhengzhou University
Zhengzhou, China

Xiang Li
East Normal China University
Shanghai, China

Xueying Zhang
Nanjing Normal University
Nanjing, China

Bolong Zheng
Huazhong University of Science
and Technology
Wuhan, China

ISSN 0302-9743   ISSN 1611-3349 (electronic)
Lecture Notes in Computer Science
ISBN 978-3-031-32909-8   ISBN 978-3-031-32910-4 (eBook)
https://doi.org/10.1007/978-3-031-32910-4

This Springer imprint is published by the registered company Springer Nature Switzerland AG
The registered company address is: Gewerbestrasse 11, 6330 Cham, Switzerland

Preface

This volume contains the papers from the 4th International Conference on Spatial Data and Intelligence (SpatialDI 2023), which was held at the Trilec International Hotel, Nanchang, during April 13–15, 2023.

SpatialDI 2023 was sponsored by the ACM SIGSPATIAL China Branch and the ACM SIGMOD China Branch, organized by Jiangxi University of Finance and Economics, and co-organized by Nanchang University, Jiangxi Normal University, East China University of Technology, Jiangxi Strategic Alliance of Virtual Reality (VR) Industrial Innovation, and the International Association of Chinese Professionals in Geographic Information Sciences.

SpatialDI mainly aims to address the opportunities and challenges brought about by the convergence of computer science, geographical information science, AI, and beyond. The main topics of SpatialDI 2023 included spatial computing and the metaverse, spatiotemporal visualization and virtual reality, high-precision automatic driving and AR navigation, computational social science and geo-computation for social sciences, human-computer interaction and spatial intelligence, spatial pattern mining and recommendation, virtual digital humans, aerospace information, and other spatial information.

This year, the conference received 68 submissions. Each submission was reviewed by at least three reviewers selected from the Program Committee in a single-blind process. Based on the reviewers' reports, 18 papers were finally accepted for presentation at the conference. The acceptance rate was 26%.

In addition to the regular papers, the conference featured a number of invited talks: Jianya Gong of Wuhan University, China, delivered a talk entitled "Realistic 3D Modeling and Urban Information Model", Philip S. Yu of the University of Illinois at Chicago, USA, addressed "On Recommendations via Deep and Broad Learning", Cyrus Shahabi of University of Southern California, USA, spoke about "Spatial Data Intelligence & Privacy: Past, Present and Future", Hui Lin of Jiangxi Normal University, China, addressed "Cognitive Shift from GIS to Virtual Geographic Environment", Haibo Li of KTH Royal Institute of Technology, Sweden, spoke about "Phenomenal Self, Space, and the Metaverse", Shijie Mao of Lenovo Research of Shanghai, China, addressed "Industrial Metaverse: A New Computing Scenario", and Liang Wu of China University of Geosciences, Wuhan, China, delivered a talk entitled "Technology Innovation and Digital Twin Application of Full-space GIS Platform".

The proceedings editors wish to thank our keynote and invited speakers and all the reviewers for their contributions. We also thank Springer for their trust and for publishing the proceedings of SpatialDI 2023.

April 2023

Xiaofeng Meng
Xiang Li
Jianqiu Xu
Xueying Zhang
Yuming Fang
Bolong Zheng
Yafei Li

Organization

Consultant Committee

Philip S. Yu   University of Illinois at Chicago, USA
Hui Lin   Jiangxi Normal University, China

General Conference Chairs

Xiaoyong Chen   East China University of Technology, China
Xing Xie   Microsoft Research Asia, China
Changxuan Wan   Jiangxi University of Finance and Economics, China

Program Committee Chairs

Xiang Li   East China Normal University, China
Jianqiu Xu   Nanjing University of Aeronautics and Astronautics, China
Xueying Zhang   Nanjing Normal University, China
Yuming Fang   Jiangxi University of Finance and Economics, China

Local Arrangements Chairs

Guoqiong Liao   Jiangxi University of Finance and Economics, China
Xiao Pan   Shijiazhuang Tiedao University, China

Publicity Chairs

Zhipeng Gui   Wuhan University, China
Lu Chen   Zhejiang University, China

Publication Chairs

Bolong Zheng   Huazhong University of Science and Technology,
                                China
Yafei Li   Zhengzhou University, China

Sponsorship Committee Chairs

Qingfeng Guan   China University of Geosciences, Wuhan, China
Xiaoping Du   Aerospace Information Research Institute,
                                Chinese Academy of Sciences, China

Thematic Forum Chairs

Kun Qin   Wuhan University, China
Lizhen Wang   Yunnan University, China

Strategic Report Chairs

Yong Li   Tsinghua University, China
Xuan Song   Southern University of Science and Technology,
                                China

Finance Chair

Zheng Huo   Hebei University of Economics and Business,
                                China

Overseas Liaison Chairs

Bin Yang   East China Normal University, China
Jilin Hu   Aalborg University, Denmark

Contents

Traffic Management

APADGCN: Adaptive Partial Attention Diffusion Graph Convolutional Network for Traffic Flow Forecasting

Bowen Zhang[1], Bohan Li[1,2,3(✉)], Jinzhan Wei[4], and Hao Wen[5]

[1] College of Computer Science and Technology, Nanjing University of Aeronautics and Astronautics, Nanjing 211106, China
bhli@nuaa.edu.cn
[2] Key Laboratory of Safety-Critical Software, Ministry of Industry and Information Technology, Beijing, China
[3] National Engineering Laboratory for Integrated Aero-Space-Ground Ocean Big Data Application Technology, Xi'an, China
[4] School of Electronic Information and Automation, Guilin University of Aerospace Technology, Guilin 541010, China
[5] College of Aerospace Engineering, Nanjing University of Aeronautics and Astronautics, Nanjing 211106, China

Abstract. Traffic flow forecasting is a core task of urban governance and plays a vital role in the development of ITS. Because of the complexity and uncertainty of traffic patterns, it is of great challenge to capture spatial-temporal correlations. Recent researches mainly focus on the pre-defined adjacency matrix based on prior knowledge as the basis of spatial-temporal correlation modeling, but the fixed graph structure cannot adequately describe the dependency between traffic sensors. To tackle this issue, a novel deep learning model framework is proposed in this paper: Adaptive Partial Attention Diffusion Graph Convolutional Network(APADGCN), which consists of three main parts: 1) the Multi-Component module that divides the historical traffic flow into recent, daily-periodic, and weekly-periodic, to capture the traffic patterns of different periodic; 2) the spatial correlation modeling which can dynamically capture node relationships and model spatial dependency, and enhance the aggregation ability of low-order information; 3) the temporal correlation modeling which models long-term time dependencies using convolution and gating. The final result is obtained by the weighted fusion of the results of the multi-components. We compared our APADGCN with various baseline models in the four real datasets from the Caltrans Performance Measurement System (PeMS). The experimental results show that the prediction accuracy of APADGCN is better than that of the baseline models.

Keywords: Traffic flow forecasting · Spatial-temporal · Graph convolution networks · Attention networks

X. Meng et al. (Eds.): SpatialDI 2023, LNCS 13887, pp. 3–20, 2023.
https://doi.org/10.1007/978-3-031-32910-4_1

1   Introduction

Traffic flow forecasting is a classic spatial-temporal task, which aims to simulate the road conditions of a certain traffic area for a period of time in the future. At present, the number of cars is growing rapidly. The growth of traffic flow has led to lots of problems, which makes the urban transportation system unbearable. Predicting the future traffic flow quickly and accurately for traffic control, road transportation, and public convenience means a lot. Figure 1 shows the spatial-temporal correlation of traffic flow. From the time dimension, the flow at different historical moments will affect the flow at other moments. Different observation points will also influence each other. A spatial association may occur even if the two nodes are far apart (this kind of spatial dependency is indicated by a dashed line). How to correlate and mine the information in traffic data needs careful consideration thoroughly. However, traffic flow is highly random and uncertain, also many other factors, such as unexpected events and weather, can affect traffic conditions, which makes it more challenging to forecast traffic flow.

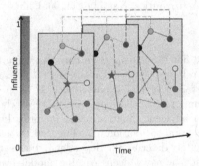

Fig. 1. The spatial-temporal correlation diagram of traffic flow.

Existing methods mainly utilized mathematical statistics, such as Kalman filter, fuzzy theory, and k-Nearest Neighbor(KNN) [1]. These algorithms achieved good results at first, but these models could not model complex traffic data nonlinearly and could not handle the spatial-temporal correlation, so most of these models relied on feature engineering. The growth of data volume and data types has increased the error of prediction results of traditional methods. In recent years, deep learning has gained attention for its ability to model high-dimensional nonlinearities for data, and it has good results in traffic flow forecasting. Recurrent Neural Network(RNN) [2] is the mainstream model for the ability to mine temporal features. However, these models are unable to extract features from the spatial attributes, leading to poor effects in traffic flow forecasting. Convolutional neural network(CNN) [3] is introduced for this. Historical traffic information is represented as a matrix, and the spatial topological links of the traffic data can be extracted by convolutional kernels. Therefore, to solve this problem, temporal correlation and spatial correlation need to be considered together. Combining CNN and RNN is a classical approach.

However, CNN is suitable for capturing spatial correlation in regular grids, which means that it is not applicable to realistic non-grid networks such as traffic networks. To address this problem, recently, spatial-temporal forecasting has been viewed as a problem of modeling, and data is usually regarded as a graph. Graph Convolutional Network (GCN) is used to discover spatial correlations in non-grid traffic networks due to its applicability to non-Euclidean spatial structures.

GCN can acquire and aggregate representations of neighbors in the vicinity of nodes, giving GCN the advantage of handling graph structures. However, there are many challenges. First, most models with GCN use the pre-defined adjacency matrix as the representation of nodes relationship, which can not truly represent the spatial relationship between nodes to a large extent. This situation is very common in traffic, where nodes are not only affected by their neighbors (such as traffic emergencies). The adjacency matrix cannot represent the dependency of nodes, which means some actual node associations are not represented in the adjacency matrix. Guo et al. [4] assigned weights to the adjacency matrix, which optimized the spatial correlation to a certain extent but still did not take into account the implicit dependency between nodes. Bai et al. [5] used points of interest(POI) to compute node similarity to represent the spatial association. Similarly, Geng et al. [6] encoded spatial associations using multigraph convolution. However, the pre-defined graph is still unable to represent node dependencies well. Because these methods rely on prior knowledge and are not available in other contexts. Wu et al. [7] embed dynamic learning of the spatial relationship between nodes and achieved good results. But relying only on the adaptive dependence matrix may ignore the attention of some inevitable node relationships. Second, when GCN aggregates information many times, the information of lower-order neighbors of nodes will be overwritten by higher-order nodes, resulting in inaccurate association. Our proposed APADGCN enhances the representation of nearby nodes in aggregation and reduces the loss of low-order neighbor information. Third, in the modeling of time correlation, previous studies mostly used recurrent neural networks such as GRU and LSTM to deal with time sequence relations. But there are some algorithm defects in the application, such as high model complexity, unstable gradients, difficulty in parallel, and so on.

To solve the above challenges, we propose Adaptive Partial Attention Spatial-Temporal Graph Convolutional Network(APADGCN). Different from previous studies, APADGCN can model the implicit spatial relationship between nodes dynamically. The problem of multiple convolution information loss is also taken into account, which enhances the aggregation ability of low-order neighbors. It also captures long-term time correlations and traffic patterns over different periods. The main contributions are as follows.

- We propose a new deep learning framework APADGCN for traffic flow prediction, which captures spatial-temporal correlation by stacking spatial-temporal layers.
- We design a new adaptive node relation matrix APA, which uses an adaptive matrix based on node embedding to capture the implicit association of nodes and propose partial attention mechanisms to enhance the aggregation ability of low-order information. Diffusion convolution is used to supplement the implied transition process and aggregate information with GCN.
- An improved gated temporal diffusion convolution is proposed, which uses diffusion convolution for long-term time dependency modeling, and incorporates the gated mechanism to control information transmission. The Multi-Component structure is used to model the traffic patterns of different periods.
- We compare our model with multiple baseline models in four real datasets, and the results of our proposed models are all better than the baseline models.

2   Related Works

2.1   Traffic Flow Forecasting

In previous studies, mathematical models were often used for traffic flow forecasting. For example, ARIMA is a classical model for forecasting [8]. Moreover, Chien et al. [9] used Kalman filtering algorithm to predict how long trips would take. Nikovski et al. [10] used Linear Regression (LR) to forecast travel time. Hou et al. [11] proposed a double-layer k-nearest neighbor (KNN) to predict the short-term traffic flow, and improved the efficiency of the model. However, these early prediction methods are mostly based on mathematics and statistics, which can not capture the intrinsic correlation between data only by relying on low-dimensional processing. This leads to the unsatisfied effect of these methods. Recently, deep learning has shown better modeling results in exploring spatial-temporal correlation [12].

Recently, deep learning has brought new solutions. Traffic flow can be modeled with long-term spatial and time dependencies. Different neural networks can be constructed to realize the learning of multidimensional representation of data. In terms of dealing with temporal correlations, early deep learning mainly uses RNN for temporal modeling. Long Short-Term Memory Neural Network (LSTM) is proposed to forecast traffic speed [13]. Cui et al. [14] proposed an SBU-LSTM framework with a data imputation mechanism, which achieved excellent prediction results for traffic data with different patterns of missing values. These methods based on RNN have some defects, such as complex parameters, low efficiency, and difficulty in parallelism. Many studies use Convolutional Neural Network(CNN) to deal with time series. Lea et al. [15] proposed a Temporal Convolutional Network(TCN) to mine spatial-temporal features in the framework of Encoder-Decoder on the temporal dimension. Liu et al. [16] proposed SCINet, which conducts sample convolution for recursive downsample to model time series effectively.

In terms of dealing with spatial correlations, CNN is often used for spatial modeling, Study [17,18] applied CNN to predict traffic speed. Wu et al. [19] construct the traffic flow prediction framework CLTFP with CNN and RNN. However, CNN is usually used for regular Euclidean graph, and the topological structure of many traffic networks is non-Euclidean. So, CNN does not apply to many traffic networks. The appearance of Graph convolutional networks (GCN) makes the study of non-Euclidean space further. GCN uses adjacency matrix to aggregate nearby nodes to achieve information dissemination. Li et al. [20] designed a diffusion graph convolution layer and completed the aggregation of information after K-hops.

2.2 Graph Neural Networks

Graph Neural Networks (GNN) was first proposed in [21], which is used to obtain topological information of non-Euclidean data. Subsequently, GCN emerged, which is one of the mainstream graph neural networks. At present, GCN is widely used because the traffic network can be represented by graph structure [22–26]. GCN is mainly divided into two categories: spectral graph convolution and spatial graph convolution [27]. In the field of spectral graph convolution, Bruna et al. [28] extended CNN to more common domains and proposed spectral convolution based on the graph Laplacian. ChebNet [29] used Chebyshev polynomials to expand and calculate the graph convolution, which avoided the calculation of the eigenvalues of the Laplacian matrix to optimize the high computational complexity of the original spectral convolution. In the field of spatial graph convolution, Micheli et al. [30] add the contextual data of the graph vertices through the traversal. The method is simple but has achieved good results. Graph Attention Network(GAT) is proposed in [31], which attached attention weight to the relationship between nodes and selectively aggregated the information of associated nodes. Wu et al. [7] proposed a Graph WaveNet that uses the node embedding algorithm to replace the pre-defined adjacency matrix with adaptive learning of the matrix, which improves the prediction accuracy of the model and training efficiency. Recently, A new adaptive matrix is proposed in [22], in which a Network Generator model is generated using the Gumbel-Softmax technique to explore the node associations.

2.3 Attention Mechanism

The attention mechanism was initially used in natural language processing to focus on the context of a word. It has since been used in many areas. At present, attention mechanism has been widely used in works, such as recommendation systems, computer vision, spatial-temporal prediction, video processing, and so on. Xu et al. [32] proposed a dual attention mechanism to classify image nodes. Liang et al. [33] added a multilevel attention network to the time series prediction, but due to a large number of parameters, the training takes a long time. In the field of graph data, there are also relevant studies to introduce the attention mechanism into the graph, through the construction of attention matrix, to achieve the function of dynamic correlation nodes. Guo et al. [4] proposed an ASTGCN, which uses the attention mechanism to dynamically compute the spatial attention weights between nodes. Zheng et al. [34] proposed a multi-attention neural network to model time steps of historical and future, based on an encoder-decoder framework. Xu et al. [35] proposed a STTN based on transformer, with the addition of spatial-temporal embedding, using attention mechanisms for time and space respectively. Jiang et al. [36] employed attention mechanism and convolution components to process long sequences.

3   Methodology

3.1   Preliminaries

In this study, we consider a traffic network as a graph $G = (V, E, A)$, where $V \in R^N$ is a set of nodes(e.g., traffic sensors) in the road network, and $E \in R^{N \times N}$ is a set of edges(e.g., the spatial connectivity between nodes); G is represented by adjacency matrix $A \in R^{N \times N}$, where $A_{i,j}$ represents the spatial connection of node i and node j, and $A_{i,j} = 1$ if $v_i, v_j \in V$ and $(v_i, v_j) \in E$.

Traffic flow forecasting can be regarded as a time series prediction task. Each node in graph G has F features at each time, and each node has the same sampling frequency. We donate $x_t^i \in R$ as the features of node i at time t. The characteristic data of all nodes at time t is expressed as $X_t = (x_t^1, x_t^2, ..., x_t^N)^T$. The historical observation traffic data are expressed as $H = (X_1, X_2, ..., X_T)$, which represents the data in T time steps of history. Our purpose is to predict the traffic flow data of the future T_{pre} time slices based on historical data H. Our task can be represented as:

$$X_{(T+1):(T+p)} = \mathcal{F}_\theta(H; G) \tag{1}$$

where $\mathcal{F}$ represents the transformation function, and θ represents all the learnable parameters in the training of the whole model.

3.2   Overview of Model Architecture

To effectively model the spatial and temporal traffic conditions, we propose a variant GCN model named APADGCN. Figure 2 depicts our proposed APADGCN, which consists of three modules: spatial Correlation module, temporal Correlation module, and Multi-Component Fusion module. We use the same association module for the recent period, daily period, and weekly period, and output the final prediction results by fusion. The spatial-temporal module is composed of APAGCN and GTCN. APAGCN is used to capture spatial correlation, and GTCN is used to explore temporal correlation.

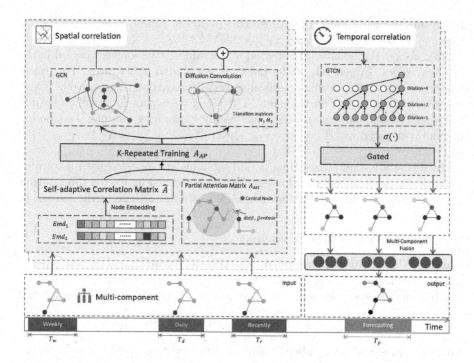

Fig. 2. Detailed framework of APADGCN.

3.3 Multi-component

Due to the strong historical periodicity of traffic flow, traffic flow often has similar
patterns to the flow in history. Therefore, in this study, to explore the periodic
patterns among the data, traffic data are divided into three time periods. Inspired
by [4], we use T_{resent}, T_{day}, and T_{week} to denote the length of time in different
period. Assume that the daily sampling frequency is T_q, the current time is
$T_{current}$, and the prediction window size is T_{pre}. The detailed representation of
the three periods is as follows:

(1) Recent Periodicity: This is the moment in history that is closest to and
closely related in time to the forecast period. The traffic at this time has an
important impact on the next time. This period of time is denoted as: $H_{recent} =
(X_{T_0-T_{recent}+1}, X_{T_0-T_{recent}+2}, ..., X_{T_0}) \in R^{N \times F \times T_{recent}}$.

(2) Daily Periodicity: This period refers to the data at the same time one day
before, and is a segment of the same time interval as the forecast period the day
before. In a fixed road section, people usually have a certain daily life pattern,
which means that traffic may show similar patterns. For example, in the morning
and evening of weekdays, there will be morning and evening peaks, which is an
obvious repeated pattern. But there are still many traffic characteristics and
patterns that we cannot intuitively recognize. So we select the daily periodicity

to capture the daily hidden features. This period of time is denoted as: $H_{day} = (X_{T_0-T_q+1}, X_{T_0-T_q+2}, ..., X_{T_0-T_q+T_{pre}}) \in R^{N \times F \times T_{day}}$.

(3) Weekly Periodicity: This period is the same as the forecast period in the last few weeks. In general, traffic patterns are similar every week. For example, there are similar traffic conditions every Friday, but there are big differences in traffic patterns on weekends. Therefore, we expect to model and study the weekly traffic patterns through the weekly Periodicity module. This period of time is denoted as: $H_{week} = (X_{T_0-7*T_q+1}, X_{T_0-7*T_q+2}, ..., X_{T_0-7*T_q+T_{pre}}) \in R^{N \times F \times T_{week}}$.

In this study, these three time period modules are modeled with a learning network and enter the network for learning respectively. Finally, the three output results are merged through the fusion module to obtain the final prediction result.

3.4   Spatial Correlation Modeling

Partial Attention Self-adaptive Correlation Matrix. The core idea of graph convolution is to aggregate the information of nodes in the graph, by which information can be updated. The basic GCN representation is as follows:

$$X^{(h)} = Conv(X^{(h-1)}) = \sigma(\widetilde{D}^{-\frac{1}{2}} \widetilde{A} \widetilde{D}^{-\frac{1}{2}} X^{(h-1)} W^{(h)}) \qquad (2)$$

where h represents the number of convolution executions, and the more h, the more information nodes aggregate. $X^{(0)} \in R^{N \times d}$ is the input feature matrix (i.e., the traffic signal data at time t_i), $\widetilde{D}$ is a diagonal matrix, $\widetilde{D}_{i,i} = \sum_j \widetilde{A}_{i,j}$. $\widetilde{A} = A + I_N \in R^{N \times N}$, where A is the adjacency matrix, I_N is the identity matrix. The matrix $W \in R^{N \times d}$ is a learnable parameter. Function $\sigma(\cdot)$ is the activation function (e.g., sigmoid or ReLU). $\widetilde{D}^{-\frac{1}{2}} \widetilde{A} \widetilde{D}^{-\frac{1}{2}}$ is a normalized adjacency matrix, which is to aggregate the information of the adjacency nodes of a node. The significance of GCN for a node is to transform the features. The data of each node in the input data are F feature signals. The function of GCN is to aggregate information and increase the features of nodes to high dimensions and discover hidden spatial features.

Traditional GCN can aggregate node information through an adjacency matrix, but it is one-sided to judge node association. Aggregation based on spatial geographical adjacency cannot reflect the real association relationship between nodes. At present, there are many pre-defined methods for adjacency matrices, but these methods are intuitive and cannot represent the real spatial association between nodes, which will lead to deviation in the forecasting results of the model. Relying on the pre-defined adjacency matrix to represent the spatial correlation makes the pre-defined method only suitable for the specific environment, which leads to poor prediction results in other models.

To discover the real spatial correlation between nodes, we design an adaptive adjacency matrix module, which can autonomously and adaptively explore the dependency relationship of nodes from data without relying on prior knowledge. We use $Emd_1, Emd_2 \in R^{N \times Emd_C}$ to represent the node embedding dictionary and initialize them randomly. The adaptive matrix is formulated as follows [7]:

$$\widehat{A} = SoftMax(ReLu(Emd_1 Emd_2^T)) \tag{3}$$

where the function of $SoftMax$ is to normalize the embeddings. $ReLu$ is the activation function, which is used to eliminate the embedded weak connection between Emd_1 and Emd_2, which will skip the calculation of the Laplace matrix to speed up the training. In addition, the adaptive adjacency matrix is also used for the data of unknown graph structures, which can mine the potential connection relationship.

Partial Attention. The spatial variation of traffic flow has great correlations. We use an adaptive adjacency matrix to dynamically model the spatial correlation. But in pure using an adaptive adjacency matrix would produce some problems, in Eq. 2, h represents the number of convolution layers. When the value of h is large, it means that the central node has been aggregated many times. Although the data of remote points are aggregated, it will also lead to the loss of low-order information, that is, the information of neighboring nodes of the central node is overwritten. To ensure that the nodes can fully obtain the high-order information without losing the association of nearby nodes, we propose an adaptive adjacency matrix with a partial attention mechanism.

Inspired by the modeling of road network distance in Gaussian kernel [37]. To strengthen the ability of the model to associate information of nearby nodes after multiple aggregations, we propose a partial attention mechanism, which only imposes attention weights on nodes within a certain range of distance from central nodes. The formula is as follows:

$$A_{att} = \begin{cases} V_s \cdot \sigma((\chi^{h-1} W_1) W_2 (W_3 \chi^{h-1})^T + b_s), \ dist(v_i, v_j) \leq k_{min} \\ 0, \hspace{5.5cm} otherwise \end{cases} \tag{4}$$

$$A'_{att_{i,j}} = SoftMax(A_{att_{i,j}}) = \frac{exp(A_{att_{i,j}})}{\sum_{j=0}^{T_r} exp(A_{att_{i,j}})} \tag{5}$$

where $\chi^{h-1} = (X_1, X_2, X_3, ..., X_{T_r}) \in R^{N \times C \times T_r}$ is the input of hth layer. $V_s, b_s \in R^{N \times N}$, $W_1 \in R^{T_r}$, $W_2 \in R^{C \times T_r}$, $W_3 \in R^C$ are the parameters to be learned. The matrix $A_{att} \in R^{N \times N}$ is the weight matrix of partial attention, $A_{att_{i,j}}$ represents the associated value between nodes i and j, and the larger the value of $A_{att_{i,j}}$ is, the stronger spatial connection between nodes i and j. We only apply attention weights to nearby nodes of the central node to strengthen the aggregation of information of nearby nodes. If attention weight is applied to all nodes, it will also lead to the loss of information of nearby nodes after multiple convolutions. It also speeds up the training process of the model by omitting many unnecessary modeling. Subsequently, we use $SoftMax$ function to normalize the attention matrix to ensure that the sum of the weights of relational nodes of node i is 1. The matrix A'_{att} is the normalized attention weight matrix.

After getting the partial attention matrix, we integrate it into the adaptive adjacency matrix. To ensure the stationarity of modeling learning, we use the average value of K training results after K repeated training as the final adjacency matrix. The formula of the adaptive adjacency matrix with partial attention mechanism is as follows:

$$A_{AP} = \frac{\lambda}{K} \sum_{i=0}^{K} \widehat{A^i} + (1 - \lambda)A'_{att} \tag{6}$$

where λ is a hyperparameter, which represents the fusion degree of the adjacency matrix with attention weight. When λ approaches 1, it means that the local attention matrix is not adopted. When λ approaches 0, it means that the local attention matrix is completely used as the node correlation matrix. A_{AP} is the partial attention adaptive adjacency matrix. The graph convolution formula with partial attention adaptive adjacency matrix is as follows:

$$X^{(h)} = Conv\_AP(X^{(h-1)}) = \sigma(\widetilde{D}^{-\frac{1}{2}} A_{AP} \widetilde{D}^{-\frac{1}{2}} X^{(h-1)} W^{(h)}) \tag{7}$$

Diffusion Convolution. The process of normalized adaptive adjacency matrix can be regarded as a transition matrix of a hidden diffusion process and can be used as a supplementary form of diffusion convolution [38]. Therefore, we introduce diffusion convolution and fuse the convolution layer with the diffusion convolution layer. The formula is as follows:

$$X^{(h)} = Conv\_AD(X^{(h-1)}) = \sigma(\widetilde{D}^{-\frac{1}{2}} A_{AW} \widetilde{D}^{-\frac{1}{2}} X^{(h-1)} W^{(h)} + Q_D) \tag{8}$$

$$Q_D = \sum_{k=0}^{R} (\theta_0 M_0^k X^{(h)} W_0 + \theta_1 M_1^k X^{(h)} W_1) \tag{9}$$

where $M_0^k = A / \sum_j A_{i,j}$ and $M_1^k = A^T / \sum_j A_{i,j_T}$ are the forward and backward transition matrices in the diffusion process, θ_0, θ_1, W_0, W_1 are the parameters matrices to learn. $M_0^2 = M_0 \cdot M_0$. The function of M_0^k and M_2^k is to represent the transition probability between nodes, and K is the number of diffusion steps. The diffusion process of convolution is simulated by the multiplication of the transition matrix. Matrix Q_D can also further enhance the ability to aggregate the information of nearby nodes to weaken the disadvantages caused by multi-layer convolution.

3.5   Temporal Correlation Modeling

GTCN. After the temporal attention layer, we have related traffic information at different moments. In this subsection, we will further merge the signals on the time slice. Recurrent neural networks, such as RNN and LSTM, have been widely used in temporal data, but there are some algorithm defects in the application.

Therefore, we follow [7] and use a dilated temporal convolutional mechanism to update the information.

$$Y^{(h)} = \begin{cases} X, & l = 0 \\ g(\theta_1 *_{d^l} Y^{(h-1)} + b) \odot \sigma(\theta_2 *_{d^l} Y^{(h-1)} + c), & l = 1, 2, 3, ..., l \end{cases} \quad (10)$$

where X is the input of DTCN, $Y^{(h-1)}$ is the input of lth layer. θ_1, θ_2 are the convolution kernels. b and c are model parameters to be learned. $\odot$ is the element-wise product. $g(\cdot)$ and $\sigma(\cdot)$ are the activation function. $d^l = 2^l - 1$ is an exponential dilation rate. We use $\sigma(\cdot)$ to control how much information can be retained. We use dilated convolution to expand the receptive field on time series, which enhances the ability to model long-time series data.

3.6   Multi-component Fusion

In this section, we integrate the results of the three time periods to get the final forecasting results. For the period to be predicted, the three periods have different impacts on it. For example, the morning peak traffic patterns on weekdays are similar, so they are greatly influenced by daily and weekly periods, so we need to pay more attention to these two periods. However, if an emergency occurs, which leads to abnormal traffic conditions, it is necessary to pay more attention to the recent period. Therefore, combined with the attention mechanism, we attach different attention weights to the forecasting results of the three time periods to achieve the purpose of different attention to the period data. The final result after the fusion of features is:

$$\widehat{Y} = Linear(Concat(\widehat{Y}_{recent}, \widehat{Y}_{day}, \widehat{Y}_{week})) \quad (11)$$

where $Linear$ is linear layer, $Concat$ means concatenation operation. $\widehat{Y}_{recent}$, $\widehat{Y}_{day}$ and $\widehat{Y}_{week}$ represent the results of the recent period, daily period, and weekly period, respectively.

4   Experiments

4.1   Datasets

To evaluate the effect of our proposed APADGCN model, we selected real highway datasets (PEMSD3, PEMSD4, PEMSD7, and PEMSD8) collected from California as experimental data. The dataset was produced by Caltrans Performance Measurement System(PeMS), which is real data on California highways and includes more than 39,000 physical sensors that integrate data every five minutes. The specific descriptions of datasets are shown in Table 1.

Table 1. Detailed information on datasets.

Dataset	PeMSD3	PeMSD4	PeMSD7	PeMSD8
Data type	Traffic flow	Traffic flow	Traffic flow	Traffic flow
Nodes(Sensors)	358	307	883	170
Edges	547	340	866	295
Time steps	26,208	16,992	28,224	17,856
Features	3	3	3	3
Data frequency	5 min	5 min	5 min	5 min

4.2 Settings

We use Z-Score normalization for the datasets we use to ensure that the inputs are of the same order of magnitude, and we divided datasets into the training set, validation set, and test set with the ratio of 6:2:2. Consecutive time slices are separated by 5 min, and a day is divided into 288 time slices. We set different data windows according to the selected period, namely T_r=24, T_d=12, T_w=24. For the three time periods, we predict the traffic flow for the next day, so the prediction window size is the same, that is, T_p=12. In APADGCN, we set the hidden dimension of graph convolution as 64, the repetition part K=6, λ=0.5. The threshold for partial attention $K_{min} = 0.12$, and the number of diffusion hops R=2. We superimposed three spatial association modules. Each TCN layer uses 64 convolution kernels. In this study, we use mean square error (MSE) as the loss function. In the stage of training, the batch size is 64 and the learning rate is 0.0001. We use the adamoptimizer and set the number of epochs to 100.

4.3 Baseline Methods

We used the following seven baselines to compare with our proposed APADGCN model.

VAR [39]: Vector Auto-Regression, which is a classical model for time series modeling.

ARIMA [40]: Autoregressive Integrated Moving Average model, which is one of the classical time series forecasting analysis methods.

LSTM [41]: Long Short Term Memory network, which is based on RNN to model timing relationships.

FC-LSTM   [42]: FullConnection-LSTM, which combines the fully connected layer and LSTM layer to predict traffic flow.

TCN   [43]: Temporal Convolution Network, which uses convolution kernel to aggregate information of time dimension for prediction.

STGCN   [44]: Spatio-Temporal Graph Convolution Network, which combines GCN and convolution to model spatial-temporal dependency.

DCRNN   [20]: Diffusion Convolutional Recurrent Neural Network, which introduces dilated convolutional to capture spatial-temporal correlation.

GraphWaveNet   [7]: Graph WaveNet, which combines adaptive convolution and dilated convolution layers using a node embedding algorithm.

4.4   Comparison and Result Analysis

Results on the PEMS Dataset. In Table 2, we compare our proposed model with the baseline on the four PEMS datasets using MAE, MAPE, and RMSE metrics. It can be seen that our APADGCN has achieved the best results in the four indicators. This shows that our model can capture the spatial and temporal dependence of traffic flow data well. In addition, we can observe that compared with other models, ARIMA and LSTM show larger prediction errors, because ARIMA and LSTM only take the temporal correlation of nodes into account and ignore the spatial correlation. Although VAR considers the spatial correlation, it is not able to capture the hidden information, so it also has a poor effect. Other models using deep learning consider the spatial-temporal correlation, thus the results of forecasting are far better than the previous two.

TCN, STGCN, DCRNN, and GraphWaveNet achieved good results on the four datasets, but the prediction accuracy was not as good as our proposed model. These baseline models use GCN to model spatial association, in which TCN and STGCN only take the network connection relationship on the real map as the adjacency matrix, and cannot associate the possible spatial relationship between nodes. Although DCRNN and GraphWaveNet use extended convolution and adaptive adjacency matrix to expand spatial correlation, their temporal correlation processing method cannot model long-term temporal dependence. Our proposed APADGCN can capture the implicit spatial correlation and the long-term temporal information. Therefore, APADGCN can better model the spatial-temporal dependency.

Table 2. Prediction Errors on the PeMSD3, PeMSD4, PeMSD7 and PeMSD8 Datasets.

Dataset	Metric	VAR	ARIMA	LSTM	FC-LSTM	TCN	STGCN	DCRNN	WaveNet	Ours
PEMSD3	MAE	23.65	33.51	20.62	21.33	19.32	17.49	17.99	19.85	**16.85**
	MAPE(%)	24.51	33.78	33.54	23.33	19.93	17.15	18.34	19.31	**16.57**
	RMSE	38.56	47.59	28.94	35.11	33.55	30.12	30.31	32.94	**29.34**
PEMSD4	MAE	23.75	33.73	26.81	27.14	23.22	22.70	21.22	25.45	**20.43**
	MAPE(%)	18.09	24.18	18.74	18.20	15.59	14.59	14.17	17.29	**13.46**
	RMSE	36.66	48.80	43.49	41.59	37.26	35.55	33.44	39.70	**32.86**
PEMSD7	MAE	75.63	38.17	29.71	29.98	32.72	25.38	25.22	26.85	**24.57**
	MAPE(%)	32.22	19.46	45.32	13.20	14.26	11.08	11.82	12.12	**10.79**
	RMSE	115.24	59.27	14.14	45.94	42.23	38.78	38.61	42.78	**37.91**
PEMSD8	MAE	23.46	31.09	22.19	22.20	22.72	18.02	16.82	19.13	**16.26**
	MAPE(%)	15.42	22.73	33.59	14.20	14.03	11.40	10.92	12.68	**10.48**
	RMSE	36.33	44.32	18.74	34.06	35.79	27.83	26.36	31.05	**25.71**

Ablation Experiment. To verify the validity of each component in our proposed model, we proposed the following variants of APADGCN which removed several modules: (1)RemSA: It removes the Self-adaptive Correlation Matrix in the APADGCN. (2)RemPA: It removes Partial Attention in the APADGCN. (3)RemAPD: It removes the Self-adaptive Correlation Matrix and Partial Attention and replaces them with a normal adjacency matrix. (4)RemDC: It removes Diffusion Convolution and replaces it with normal GCN. We compare these four variants with our proposed APDGCN model on PEMS04. We used MAE, MAPE, and RMSE as metrics. In Fig. 3, the comparison results of the models are shown in detail.

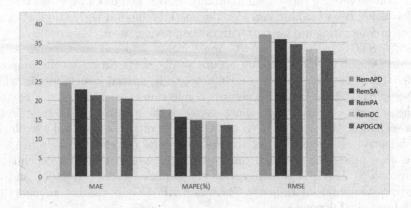

Fig. 3. Details of Ablation experiment.

Figure 3 shows the prediction accuracy of each model. It can be seen that the accuracy of the four variant models is lower than APADGCN. RemAPD has the worst prediction effect. It can be found that our proposed SEPA module has the function of dynamically capturing node association, which indicates the importance of node spatial correlation. By comparing RemPA and RemSA, it can be found that the performance of PA is inferior to SA, which means that the adaptive correlation matrix is better than the attention mechanism in capturing spatial correlation. The performance of RemDC is worse than APADGCN, which indicates that the transition matrix in diffusion convolution can enhance the function of capturing the spatial relationship of nodes.

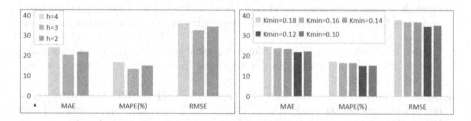

Fig. 4. Network configuration analysis. In these two images, we have different configurations for the hyperparameter. Where h is the number of spatial convolution layers, K_{min} is the distance threshold of partial attention.

Effect of Different Network Configurations. To explore the influence of hyperparameters in the model on the prediction results, we conducted experiments on the networks with different hyperparameters. All parameters are the same as those in 4.2. Only the parameters for comparison are adjusted. Figure 4 shows the experimental results for different configurations of the hyperparameter. It can be seen that (1) When the convolution layer is expanded from two layers to three layers, no information loss is caused because we set part of the attention mechanism, so more node information is aggregated to achieve the best effect; (2) The expansion of the distance threshold of some attention increases the number of nodes aggregated, but decreases the effect. When the threshold is close to 1, it is the global attention mechanism and cannot enhance the near-point representation.

5   Conclusion

In this paper, we propose a novel traffic flow forecasting model APADGCN based on deep learning. We use a node embedding algorithm and partial attention mechanism to build an adaptive node association matrix and combine graph convolution and diffusion convolution to aggregate node information to capture spatial association. This approach can represent the node association without the pre-defined adjacency matrix and enhance the representation of the hidden dependency of nodes and the attention to nearby nodes. We introduce Multi-component to model traffic patterns in the different periods. Therefore, our model can better capture the spatial-temporal correlation of traffic flow. We conduct sufficient comparisons with some baseline models on four public datasets, and the results show that our proposed APADGCN is superior to the baseline model and has good performance. In the future, we will consider adding information such as weather to assist traffic flow forecasting and enhance the versatility of the model in different scenarios.

References

1. Pang, X., Wang, C., Huang, G.: A short-term traffic flow forecasting method based on a three-layer k-nearest neighbor non-parametric regression algorithm. J. Transp. Technol. **6**(4), 200–206 (2016)
2. Laptev, N., Yosinski, J., Li, L.E., Smyl, S.: Time-series extreme event forecasting with neural networks at uber. In: International Conference on Machine Learning, vol. 34, pp. 1–5 (2017)
3. Dong, C., Loy, C.C., He, K., Tang, X.: Learning a deep convolutional network for image super-resolution. In: Fleet, D., Pajdla, T., Schiele, B., Tuytelaars, T. (eds.) ECCV 2014. LNCS, vol. 8692, pp. 184–199. Springer, Cham (2014). https://doi.org/10.1007/978-3-319-10593-2_13
4. Guo, S., Lin, Y., Feng, N., Song, C., Wan, H.: Attention based spatial-temporal graph convolutional networks for traffic flow forecasting. Proceed. AAAI Conf. Artif. Intell. **33**(01), 922–929 (2019)
5. Bai, L., Yao, L., Kanhere, S.S., Yang, Z., Chu, J., Wang, X.: Passenger demand forecasting with multi-task convolutional recurrent neural networks. In: Yang, Q., Zhou, Z.-H., Gong, Z., Zhang, M.-L., Huang, S.-J. (eds.) PAKDD 2019. LNCS (LNAI), vol. 11440, pp. 29–42. Springer, Cham (2019). https://doi.org/10.1007/978-3-030-16145-3_3
6. Geng, X., et al.: Spatiotemporal multi-graph convolution network for ride-hailing demand forecasting. Proceed. AAAI Conf. Artif. Intell. **33**(01), 3656–3663 (2019)
7. Wu, Z., Pan, S., Long, G., Jiang, J., Zhang, C.: Graph waveNet for deep spatial-temporal graph modeling. arXiv preprint arXiv:1906.00121 (2019)
8. Ahmed, M.S., Cook, A.R.: Analysis of freeway traffic time-series data by using box-Jenkins techniques (1997)
9. Chien, S.I.-J., Kuchipudi, C.M.: Dynamic travel time prediction with real-time and historic data. J. Transp. Eng. **129**(6), 608–616 (2003)
10. Nikovski, D., Nishiuma, N., Goto, Y., Kumazawa, H.: Univariate short-term prediction of road travel times. In Proceedings.: IEEE Intelligent Transportation Systems, vol. 2005, pp. 1074–1079 (2005). IEEE (2005)
11. Xiaoyu, H., Yisheng, W., Siyu, H.: Short-term traffic flow forecasting based on two-tier k-nearest neighbor algorithm. Procedia. Soc. Behav. Sci. **96**, 2529–2536 (2013)
12. Li, Z., Ren, Q., Chen, L., Sui, X., Li, J.: Multi-hierarchical spatial-temporal graph convolutional networks for traffic flow forecasting. In: 2022 26th International Conference on Pattern Recognition (ICPR), pp. 4913–4919. IEEE (2022)
13. Ma, X., Tao, Z., Wang, Y., Yu, H., Wang, Y.: Long short-term memory neural network for traffic speed prediction using remote microwave sensor data. Transp. Res. Part C: Emerg. Technol. **54**, 187–197 (2015)

14. Cui, Z., Ke, R., Pu, Z., Wang, Y.: Stacked bidirectional and unidirectional LSTM recurrent neural network for forecasting network-wide traffic state with missing values. Transp. Res. Part C: Emerg. Technol. **118**, 102674 (2020)
15. Lea, C., Flynn, M.D., Vidal, R., Reiter, A., Hager, G.D.: Temporal convolutional networks for action segmentation and detection In: proceedings of the IEEE Conference on Computer Vision and Pattern Recognition, pp. 156–165 (2017)
16. Liu, M., Zeng, A., Xu, Z., Lai, Q., Xu, Q.: Time series is a special sequence: forecasting with sample convolution and interaction. arXiv preprint arXiv:2106.09305 (2021)
17. Ma, X., Dai, Z., He, Z., Ma, J., Wang, Y., Wang, Y.: Learning traffic as images: a deep convolutional neural network for large-scale transportation network speed prediction. Sensors **17**(4), 818 (2017)
18. Zhang, J., Zheng, Y., Qi, D.: Deep Spatio-temporal residual networks for citywide crowd flows prediction. In: Thirty-first AAAI Conference on Artificial Intelligence (2017)
19. Wu, Y., Tan, H.: Short-term traffic flow forecasting with spatial-temporal correlation in a hybrid deep learning framework. arXiv preprint arXiv:1612.01022 (2016)
20. Li, Y., Yu, R., Shahabi, C., Liu, Y.: Diffusion convolutional recurrent neural network: data-driven traffic forecasting. arXiv preprint arXiv:1707.01926 (2017)
21. Gori, M., Monfardini, G., Scarselli, F.: A new model for learning in graph domains. In: Proceedings. 2005 IEEE International Joint Conference on Neural Networks, vol. 2, no. 2005, pp. 729–734 (2005)
22. Kong, X., Zhang, J., Wei, X., Xing, W., Lu, W.: Adaptive spatial-temporal graph attention networks for traffic flow forecasting. Appl. Intell. **52**(4), 4300–4316 (2022)
23. Zhang, C., et al.: Augmented multi-component recurrent graph convolutional network for traffic flow forecasting. ISPRS Int. J. Geo Inf. **11**(2), 88 (2022)
24. Wang, Y., Jing, C., Xu, S., Guo, T.: Attention based spatiotemporal graph attention networks for traffic flow forecasting. Inf. Sci. **607**, 869–883 (2022)
25. Zhang, W., Zhu, K., Zhang, S., Chen, Q., Xu, J.: Dynamic graph convolutional networks based on spatiotemporal data embedding for traffic flow forecasting. Knowl.-Based Syst. **250**, 109028 (2022)
26. Zhang, S., Guo, Y., Zhao, P., Zheng, C., Chen, X.: A graph-based temporal attention framework for multi-sensor traffic flow forecasting. IEEE Trans. Intell. Transp. Syst. **23**(7), 7743–7758 (2021)
27. Wu, Z., Pan, S., Chen, F., Long, G., Zhang, C., Philip, S.Y.: A comprehensive survey on graph neural networks. IEEE Trans. Neural Netw. Learn. Syst. **32**(1), 4–24 (2020)
28. Bruna, J., Zaremba, W., Szlam, A., LeCun, Y.: Spectral networks and locally connected networks on graphs. arXiv preprint arXiv:1312.6203 (2013)
29. Defferrard, M., Bresson, X., Vandergheynst, P.: Convolutional neural networks on graphs with fast localized spectral filtering. In: Advances in Neural Information Processing Systems, vol. 29 (2016)
30. Micheli, A.: Neural network for graphs: a contextual constructive approach. IEEE Trans. Neural Networks **20**(3), 498–511 (2009)
31. Veličković, P., Cucurull, G., Casanova, A., Romero, A., Lio, P., Bengio, Y.: Graph attention networks. arXiv preprint arXiv:1710.10903 (2017)
32. Xu, K., et al.: Show, attend and tell: neural image caption generation with visual attention. In: International Conference on Machine Learning, pp. 2048–2057. PMLR (2015)
33. Liang, Y., Ke, S., Zhang, J., Yi, X., Zheng, Y.: GeoMAN: multi-level attention networks for geo-sensory time series prediction. IJCAI **2018**, 3428–3434 (2018)

34. Zheng, C., Fan, X., Wang, C., Qi, J.: GMAN: a graph multi-attention network for traffic prediction. Proceed. AAAI Conf. Artif. Intell. **34**(01), 1234–1241 (2020)

35. Xu, M., et al.: Spatial-temporal transformer networks for traffic flow forecasting. arXiv preprint arXiv:2001.02908 (2020)

36. Jiang, S., Zhu, M., Li, J.: Traffic flow forecasting using a spatial-temporal attention graph convolutional network predictor. In: Meng, X., Xie, X., Yue, Y., Ding, Z. (eds.) SpatialDI 2020. LNCS, vol. 12567, pp. 107–121. Springer, Cham (2021). https://doi.org/10.1007/978-3-030-69873-7_8

37. Shuman, D.I., Narang, S.K., Frossard, P., Ortega, A., Vandergheynst, P.: The emerging field of signal processing on graphs: extending high-dimensional data analysis to networks and other irregular domains. IEEE Signal Process. Mag. **30**(3), 83–98 (2013)

38. Qi, J., Zhao, Z., Tanin, E., Cui, T., Nassir, N., Sarvi, M.: A graph and attentive multi-path convolutional network for traffic prediction. IEEE Transactions on Knowledge and Data Engineering (2022)

39. Hamilton, J.D.: Time series analysis. Princeton University Press (2020)

40. Williams, B.M., Hoel, L.A.: Modeling and forecasting vehicular traffic flow as a seasonal Arima process: theoretical basis and empirical results. J. Transp. Eng. **129**(6), 664–672 (2003)

41. Hochreiter, S., Schmidhuber, J.: Long short-term memory. Neural Comput. **9**(8), 1735–1780 (1997)

42. Sutskever, I., Vinyals, O., Le, Q.V.: Sequence to sequence learning with neural networks. In: Advances in Neural Information Processing Systems, vol. 27 (2014)

43. Bai, S., Kolter, J.Z., Koltun, V.: An empirical evaluation of generic convolutional and recurrent networks for sequence modeling. arXiv preprint arXiv:1803.01271 (2018)

44. Yu, B., Yin, H., Zhu, Z.: Spatio-temporal graph convolutional networks: a deep learning framework for traffic forecasting. arXiv preprint arXiv:1709.04875 (2017)

DeepParking: Deep Learning-Based Planning Method for Autonomous Parking

Yunxiao Shan[1,2], Ziwei Zhong[1], Li Fan[1], and Huang Kai[1(⊠)]

[1] Sun Yat-sen University, Guangzhou, China
huangk36@mail.sysu.edu.cn
[2] The Shenzhen Institute, Shenzhen, China

Abstract. Planning methods for parking are an important topic in the realm of autonomous driving. To achieve successful parking, complicated maneuvers are required to be reasonably performed in a very limited space. Moreover, since unstructured parking scenarios are lack of significant common features, creating useful heuristics manually to adapt to changing conditions is a non-trivial task. Therefore, we propose a two-stage scheme, Deep Neural Networks based path prediction for the first stage and sampling-based optimization for the second stage. Specifically, a customized network is used for predicting a feasible path with a high successful rate and the prediction error is modeled by Gaussian in the second stage. With the modeled error, a variant Bi-RRT* method is specially-designed to correct the possible prediction error and further improve the path quality. We carry out experiments to validate the performance of the proposed scheme and compare it to existing methods. Experimental results demonstrated that our planning scheme can infer a path by neural networks within 25 ms and plan a final path around 75 ms.

Keywords: autonomous parking · path planning · deep learning

1 Introduction

Planning methods play an important role in autonomous driving systems [13] [3]. A successful planning strategy should guarantee planning a safe trajectory from a initial state to a goal state while complying with many interior and exterior constraints. Since most of the driving conditions are structured, a planning task can be achieved in structured environments by just following a road center or lane marks. However, difficulties may arise when parking a car. A planning method should perform complicated maneuvers without significant guides in such unstructured or semi-unstructured parking environments. Therefore, it is important to study the planning methods for parking.

Compared with driving in structured environment, the parking problem imposes extra difficulties on planning strategies. On the one hand, forward and backward maneuvers are needed to be combined optimally to accomplish a successful parking task. Once one of maneuvers is not correctly operated, a failure may be inevitable regardless of efforts afterward. On the other hand, unlike the similarity of structured scenarios, the working space in different parking scenarios varies remarkably. For instance, the planning space in parallel parking is different from that of perpendicular parking.

For the purpose of planning in parking scenarios, it is a common and reasonable choice for existing planning methods to integrate heuristics to improve planning efficiency and reduce the failure probabilities. Liu et al. [9] proposed a lattice A* based searching method with boundary layer heuristics to minimize the length of the path as well as the number of gear shifts in parking maneuvers. Chen et al. [2] considered the orientation of a vehicle in a space exploration phase as heuristics for the latter-on searching. Nevertheless, selection heuristics based on one or several handcraft features for guiding the planner to converge to a goal are over-dependent on the experiences of experts, which may lead to unstable planning performance. Recently, more appealing solutions are based on deep learning to learn the deep features of planning scenarios for predictions and then use the predictions as heuristics. Higueras et al. [10] deployed Fully Convolutional Networks (FCNs) to learn a prediction trajectory for the planning task of mobile robots and Banzhafe et al. [1] also used FCNs to predict the feasible regions for the planner of autonomous vehicles in unstructured scenarios. Du et al. [5] proposed a reinforcement learning based method to achieve automated parking systems.

Due to the complexity of planning in parking environment, it is still an open issue for planning research to improve planning efficiency and success rate in limited time. Although previous work improves the planning performance by predicting feasible regions for later-on optimization, the prediction results cannot be used straightforwardly due to low prediction accuracy. Moreover, the latter-on optimization methods are all based on the assumption that the prediction errors are in reasonable ranges and cannot adjust the planning space according to the prediction errors.

Being aware of the aforementioned problems, this paper presents a planning scheme with a deep neural networks that can infer path with a high successful rate and a later-on optimization method that can adaptive change planning space with the prediction errors. In our scheme, unlike the approaches in [1] and [10], a novel network is proposed to predict a feasible path with a high success rate and can be be directly used for real-time parking. Afterward, a Bi-RRT* [7] based method is deployed for later-on optimization and an efficient sampling strategy is achieved by making use of that best-fit Gaussian model to model the prediction errors from the previous pipeline. In order to evaluate our scheme, experiments based on CARLA were carried out to validate our planning ability in a variety of parking scenarios. The main contributions of this paper are as follows:

- A two-stage planning scheme is proposed to real-time plan the parking path while guaranteeing the success rate and path quality.
- A deep neural network is customized to infer an admissible path directly with a high success rate.

– A Bi-RRT* based optimization method is specially-designed with an adaptive sampling strategy guided by the modeled prediction error of the customized pipeline.

2 Our Approach

A two-stage planning method is customized for autonomous parking, as shown in Fig. 1. In our method, a rough path is predicted by a deep neural network and then a Bi-RRT* based traditional planning method is proposed to improve the quality of the predicted path.

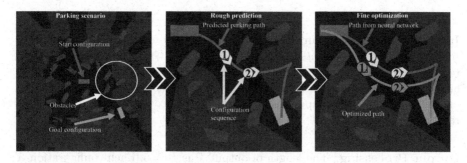

Fig. 1. parking path planning system. The scenario is firstly encoded into a RGB image (left) and then input to the prediction network to predict the parking path (middle). With the predicted path, a customized sampling-based method is deployed to further optimize (right).

2.1 Stage1: Rough Prediction

For a given autonomous vehicle, a parking scenario can be defined as a tuple $\mathcal{S} = (\mathcal{X}_{start}, \mathcal{X}_{goal}, \mathcal{W})$, where $\mathcal{X}_{start}$ and $\mathcal{X}_{goal}$ denote the start and goal configurations, $\mathcal{W}$ denotes the workspace. The path prediction by a deep neural network can be seen as a mapping process to build a map from tuple $\mathcal{S}$ to $\mathcal{P} = (\mathcal{X})_{i=1}^{n}$, which is a sequence of configurations and equivalent to a path. Therefore, a deep convolutional neural network is constructed (Fig. 2) for mapping paths. Just like many one-stage object detection networks, the prediction pipeline is based on DarkNet from YOLO [11] with the input shape is $480 \times 480 \times 3$ and the output shape is $1 \times 1 \times 20$. Following DarkNet, we use batch normalization after each convolutional layer. For the backbone, VGG is used in our network since it can guarantee large receptive field with deep network structure and smaller convolution kernel.

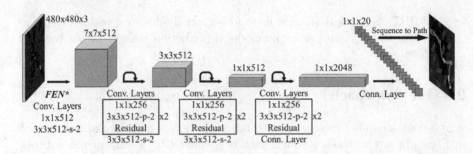

Fig. 2. The Architecture of proposed prediction network. FEN denotes the VGG based feature extraction backbone. In the 'Sequence to Path' process, Reeds-Shepp curves are used to connect configurations to generate the parking path.

Input Processing. In our network, the inputs are encoded into a 600×600 RGB image. $\mathcal{W}$ is represented by OGM (Occupancy Grid Map) (size 600×600, resolution $0.1\,\mathrm{m/cell}$, grayscale image) and put on R channel. $\mathcal{X}_{start}$ and $\mathcal{X}_{goal}$ are represented by rectangles (width and length are the same as the automobile) on the OGM and their shapes and orientation are encoded on G and B channels respectively.

Output Processing. The length of output $\mathcal{P}$ is $B = 5$. Each configuration $\mathcal{X}$ in $\mathcal{P}$ consists of 4 predictions: x, y, ϕ, and p. p is a confidence score reflects the probability that the predicted $\mathcal{X}$ belongs to the ground true sequence $\hat{\mathcal{P}}$. (x, y, ϕ) denote the coordinates of $\mathcal{X}$ and they are normalized as shown in Eq. 1.

$$[x,y,\phi] = ([\tilde{x},\tilde{y},\tilde{\phi}] + [\frac{W}{2}, \frac{H}{2}, \pi]) \circ [\frac{1}{W}, \frac{1}{H}, \frac{1}{2\pi}] \tag{1}$$

where $[x,y,\phi]$ denoted normalized value, $[\tilde{x},\tilde{y},\tilde{\phi}]$ denoted the origin value, $\circ$ operator denotes the Hadamard product, W and H denote the width and height of the OGM.

Loss Function. The loss defined by Eq. 2 consists of two parts: coordinate loss $\mathcal{J}_r$ and classification loss $\mathcal{J}_c$. The parameter λ_r is used to balance the convergence of J_r and J_c. Specifically, we use $\lambda_r = 10^4$ to balance.

$$J = \lambda_r \mathcal{J}_r + \mathcal{J}_c$$
$$= \lambda_r \sum_b^B \hat{p}_b \, \mathrm{BCE}([\hat{x}_b, \hat{y}_b, \hat{\phi}_b], [x_b, y_b, \phi_b]) + \sum_b^B \mathrm{BCE}(\hat{p}, p_b) \tag{2}$$

where $\hat{x}$, $\hat{y}$, $\hat{\phi}$, and $\hat{p}$ are the ground truths of x, y, ϕ, and p. BCE($\bullet$) denotes binary cross-entropy function.

It is noted that we use Binary Cross-entropy (BCE) function to calculate the coordinate loss instead of widely-used Mean Squared Error (MSE) function. The basic reason for the replacement is that using BCE makes the loss calculation method of J_r and J_c are the same, thus the changing of their gradient is similar. With similar gradient, the imbalance problem can be alleviated.

2.2   Stage2: Fine Optimization

Although the path predicted by the deep neural network can infer the path, complicated parking scenarios make it difficult to guarantee high quality of path. A normal method is to develop a more complex network, but it is costly to make step toward higher performance by optimizing networks. Therefore, tradition optimization methods are used in our scheme, namely second-stage optimization. Specifically, a Bi-RRT* based optimization method is used in our second-stage optimization.

Bi-RRT* Based Optimization. For the selection of Bi-RRT*, on the one hand, RRT variants provide established framework (sampling process) to incorporate the predicted path [8]. On the other hand, the used bi-direction extensions in Bi-RRT* will accelerate the convergence for the planning problem in such unconstructed parking scenarios [7]. Our variant method keeps similar process with original framework of Bi-RRT* except for the sampling process and cost metric. Details of Bi-RRT* can be referred to [7] and only sampling strategy and cost metric will be detailed illustrated in this paper.

The purpose of improving sampling strategy is to make up the prediction error and correct possible failures. In order to model the prediction error, we firstly make a statistic analysis. For the results of validation dataset, the prediction error of coordinates (x, y, ϕ) is defined by Eq. 3. We treat each component of E as an independent random variable. The probability density function (PDF) and cumulative distribution function (CDF) curve of E are shown in Fig. 3. It can be observed that the distribution of E is exactly similar to Gaussian.

$$E = (X_e, Y_e, \Phi_e) = (\hat{x} - x, \hat{y} - y, \hat{\phi} - \phi), \quad \hat{p} = 1 \qquad (3)$$

where E denotes the coordinate generalization error. x, y, and ϕ denote the coordinates of a configuration output by the prediction network, $\hat{x}$, $\hat{y}$, and $\hat{\phi}$ denote the coordinates of the ground truth configuration. Therefore, a gaussian model is deployed to show the distribution of prediction error and the P-P plot [6] (probability-probability plot) method is used to model gaussian on each dimension on the assumption x, y, and ϕ are uncorrelated. We take X_e as an example to illustrate the modeling process, as shown in Fig. 4. Specifically, we firstly plot X_e against the theoretical quantiles of the standard Gaussian distribution and then fit a least-squares regression (best-fit) line to X_e to obtain the Best-fit Gaussian model. Finally, we extract the slope and y-intercept of the best-fit line as the deviation and mean of the best-fit Gaussian model.

In order to prove the fitting performance, the modeling result of X_e is shown in Fig. 5. It can be seen that our model can fit the distribution of X_e accurately when the theoretical quantiles are in the range $[-2, 2]$. For the deviation beyond

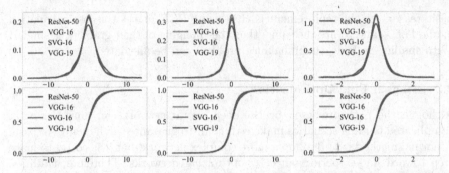

(a) PDF (top) and CD-F (bottom) of random variable X_e.

(b) PDF (top) and CD-F (bottom) of random variable Y_e.

(c) PDF (top) and CD-F (bottom) of random variable Φ_e.

Fig. 3. Probability Density Function (PDF) and Cumulative Distribution Function (CDF) Curve of the prediction error. Different backbones are tested to show the consistence of the distribution of prediction error.

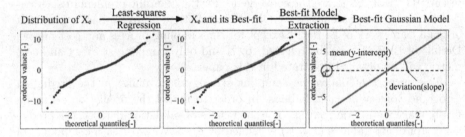

Fig. 4. Modeling procedure of the prediction error.

the range, according to our analysis, the main reason is that the prediction pipeline may predict an alternative feasible solution which are different from the ground truth path, shown as Fig. 6. Therefore, the large deviation does not mean the unfeasible path, which will not affect the sampling process.

With the customized gaussian model of prediction error, the sampling process is developed in Algorithm 1. In Algorithm 1, we firstly obtain the gaussian model from the validation dataset, $\Delta x \sim \mathcal{N}_x(\mu_x, \sigma_x)$, $\Delta y \sim \mathcal{N}_y(\mu_y, \sigma_y)$, $\Delta\theta \sim \mathcal{N}_\theta(\mu_\theta, \sigma_\theta)$. Afterwards, a random configuration (x, y, θ) is selected from the predicted path $\mathcal{P}$ (line 1). Finally, $\mathcal{X}_{rand}$ is obtained by deviating $\Delta x, \Delta y \Delta\theta$ from (x, y, θ) (line 4). Table 1 shows all the parameters of gaussian models of X_e, Y_e, θ_e.

For the case of cost metric, we use the Reed-Shepp curve [12] length as our metric function instead of the straight-line Euclidean distance used in [7]. Compared with widely used Dubins path, Reed-Shepp curve can represent the reverse direction which is a common maneuver in parking scenarios.

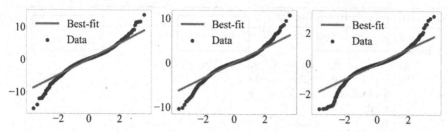

(a) X_e and its Best-fit. (b) Y_e and its Best-fit. (c) Φ_e and its Best-fit.

Fig. 5. The modeling result with the backbone VGG-19.

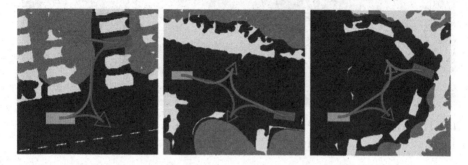

Fig. 6. The Prediction path which is different from ground truth but still be feasible. The red curves and green curves represent the predicted paths and ground-truth paths respectively. The red triangles and green triangles represent the predicted configurations and ground-truth configurations respectively. The purple, cyan, and yellow area represent the feasible, unknown, and obstacle area. The cyan and green rectangles represent the start and goal configurations. (Color figure online)

2.3 Parking Scenarios Dataset

In order to train and validate our pipeline, we make use of CARLA [4] simulator to create a dataset including various and realistic parking scenarios. The dataset consists of four types of scenarios (shown in Fig. 7): regular parking, Semi-regular parking, rural area parking and open field parking. Those basically cover all the typical parking scenarios in real-world.

Algorithm 2 explains building process of the dataset. Firstly, we manually generate a basic parking scenario set including 87 scenarios and each scenario consists of three components: start configuration, goal configuration and the

Table 1. Gaussian parameters of X_e, Y_e, θ_e.

μ_x [m]	σ_x [m]	μ_y [m]	σ_y [m]	μ_ϕ [rad]	σ_ϕ [rad]
0.087	2.436	0.052	1.659	−0.014	0.500

Algorithm 1. SampleFromPath($\mathcal{P}, \mathcal{W}$)

1: $(x, y, \theta) \leftarrow$ SelectConfigurationFromSequence($\mathcal{P}$)
2: **loop**
3:     $\Delta x \leftarrow \mathcal{N}_x(\mu_x, \sigma_x), \Delta y \leftarrow \mathcal{N}_y(\mu_y, \sigma_y), \Delta \theta \leftarrow \mathcal{N}_\theta(\mu_\theta, \sigma_\theta)$
4:     $\mathcal{X}_{rand} \leftarrow (x, y, \theta) + (\Delta x, \Delta y, \Delta \theta)$
5:     **if** CollisionFree($\mathcal{X}_{rand}, \mathcal{W}$) **then**
6:         **break**
7:     **end if**
8: **end loop**
9: **return** $\mathcal{X}_{\text{rand}}$

(a) Regular park-(b) Semi-regular(c) Rural area(d) Open field
ing.   parking.   parking.   parking.

Fig. 7. Four types of scenarios in dataset. Red and green rectangles represent the automobile on the start and goal configurations. (Color figure online)

Algorithm 2. procedure of collecting dataset

1: $Scenarios \leftarrow CARLA_{simulator}$
2: $Scenarios \leftarrow Augment(Scenarios)$
3: **for** $scenario \in Scenarios$ **do**
4:     $Input\_image \leftarrow Depth\_cameras$
5:     $Ground\_truth \leftarrow Best(GBS\_RRT^*, OSE\_RRT^*)$
6: **end for**

distribution (posture and vehicle type) of obstacle vehicles (Line 1). Secondly, we augment the size of the basic set 160 times through randomly biasing the start configuration and changing the distribution of obstacle vehicles (line 2). Afterwards, we build a virtual automobile and a depth camera array to collect sensor data from the parking scenes. The configurations of the used automobile car and the camera array are shown in Fig. 8. Making use of the virtual depth cameras can rapidly produce high-quality 3D point clouds and thus accelerate to generate high-quality occupancy grid maps. Based on the collected sensor data, we then generate the RGB image input (line 4) and the ground truth parking paths. To generate high-quality ground truth path, we make use of two Bi-RRT* [7] planners to plan the parking paths, one is guided by Gaussian Biased

Sampling (GBS) [8] heuristic and the other is guided by Orientation-aware Space Exploration (OSE) [2] heuristic. Finally, we choose the best of the outputs from the two planners as the ground truth path (line 5).

Fig. 8. Used automobile car and depth camera array in CARLA Simulator. For mounted cameras, "[]" contains the Euler angles of a camera and "()" contains the location.

3   Experiments

Firstly, we compare our two-stage method to two state-of-the-art methods: the OSE guided Bi-RRT* [7] and the Bi-RRT* using GBS heuristic, which provide ground-truth path for our prediction network. Secondly, we investigate the performance of our planning method.

3.1   Experimental Setup

We firstly compare with existing other traditional methods to validate our planning effects and then prove that our proposed method is better in planning efficiency and path quality. Afterwards, our planning method will be further analyzed, especially the effects of backbones and the proposed sampling strategy.

3.2   Implementation Details

Both our method and comparison counterparts are implemented in Python and run on a single core of Intel Xeon E5@3.20 GHz. Table 2 lists several important parameters for training and testing the neural network.

Table 2. Parameters for the prediction network

Parameters	Value
size of training dataset	8221 (images)
size of test dataset	2741 (images)
Batch Size	16
Training platform	NVIDIA Tesla P100

3.3 Metrics

Normally, there are two metrics to evaluate the planning performance, the efficiency and quality. For the purpose to evaluate efficiency, we define two metrics:

- mTTFP denotes the mean Time To the First (feasible) Path.
- mTTFP* denotes the mTTFP which doesn't include the run time of the OSE heuristic in OSE guided Bi-RRT* or deep convolutional network in our method.

For the case of path quality, two metrics are used as follows:

- mLOFP denotes the mean Length Of the First Path.
- SR denotes the planning Success Rate of the planner over the test set (including 2741 scenarios)

3.4 Comparison to Other Planning Methods

We compare our method to two methods, OSE guided Bi-RRT* and GBS guided Bi-RRT*. Both OSE guided Bi-RRT* and GBS guided Bi-RRT* are competitive, especially when comparing with learning based methods [1]. For the parameters used in these two methods, we optimize them and make sure they can reach to state-of-the-art performance in our scenarios.

Table 3. Planning performance comparison.

Method	SR [%]	mTTFP [ms]	mLOFP [m]	mTTFP* [ms]
Our method	**99.8**	**76.81**	**24.92**	**53.58**
OSE+Bi-RRT*	99.1	530.44	25.02	74.70
GBS+Bi-RRT*	98.1	166.50	26.83	–

The experimental results are shown in Table 3. It can be observed that our method significantly outperforms two other approaches. Our method not only achieves the highest success rate of 99.8 % but also averagely spends the least time to plan the first feasible paths. For the sampling model used in our method, the best fit parameters of Table 5 are used in our method. Although OSE can achieve similar quality of path with our method, they need to spend more time since it is costly to uniformly sample in the complicated parking scenarios. Moreover, it can also be observed that gaussian sampling strategy which is used both in our method and GBS+Bi-RRT* makes a better trade-off between the time consumption and path quality. Moreover, our scheme outperforms the GBS+Bi-RRT* in computation efficiency and saves nearly 20ms in average. The reason for the high efficiency is the prediction network in our scheme, which can rapidly infer a feasible path from a scenario and has better scenario adaptability. Figure 9 shows several planning samples of our proposed method in different parking scenarios, which further proves our planning scheme can adapt to complicated unstructured environment.

(a) Regular Parking Scenario.   (b) Semi-regular Parking Scenario.

(c) Rural Area Parking Scenario.   (d) Open Field Parking Scenario.

Fig. 9. Planning results of our scheme in different challenging scenarios. Green curves are the planned path and blue and green rectangles represent the start and goal configurations repectively. (Color figure online)

3.5   Planning Performance Analysis

We firstly investigate the impacts of different backbones and then show the effects of gaussian sampling model used in our method.

Impacts of Backbones. The performance of our method with different backbones is shown in Table 4. It can be observed that different backbones mainly influence the planning speed and VGG-19 backbone can bring about 20 ms reduction in the average time to plan the first path when comparing to the ResNet-50 backbone. Therefore, VGG-19 is adopted as our backbone.

Table 4. The performance of prediction network with different backbones.

Backbone	SR [%]	mTTFP [ms]	mLOFP [m]	mTTFP* [ms]
VGG-19	**99.8**	**76.81**	**24.92**	**53.38**
VGG-16	99.7	81.89	25.02	62.31
SVG-16	99.7	84.37	24.97	64.31
ResNet-50	99.5	96.70	25.13	79.22

Effects of Gaussian Sampling Model. In order to show the effects of gaussian sampling model, we compare our model to three other Gaussian sampling models with empirical parameters. Specifically, we manually change the variance of different gaussian models to make the samples deviate from the predicted path to varying degrees. As shown in Table 5, large, middle and small deviation are defined to compare with our established model. The first observation is that our gaussian sampling model can balance the computation efficiency and path quality. When we increase the deviation, a low-quality path is planned and will consume more time to get a path when the deviation is limited to a small range. When we narrow down the sampling space (small), the path quality is increased. However, the successful rate is decreased since excessively limited sampling space may not avoid collision.

Table 5. Comparison of different sampling models. $X(\mu_x,\sigma_x)$, $Y(\mu_y,\sigma_y)$, and $\phi(\mu_\phi,\sigma_\phi)$ denote the (mean, deviation) on x, y, and ϕ dimension of a sampling model.

Model	$X/Y/\phi$	mTTFP [ms]	mLOFP [m]
Best-Fit	$(0.13,2.44)/(0.07,1.78)/(-0.03,0.51)$	**62.31**	25.02
Large	$(0.00,4.00)/(0.00,4.00)/(0.00,1.05)$	66.35	28.04
middle	$(0.00,2.00)/(0.00,2.00)/(0.00,0.52)$	67.98	24.94
small	$(0.00,1.00)/(0.00,1.00)/(0.00,0.26)$	124.54	**23.66**

4   Conclusion

This paper shows that our proposed method can successfully plan feasible and high-quality path in complicated parking scenarios. Nevertheless, we assume that the working environment is rather static and completely known environment. But in real-world, environment is always changing and it is hard to completely sense and model the parking scenario before planning. Thus, dealing with stream input and efficiently replan in dynamic and partially-known environment is an important future task.

Acknowledgement. This research is supported partly by GuangDong Basic and Applied Basic Research Foundation (2020A1515110199), partly by Guangdong HUST Industrial Technology Research Institute Guangdong Provincial Key Laboratory of Manufacturing Equipment Digitization (2020B1212060014) and partly by Shenzhen science and technology program (JCYJ20210324122203009, JCYJ20180508152434975).

References

1. Banzhaf, H., et al.: Learning to predict ego-vehicle poses for sampling-based non-holonomic motion planning. IEEE Robot. Autom. Lett. **4**(2), 1053–1060 (2019)
2. Chen, C., Rickert, M., Knoll, A.: Path planning with orientation-aware space exploration guided heuristic search for autonomous parking and maneuvering. In 2015 IEEE Intelligent Vehicles Symposium (IV), pp. 1148–1153. IEEE (2015)
3. Chen, G., et al.: Multiobjective scheduling strategy with genetic algorithm and time-enhanced a* planning for autonomous parking robotics in high-density unmanned parking lots. IEEE/ASME Trans. Mechatron. **26**(3), 1547–1557 (2021)
4. Dosovitskiy, A., et al.: CARLA: an open urban driving simulator. arXiv preprint arXiv:1711.03938 (2017)
5. Zhuo, D., Miao, Q., Zong, C.: Trajectory planning for automated parking systems using deep reinforcement learning. Int. J. Automot. Technol. **21**(4), 881–887 (2020)
6. Gibbons, J.D., Chakraborti, S.: Nonparametric Statistical Inference: revised and Expanded. CRC Press (2014)
7. Jordan, M., Perez, A.: Optimal bidirectional rapidly-exploring random trees (2013)
8. Kuwata, Y., et al.: Motion planning for urban driving using RRT. In: 2008 IEEE/RSJ International Conference on Intelligent Robots and Systems, pp. 1681–1686. IEEE (2008)
9. Liu, C., Wang, Y., Tomizuka, M.: Boundary layer heuristic for search-based non-holonomic path planning in maze-like environments. In: Intelligent Vehicles Symposium (2017)
10. Pérez-Higueras, N., Caballero, F., Merino, L.: Learning human-aware path planning with fully convolutional networks. In: 2018 IEEE International Conference on Robotics and Automation (ICRA), pp. 1–5. IEEE (2018)
11. Redmon, J., Farhadi, A.: YOLOv3: an incremental improvement. arXiv preprint arXiv:1804.02767 (2018)
12. Reeds, J., Shepp, L.: Optimal paths for a car that goes both forwards and backwards. Pac. J. Math. **145**(2), 367–393 (1990)
13. Tian, W., Salscheider, N.O., Shan, Y., Chen, L., Lauer, M.: A collaborative visual tracking architecture for correlation filter and convolutional neural network learning. IEEE Transactions on Intelligent Transportation Systems (2019)

Recommendations for Urban Planning Based on Non-motorized Travel Data and Street Comfort

Linfeng Xie, Zhiyong Yu, Fangwan Huang, and Daoye Zhu[✉]

College of Computer and Data Science, Fuzhou University, Fuzhou 350108, China
zhudaoye@fzu.edu.cn

Abstract. Urban open spaces provides various benefits to citizens, but the thermal environment under this space is being affected by the accelerated urbanization and global warming. Based on this, this paper is dedicated to conducting research on improving the attractiveness of outdoor environmental spaces and improving outdoor thermal comfort. The main work of this paper is first to propose a street comfort model by considering both environmental and climatic factors, which is trained to learn using indirect data. Secondly, the comfort level of each street is combined with the frequency of non-motorized trips on that street to obtain the urgency index of rectification for that street and to achieve accurate recommendations for urban planning. Considering the public accessibility of the data in the paper in cities across China, this study can be easily deployed to other cities to support urban planning and provide useful recommendations for improvement of urban open spaces.

Keywords: Indirect learning · Street solar radiation value · Street comfort model · Street rectification urgency index

1 Introduction

With warming and urbanization, heat is increasing globally, especially in large cities with high population mobility. One of the biggest difficulties for future urban planning is to develop and protect cities to make them livable and sustainable. Outdoor comfort is an important evaluation indicator for urban planning as well as for architectural design. An increase in outdoor comfort is often accompanied by an increase in the number of hours residents spend outdoors, which also means an increase in urban vitality. As the research on urban climate has intensified, scholars have also paid more attention to how to create more comfortable outdoor spaces in order to improve the service efficiency of urban outdoor spaces.

Most of the studies on urban outdoor comfort have been conducted on the whole city or the whole area. However, this paper considers that after excluding parks and amusement parks, which are open-air entertainment and recreation places, the traffic axis is the largest piece of urban open spaces, so this paper locks the scope to the street level to study the comfort of streets. The work in this paper can be divided into the following two steps: 1. Integrate both environmental and climatic factors to propose a street comfort model. 2. Combine the comfort level of each street with the frequency of non-motorized trips on that street to get the urgency index of rectification for that street and achieve accurate recommendation for urban planning.

In terms of environmental factors, this paper considers the degree of street greenery. Greenery is one of the effective means to promote the adoption of non-motorized travel activities by citizens, and exists in various forms in streets, including trees, environmental zones, and green walls. Traditional urban greenery measurement methods cannot encompass all forms of greenery and cannot accurately reflect the degree of pedestrian visibility of greenery. Therefore, this paper uses the panoramic image and semantic segmentation method of Baidu Street View (BSV) to calculate the Green View Index (GVI) with reference to the pedestrian's visual perspective to improve the comprehensiveness of the quantitative representation of street greenery. As for the climatic factors, in addition to the conventional temperature and humidity, this paper also considers the street-level solar radiation. It depicts the horizontal solar radiation of each street per hour, which can well represent the exposure of residents to sunlight. Considering that the street orientation has a significant effect on the radiation value, this paper first obtains the street orientation by road network calculation, and then adds it to the existing radiation estimation method based on street images [1] to improve the accuracy of estimating the street-level solar radiation value. Finally, the comfort value of each street is obtained by using a street comfort model by considering both environmental and climatic factors.

In urban planning, considering that both street comfort and non-motorized travel data are spatio-temporally heterogeneous and can reflect the detailed situation of each street at each time, this paper combines the comfort value of each street and the frequency of non-motorized travel of that street to obtain a reasonable street rectification urgency index. Finally, using the ranking of this index and combining detailed research and discussion analysis, we propose targeted suggestions for the rectification of existing roads in the city.

2 Related Work

2.1 Estimation of Street Solar Radiation Values

For the calculation of street solar radiation values, the two main traditional methods are inversion by remotely sensed data and calculation by digital urban models. Different metrics such as canopy cover and vegetation index can be calculated from remotely sensed images to indicate the microclimate regulation of urban vegetation [2] and added to the estimation of solar radiation at ground level. However, it is difficult to simulate the solar radiation reaching the ground with only the remote sensing data overhead. This is because the vertical structure of the street canopy and other urban features under the street canopy affect the solar radiation within the street, which are not reflected in the high-view remote sensing data [3]. On the other hand, with the advent of high-resolution digital city models, it is possible to simulate the transmission of solar radiation within the streets. However, most digital city models oversimplify the complex geometry within the city streets [4]. Recently, street view images provided by online maps such as Google Maps, Baidu Maps, Tencent Maps, and Mapillary have provided a novel and low-cost data source for urban studies. These street view image data enable a more comprehensive description of high-density street patterns to address the shortcomings of the two traditional methods mentioned above. This computational approach first originated from the thermal comfort model proposed by RayMan [5] in 2007, who converted the manually taken streetscape photos into Sky View Factor (SVF) and then added the calculation of horizontal street radiation. Since then, with the development of deep learning technology and the opening of street view images on the Internet, more studies based on this idea have started to study the distribution of street level radiation throughout the city [1, 6] and use it to make suggestions for urban planning. In this paper, borrowing from Deng Mingyu et al.'s method [7], we use deep learning techniques to process Baidu street view images so as to derive the sky visibility, and then use this parameter to estimate the solar radiation at street level, while the innovation is to include the preprocessing of street direction in the calculation process.

2.2 Comfort Model

Currently available comfort models use two main types of objective elements: local climatic factors and urban environmental parameters. Unfortunately, the existing models model only one of these categories and do not consider both at the same time. For example, the Physiological Equivalent Temperature (PET) [8], the Predicted Mean Vote (PMV) [9], the Universal Thermal Climate Index (UTCI) [10] and Standard Effective Temperature (SET) [11] are the four most commonly used comfort assessment models [12], all of which use only climatic factors in the objective elements part. While studies by Mohammad Fahmy [13] and Hongxuan Zhou [14] et al. used only urban environmental parameters.

For traditional modeling of comfort models, there are mainly empirical modeling based on theoretical knowledge and traditional supervised learning methods, which often require large costs to acquire data. For example, the fully connected neural network model used by Dyvia [15] and the K-Nearest Neighbor (KNN) used by Lei Xiong [16] are trained based on known PMV values. However, the comfort model proposed in this paper is characterized by parameter diversity, and if supervised learning is used, a large number of questionnaire research results are required to label the data, which is time-consuming and labor-intensive. In order to solve the above problems, this paper proposes to construct a complete closed network model based on indirect data first, and then extract the intrinsic relationship between street environment factors and street comfort through the overall model, so that the comfort model to be constructed can be obtained.

3 Method

The purpose of this paper is to construct a street comfort model that considers both environment and climate, and to combine it with street pedestrian flow to generate street rectification urgency indicators to provide reliable suggestions for urban planning and rectification. The methodological framework of this study is shown in Fig. 1 and consists of three main stages. In the first stage, SVF and GVI are first estimated from Baidu Street View panoramic images, and then SVF is combined with street direction, sun path and extraterrestrial solar radiation to calculate street-level solar radiation values. In the second stage, a neural network is constructed based on indirect learning with environmental factors, climate factors, and non-motorized travel data as inputs, from which a comfort model is extracted. In the third stage, a set of streets with low comfort level and high pedestrian traffic is obtained by constructing a street rectification urgency index and fed back to the city planning department.

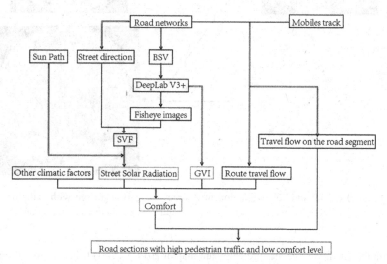

Fig. 1. Research framework for urban planning recommendations based on non-motorized travel data and street comfort.

3.1 Estimation of Street Solar Radiation Values Based on Baidu Street View Map

In this section, the method of using BSV images to estimate the street solar radiation values will be described. It consists of three main parts: (1) generating fisheye images from BSV panoramic images and calculating SVF, (2) obtaining solar irradiation from sun path map and fisheye images, and (3) estimating street solar radiation values.

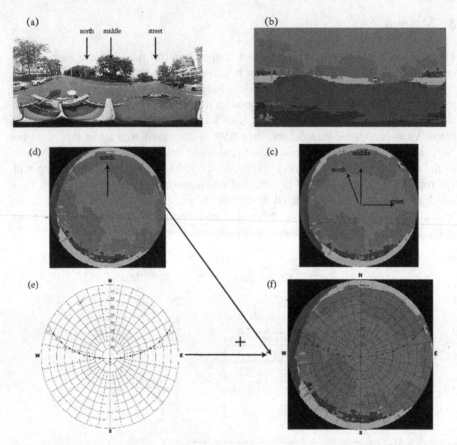

Fig. 2. Flow of calculating solar radiation of a street using BSV image with sampling point (119.2845351, 26.0041302) as an example. (a) panoramic image obtained using Baidu Map API; (b) panoramic map obtained by DeepLab V3+; (c) fisheye map converted from the panoramic map; (d) fisheye map obtained by considering the street direction and rotating figure (c) to face upward in the due north direction; (e) sun path map of 2017-6-15; (f) fisheye map (d) with the street direction considered and the sun path diagram (e) superimposed on the diagram.

3.1.1 Generate Fisheye Images from BSV Panoramic Images and Calculate Sky Visibility

In real roads, the solar radiation values reaching the ground are influenced by shading such as buildings and trees. The traditional way to calculate radiation is to use remote sensing data or urban modeling to estimate it, but both of them use top-down calculation, which does not describe the shading of trees and buildings in the street well. Based on this, this paper proposes to use a bottom-up approach to calculate solar radiation values.

The SVF measures the proportion of the sky seen at a location in the street; a smaller SVF means more occlusion at that location point, and vice versa means less occlusion. Using fisheye images to calculate the SVF is more in line with the real street view [7]. Taking Fig. 2 as an example, the specific approach is as follows: (1) the panoramic image of Fig. 2(a) is obtained using Baidu Map API; (2) the extraction of street elements such as trees, green, sky, and buildings is completed by DeepLab V3+ model [17], as shown in Fig. 2(b), where orange represents the sky, black represents the background, and green, red, etc. represent other street elements; (3) according to the method proposed by XiaoJiang Li [6], the panoramic image is converted into a fisheye image, as shown in Fig. 2(c); (4) SVF can be expressed by the percentage of pixels representing the sky in the fisheye image, and the calculation equation is as follows.

$$\text{SVF} = \frac{\text{number of sky pixels}}{\text{number of total pixels } - \text{ number of background pixels}} \tag{1}$$

3.1.2 Acquisition of Solar Irradiation from Sun Path and Fisheye Images

Street alignment affects the timing of exposure to direct sunlight. In north-south oriented streets, the street surface will be exposed to direct sunlight near noon, but will be influenced by shading at other times. However, in east-west oriented streets, it is more likely to be exposed to direct sunlight all day from morning to afternoon [1]. In order to reduce the effect of street orientation, the literature [6] proposes to rotate the fisheye map so that it has the same coordinate system as the sun path map. This method uses the Google Street View (GSV) panoramic image because Google Maps has an interface to provide the return street orientation. However, the coverage of GSV panoramic image for Chinese road network is seriously insufficient, so this paper uses BSV panoramic image, which has significantly higher coverage than GSV panoramic image, see Fig. 3 for details. Unfortunately, Baidu map does not provide the street direction data, so this paper proposes a processing method to obtain the street direction.

First, sampling points are generated on the road network at 50 m equal intervals, as shown in Fig. 4(a). Then the road network is segmented with these sampling points on the arcgis software, and a road section is generated between every two adjacent sampling points, followed by the direction line of the road section, as shown in Fig. 4(b), from which the street orientation $\theta°$ can be obtained. The clockwise deflection $\theta°$ in the due north direction is the direction of the street where it is located. Finally, the fisheye image in Fig. 2(c) is rotated by $(450°-\theta°)\%360°$ ("%" means taking the remainder) to obtain Fig. 2(d). The rotated fisheye image will have the same coordinate system as the sun path map.

The sun path map is generated by Rayman software [5] after inputting the position and date, as shown in Fig. 2(e), where the points in the map represent the position of the sun at a given moment. Finally, overlaying the sun path diagram with a fisheye diagram considering the street direction yields Fig. 2(f), so that the sun exposure at each moment (i.e., whether the sun is blocked or not) can finally be determined.

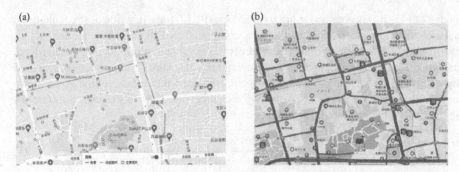

Fig. 3. Coverage of panoramic images in Google Maps and Baidu Maps. (a) Google Maps, the locations marked with circles represent the presence of panoramic images; (b) Baidu Maps, the road sections marked with dark blue represent the presence of panoramic images.

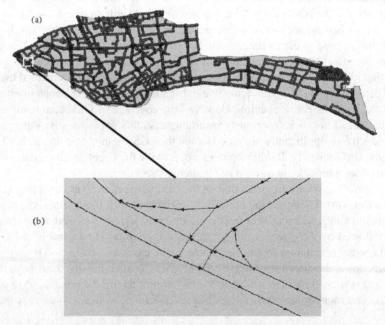

Fig. 4. Street directions (a) Sampling points generated along a street; (b) Street directions generated by a subregion based on a road segment.

3.1.3 Estimated Street Solar Radiation Values

Solar radiation in the transmission process can be divided into direct radiation, reflected radiation and diffuse radiation. Since the reflected radiation accounts for a very small proportion of the total radiation, the total radiation (G_{street}) is often equivalent to the sum of direct radiation (I_{street}) and diffuse radiation (D_{street}) [7], as shown in Eq. (2).

$$G_{street} = I_{street} + D_{street} \qquad (2)$$

The formula for calculating I_{street} is as follows.

$$I_{street} = I_{open} * f \tag{3}$$

I_{open} is the direct radiation under the free field of view, the calculation method can be found in the literature [1]; f is a binary variable, as shown in Fig. 2(f), if a point belonging to a moment in the sun path diagram is in the region where the sky is located (i.e., the moment point is in the orange region), it represents not blocked by obstacles, at this time the value is 1, anyway, it is 0.

The formula for calculating D_{street} is as follows.

$$D_{street} = D_{iso\_open} * \psi_{sky} + D_{aniso\_open} * f + D_{cloud\_open} * \psi_{sky} \tag{4}$$

D_{iso_open} is the isotropic diffuse radiation on the horizontal surface in the free horizon; D_{aniso_open} is the anisotropic diffuse radiation on the horizontal surface in the free horizon, which tends to concentrate near the Sun and is distinguished according to whether the Sun is directly visible or not; D_{cloud_open} is the diffuse radiation on the horizontal surface in the free horizon due to cloud cover; The calculation of the above three can be found in the literature [1]. ψ_{sky} is the SVF, and the specific calculation procedure is described in Subsect. 3.1.1; The description of f is detailed in Eq. (3).

3.2 Model for Calculating GVI

Urban greening will provide a variety of benefits to citizens, including physical, environmental and social benefits, thus promoting urban livability and vitality [19] and making urban open spaces more attractive. Among them, the impact of street greening on comfort is mainly reflected in two aspects: 1. Street greening, as an important part of street spaces planning and design, has been proven by numerous studies to be an important way to improve the thermal comfort of street spaces [20]. Therefore, it is important to investigate the mechanism of the effect of street greening on outdoor comfort to better utilize street planting design to improve pedestrian thermal comfort. 2. Studies have shown that residents' exposure to natural and semi-natural environments, whether long-term or short-term, can have certain benefits on physical and mental health [21]. A Japanese study analyzed the 5-year survival rate of 3144 elderly people and concluded that walkable urban green spaces have a positive impact on extending the life expectancy of urban elderly [22]. In addition to physical health benefits, urban greenery can also provide a sense of social support to residents. by measuring social contact and health status of 10,089 residents in the Netherlands, Maas et al. found that a large number of outdoor green spaces can reduce loneliness [23], as well as enhance the quality of life and well-being of residents [24, 25].

GVI is the proportion of greenery visible from a given location. In this paper, GVI will be used to quantify street greenery. Since GVI is mainly for green vegetation within the visual range of pedestrians on the street, and the top and bottom of the panoramic image also have more serious distortion, it is necessary to set the range of the visual fence and keep the middle part of the image with less distortion. In this paper, the method of Yin et al. [2] is adopted, and the part of the panoramic image corresponding to the pedestrian view with less distortion is cropped and utilized, as shown in Fig. 5.

Fig. 5. A figure caption is always placed below the illustration. Short captions are centered, while long ones are justified. The macro button chooses the correct format automatically.

The GVI can be calculated by Eq. (5), and the total number of pixels and the number of green pixels are for the blue area in Fig. 5. The GVI of the sampled points is calculated and then correlated to the road of the area where they are located, and the GVI distribution of the whole area can be obtained, as shown in Fig. 6.

$$GVI = \frac{\text{number of green pixels}}{\text{number of total pixels}} \tag{5}$$

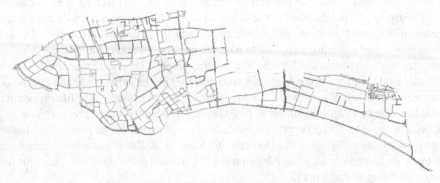

Fig. 6. GVI distribution of the whole region.

3.3   Indirect Learning Based Comfort Model Construction

Traditional outdoor comfort models mainly focus on thermal comfort as well as visual comfort, but less consider these two together. Based on this, this paper proposes a neural network model based on indirect learning to construct a new comfort model. First, the constructed comfort model considers both visual and thermal comfort factors, and concentrates on the street level, which is finer in granularity than previous work. Second, unlike previous supervised learning methods or empirical modeling based on theoretical knowledge, the comfort model proposed in this paper uses indirect learning to extract the intrinsic relationship between street environment factors and street comfort. This approach was mainly used in cases where experimental results require large computational costs or where experimental results are more difficult to obtain [26]. Given the very high cost and operational difficulty of obtaining street comfort by means of questionnaires, this paper adopts an indirect learning-based approach to construct a street comfort model. This is done by treating the street comfort model as a sub-network of the overall model, and the overall model is obtained using supervised learning. When the training of the overall model is completed, it can be approximated that its sub-network has also completed training.

In this section, the closed-form solution of the comfort model will be illustrated, discussing the overall model construction process. First of all, it is necessary to explain that residents receive two main factors for travel, which are subjective travel purpose and objective external factors. The subjective travel purpose can be reflected in the individual's travel intentions or in the trajectory data by the routes connected to the origin and destination points. For example, trips to work are generally not affected by personal travel intentions and usually have an inherent travel route from home to work, while trips for leisure purposes such as walking and exercising are more affected by personal travel intentions and usually have a route from the leisure place to other locations. Thus, this paper considers that travel trajectories with the same origin and destination points have the same travel purpose. The objective external factors are considered as climate factors and street environment factors.

Since the final travel data will be influenced by both subjective and objective factors, and the comfort model proposed in this paper is only influenced by objective factors, the influence of subjective factors needs to be quantified in the process. From the description in the previous paragraph, it can be seen that the subjective factors can be quantified by the origin and destination points, i.e., the influence of subjective factors can be considered fixed under the premise of having the same origin and destination points or the same travel routes. From this, two data features can be further elicited, the length of the travel route and y_{ideal}, y_{ideal} represents the ideal number of people traveling under a particular travel route. For y_{ideal}, it can be understood that the ideal value of the number of travelers on a certain route, under the condition that the external environment is all in ideal conditions, should satisfy $y_{ideal} \geq y_{realty}$, y_{realty} is the actual number of travelers on a certain route at a certain moment. Given that y_{realty} is unavailable data, the maximum value of $\max(y_{realty})$ will be used as an approximation of y_{ideal} in the subsequent study of this paper.

In summary, this paper proposes a solution that allows the measurement of the relationship between street environmental factors and street comfort ontology and is represented as a neural network, as shown in Fig. 7. The overall model of the solution is constructed by the two modules F1 and F2 together. One of the modules, F1, is the comfort model to be constructed in this paper, and its output node values are the comfort values. As mentioned in the previous paragraph, residents' trips are mainly influenced by subjective trip purpose y_{ideal} and objective external factors, while the F2 module constructs the relationship between these data features in the form of a neural network. The y_{realty} is a quantitative representation of the residents' travel data; the weeks represent the weeks of the year, expressing the temporal order of the input data; the path length represents the length of a travel route.

Although the purpose of this paper is to construct a comfort model, the participation of the real values of comfort is not required in the model training process, but the comfort model is obtained indirectly by learning from the other data features mentioned above. In this paper, we first perform supervised learning of the overall model, with the six objective factor features in the F1 model and the three features y_{ideal}, weeks and path length in the F2 module as input features, and y_{realty} as output features. Wait for the overall model training to converge before extracting the weights of the F1 module, and use the network model of the F1 module as the final comfort model.

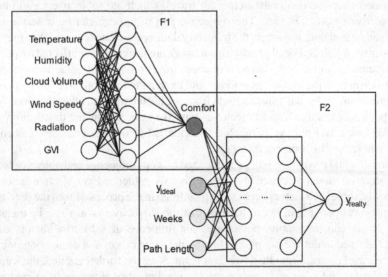

Fig. 7. Overall model including comfort model.

3.4 Methodology for Estimating Street Correction Urgency Indicators

The purpose of calculating the street correction urgency indicator is to identify a set of road sections with high pedestrian flow and low comfort level, and to provide targeted suggestions for the street component of urban planning. For this indicator, two main factors are considered, count and comfort, where count is obtained statistically and refers to the pedestrian flow of a road section over a certain period of time, and comfort is calculated by the comfort model constructed in Subsect. 3.3. Since the range of values of the two results for count and comfort may be very different, the two features are first normalized in this paper. Then each is classified into 5 levels according to the values, as shown in Eq. (6). The final street improvement urgency index is obtained by multiplying the ranks of these two features, as shown in Eq. (7). Urgency is larger to indicate that the street improvement is more urgent.

$$F(x) = \begin{cases} 1, & \text{MinmaxScaler}(x) \in [0, 0.2) \\ 2, & \text{MinmaxScaler}(x) \in [0.2, 0.4) \\ 3, & \text{MinmaxScaler}(x) \in [0.4, 0.6) \\ 4, & \text{MinmaxScaler}(x) \in [0.6, 0.8) \\ 5, & \text{MinmaxScaler}(x) \in [0.8, 1] \end{cases} \tag{6}$$

where MinmaxScaler(.) is the normalization function.

$$\text{urgency} = F(\text{comfort}) * F(\text{count}) \tag{7}$$

4 Experimental Design and Results Analysis

4.1 Experimental Design

4.1.1 Study Area

In this paper, relevant experiments were conducted in Taijiang District, Fuzhou City, Fujian Province. Fuzhou City is located in the eastern part of Fujian Province and has a typical subtropical monsoon climate. According to the Statistical Bulletin of National Economic and Social Development of Fuzhou City in 2021, the resident population of Fuzhou is 8.42 million. As a typical representative city with hot summers and warm winters, Fuzhou has an annual average of 32.6 days of high temperature in the past 30 years, and has been crowned as the "top furnace city". According to the data provided by Fujian Meteorological Bulletin, Fujian Province experienced 13 high temperature processes in 2020, with the highest extreme temperature in the province occurring in Fuzhou City [27]. The large resident population and the hot climate factors make Fuzhou city a suitable area for this paper to study summer comfort.

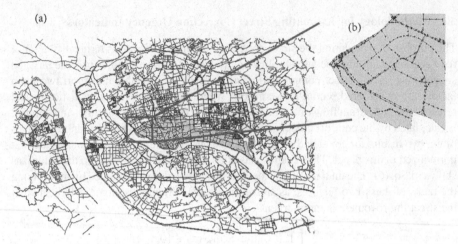

Fig. 8. Location and map of the study area (a) Location of the main urban areas in Fuzhou City, the area marked in green is the Taijiang District to be studied in this paper. (b) Sampling points generated along the streets with 50 m interval, total 5361 points.

4.1.2 Data Collection

The datasets used in this paper include (1) Fuzhou city street vector map, as shown in Fig. 8(a), from OpenStreetMap (https://www.openstreetmap.org). (2) Hourly meteorological data from June 2017 to September 2017, including temperature, humidity, wind speed, and cloudiness, from World Weather (https://rp5.ru/). (3) Hourly total solar radiation as well as direct radiation in Fuzhou City from June 2017 to September 2017 were obtained from the Xiehe Energy Platform (https://www.xihe-energy.com/). (4) Solar zenith angle and extraterrestrial radiation data. They can be obtained by entering the location, time zone, and date in the interface provided by the National Renewable Energy Laboratory (https://midcdmz.nrel.gov/solpos/solpos.html). (5) Trajectory data of pedestrians traveling with Mobiles, provided by the Fuzhou Municipal Bureau of Transportation. (6) Panoramic image of Baidu street view.

The BSV panoramic image is acquired in two steps: (1) Generate sampling points along the street with an average sampling distance of about 50 m, as shown in Fig. 8(b). (2) The BSV panoramic images of each sampling point are acquired using the API interface provided by Baidu Maps (https://lbsyun.baidu.com/index.php?title=viewstatic). Finally, 5361 valid street panoramas were obtained.

4.2 Experimental Results

4.2.1 Validation of the Effect of Street Direction Treatment

Buildings and trees along the street can block the sun's rays. The sun rises in the east and sets in the west, so this phenomenon is especially obvious for streets running north-south, while streets running east-west are less affected by this phenomenon, so the street orientation is a factor that cannot be ignored when calculating solar radiation at the street level. This section will verify the validity of the street orientation treatment proposed in Subsect. 3.1.2.

Figure 9 shows the data for location point 5 in Fig. 10, which is located on a street that runs east-west and has a dormitory building on one side of the road. From Fig. 9(c), it can be seen that the estimated solar radiation before 8 o'clock is significantly lower when street direction processing is not added. The reason for this is that if the solar radiation value is estimated directly from the fisheye map obtained from the Baidu Map street view image (i.e., Fig. 9(a)), the solar radiation before 8:00 is considered to be blocked by buildings. However, the street actually runs east-west and the sunlight is not blocked in the morning. Figure 9(b) shows the fisheye diagram generated by adding the street orientation processing, from which the estimated solar radiation is obtained as shown in the orange curve in Fig. 9(c). It is clear that the orange curve can better fit the true value of solar radiation during the 6:00–9:00 h.

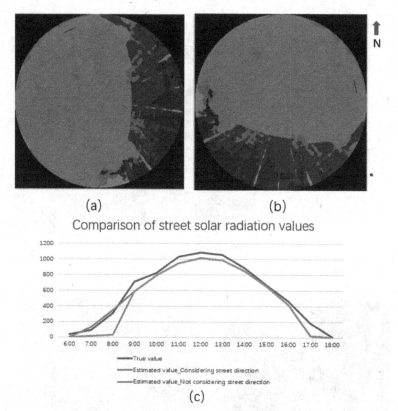

(a)   (b)

Comparison of street solar radiation values

True value
Estimated value_Considering street direction
Estimated value_Not considering street direction

(c)

Fig. 9. Street direction (a) Fisheye map obtained by direct processing from Baidu Map Street View image without additional consideration of street direction; (b) Fisheye map obtained by additional processing with street direction on top of Baidu Map Street View image; (c) Comparison of street-level solar radiation values. (Color figure online)

48   L. Xie et al.

4.2.2 Performance Evaluation of Methods for Estimating Solar Radiation Values in Streets

In this section, the BSV-based solar radiation estimation method will be evaluated using data measured in the field. The authors measured the real data of street solar radiation with solar radiation detection instruments on the campus of Fuzhou University on two days, 2022.07.26 and 2022.07.30. Due to the problem of rainfall, radiation data were not collected for the intermediate days. The measurement location points are shown in Fig. 10(a), there are 6 location points, and each location corresponds to the measurement reality as shown in Fig. 10(b). The following two factors are taken into consideration when selecting the location points: the street direction and the blockage of solar radiation by the buildings beside the road. As shown in Fig. 10(a), location 2, 4, and 6 are located in the north-south direction, and trees are planted on both sides of location 2 and 4, which will block the sunlight in the morning or evening. The trees on the right side of location

(a)   (b)

(c)   (d)

Fig. 10. Live map of the measurement sites located on the Fuzhou University campus. (a) Location of the measurement site on the map; (b) live street view of the corresponding location point; (c) live street view of location point 1 in 2019; (d) live street view of location point 1 in 2022.

6 and the dormitory building on the left side also block the sunlight in the morning and evening. Locations 1, 3, and 5 are located in the east-west direction, but location 1 has a thicker tree shade, location 3 has almost no shade, and there is a dormitory building on the side of location 5.

Figures 11 and 12 show the differences between the real and estimated values of street solar radiation for two days, 2022.07.26 and 2022.07.30, respectively. From the figures, it can be seen that the estimated street radiation values at locations 3 and 5 can fit the true values well. The true values of position 4 at 9:00 and position 5 at 10:00 in Fig. 11 are significantly lower than the estimated values, which may be caused by the sudden passing of clouds in the sky. The deviation between the estimated and true values of location 1, 2 and location 6 at 14:00 may be due to the fact that the street view image in Baidu Maps was updated in 2019, and the trees have grown during these years, thus blocking more sunlight and reducing direct radiation, which in turn causes the true value of radiation to be lower than the estimated value at some times. Taking location 1 as an example, Fig. 10(c) and Fig. 10(d) represent the actual road map of location 1 in 2019 and 2022 respectively, and it can be clearly seen that the trees on both sides of the road in 2022 have grown very densely compared to the road condition in 2019, leaving only a small gap for direct sunlight to pass through.

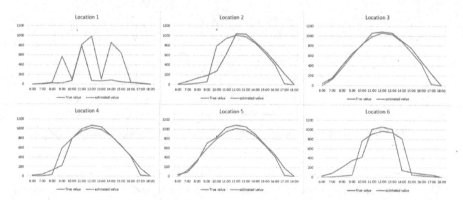

Fig. 11. 2022.07.26 Comparison plot of the real and BSV-based solar radiation estimates of street solar radiation detected at measurement sites located on the Fuzhou University campus.

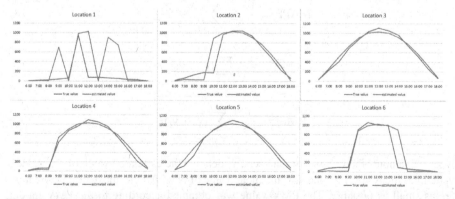

Fig. 12. 2022.07.30 Comparison plot of the true and BSV-based solar radiation estimates of street solar radiation detected at measurement sites located on the Fuzhou University campus.

4.2.3 Constructing a Comfort Model Based on Indirect Data for Performance Evaluation

Since the proposed multiparameter comfort model in this paper lacks labels for supervised learning and performance evaluation, this section will demonstrate the effectiveness of the multiparameter comfort model by verifying the feasibility of the method of constructing a comfort model based on indirect learning. Based on the fact that most outdoor comfort models refer specifically to thermal comfort models, this paper will first construct the conventional thermal comfort model (shown in Fig. 13) through indirect learning and compare its performance with the supervised model proposed by Dyvia.

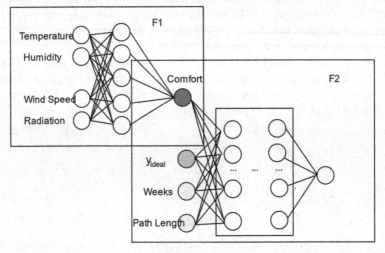

Fig. 13. Construction of thermal comfort model based on indirect learning.

The evaluation indexes used in this paper include: Mean Absolute Percentage Error (MAPE), Mean Absolute Error (MAE) and Root Mean Square Error (RMSE), which are calculated as follows.

$$\text{MAPE} = \frac{100\%}{N} \sum_{i=1}^{N} \left| \frac{\tilde{y}_i - y_i}{y_i} \right| \tag{8}$$

$$\text{MAE} = \frac{1}{N} \sum_{i=1}^{N} |\tilde{y}_i - y_i| \tag{9}$$

$$\text{RMSE} = \sqrt{\frac{1}{N} \sum_{i=1}^{N} (y_i - \tilde{y}_i)^2} \tag{10}$$

where N denotes the number of data sets, $\tilde{y}_i$ denotes the estimated value of the model, y_i denotes the true value, and $\bar{y}_i$ is the mean value of N y_i. All the above three indicators are as small as possible. The PMV value was obtained according to the PMV model proposed by Professor P.O. Fanger from Denmark. The PMV value is an evaluation index characterizing the human thermal response (hot and cold sensation) and represents the average hot and cold sensation of most people in the same environment. This index takes into account six factors such as human activity level, clothing thermal resistance, air temperature, air humidity, average radiation temperature, and air flow rate, etc. Rayman et al. [5] developed a software for calculating PMV values based on this, which will also be used in this paper. When processing the input data, this paper fixes the values affected by individual factors to ensure that the generated PMV values are only affected by four external environmental factors: temperature, humidity, wind speed, and radiation. The final 122 data were generated, containing 61 PMV values at 8:00 am for each day from June to July 2017 and 61 PMV values at 14:00 pm for each day from June to July 2017.

It should be noted that since the comfort value and pedestrian flow are treated in a graded manner during the subsequent calculation of the street rectification urgency index, the evaluation requirement of the comfort model in this paper is to ensure that the comfort value is on the correct grade. Based on this, both $\tilde{y}_i$ and y_i are normalized and graded in this paper before calculating the three evaluation indexes mentioned above. The experimental results are shown in Table 1. It is easy to find that although there is a certain gap between the estimated values of the comfort model constructed based on indirect learning and the estimated values of the model constructed by the supervised learning method, the gap is within an acceptable range. The supervised learning-based network model has real PMV values as labels for network training, while the indirect learning-based network model does not have PMV values as labels, so it is normal for the supervised learning-based method to outperform the indirect learning-based method. Given the small difference in the evaluation metrics calculated by the two models, it shows the feasibility of the indirect learning-based approach to constructing the comfort model.

Table 1. Comparison of model estimates with PMV values.

Contrast Model	MAPE	MAE	RMSE
Thermal comfort model constructed based on indirect learning	20.6844	0.4475	0.7114
Thermal comfort model constructed based on supervised learning	12.7951	0.2508	0.5182

4.2.4 Validation of the Effectiveness of Street Correction Urgency Indicators

The road network in Taijiang District, Fuzhou City, is divided at 50 m intervals to obtain 1962 road sections, and then the score of each road section is calculated according to the calculation of the street improvement urgency index in Sect. 3.4. The top 100 road sections are first taken, marked in red and visualized in the road network to obtain Fig. 14(b). Figure 14(a) shows the distribution of pedestrian flow on the street, the darker the color of the road section means the higher the pedestrian flow, and several road sections with particularly high pedestrian flow also show obvious red color in

Fig. 14(b), indicating that the high value of the urgency of improvement index of these road sections is mainly caused by the abnormally high pedestrian flow.

After excluding the above-mentioned high-traffic streets, five locations were randomly selected, as shown in Fig. 14(b), and it can be seen that these locations are characterized by less vegetation on both sides and wider roads. From the left side to the right side of the map, the five locations have office buildings, intersections, Wuyi Square, schools, and Wanda Square next to each other, and the pedestrian flow in these locations is obviously larger than that in other unusual streets. This result proves that the calculation of the street improvement urgency index is reasonable.

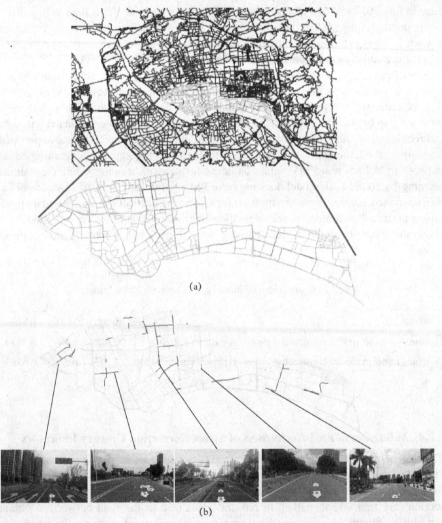

(a)

(b)

Fig. 14. (a) Street traffic distribution map. (b) Visualization of street rectification urgency indicators.

5 Summary

This paper develops a computational framework for constructing an outdoor comfort model and depicting the urgency indicators of street rectification. The framework has several advantages: (1) The construction of the street comfort model is based on indirect data for modeling, which can well solve the problems of difficulty in obtaining comfort values and high cost of obtaining them. (2) The street comfort model takes into account both visual and environmental factors and is more comprehensive. (3) In terms of environmental factors, street-level solar radiation, a weather data, is used to capture the dynamic changes of urban streets in a more fine-grained manner. (4) The street-level solar radiation is made more accurate by adding the processing of street direction in the estimation of street-level solar radiation based on BSV. (5) The proposed street rectification urgency index can reveal the road sections with high pedestrian flow and low street comfort, which facilitates urban planning. The accuracy and validity of the method are verified by taking Taijiang District, Fuzhou, China, as an example.

The public nature of the data in this paper and the proposed low-cost and efficient modeling approach make it applicable to other cities. At the same time, the generated data and maps provide a useful dataset for understanding complex urban systems.

References

1. Gong, F.-Y., Zeng, Z.-C., Ng, E., Norford, L.K.: Spatiotemporal patterns of street-level solar radiation estimated using Google Street View in a high-density urban environment. Build. Environ. **148** (2019)
2. Kong, F., Yin, H., Wang, C., Cavan, G., James, P.: A satellite image-based analysis of factors contributing to the green-space cool island intensity on a city scale. Urban For. Urban Green. **13**(4), 846–853 (2014a)
3. Li, X., Ratti, C., Seiferling, I.: Quantifying the shade provision of street trees in urban landscape: a case study in Boston, USA, using Google Street View. Landsc. Urban Plan. **169**, 81–91 (2018)
4. Carrasco-Hernandez, R., Smedley, A.R., Webb, A.R.: Using urban canyon geometries obtained from Google Street View for atmospheric studies: potential applications in the calculation of street level total shortwave irradiances. Energy Build. **86**, 340–348 (2015)
5. Matzarakis, A., Rutz, F., Mayer, H.: Modelling radiation fluxes in simple and complex environments: basics of the RayMan model. Int. J. Biometeorol. **54**(2) (2010)
6. Li, X., Ratti, C.: Mapping the spatio-temporal distribution of solar radiation within street canyons of Boston using Google Street View panoramas and building height model. Landsc. Urban Plan. **191**(C) (2019)
7. Deng M., Yang, W., Chen, C., Wu, Z., Liu, Y., Xiang, C.: Street-level solar radiation mapping and patterns profiling using Baidu Street View images. Sustain. Cities Soc. **75** (2021)
8. Höppe, P.: The physiological equivalent temperature – a universal index for the biometeorological assessment of the thermal environment. Int. J. Biometeorol. **43**, 71–75 (1999)
9. Fanger, P.O.: Thermal Comfort. McGraw Hill, New York (1970)
10. Jendritzky, G., de Dear, R., Havenith, G.: UTCI–why another thermal index? Int. J. Biometeorol. **56**, 421–428 (2012)
11. Gagge, A.P., Fobelets, A.P., Berglund, L.G.: A standard predictive index of human response to the thermal environment. ASHRAE Trans. **92** (1986)

12. Lai, D., et al.: A comprehensive review of thermal comfort studies in urban open spaces. Sci. Total Environ. **742** (2020, prepublish)
13. Fahmy, M., Kamel, H., Mokhtar, H., et al.: On the development and optimization of an urban design comfort model (UDCM) on a passive solar basis at mid-latitude sites. Climate **7**(1), 1 (2019)
14. 周宏轩, 陶贵鑫, 炎欣烨, 等.: 绿量的城市热环境效应研究现状与展望. Yingyong Sheng-tai Xuebao **31**(8) (2020). (in Chinese)
15. Dyvia, H.A., Arif, C.: Analysis of thermal comfort with predicted mean vote (PMV) index using artificial neural network. In: IOP Conference Series: Earth and Environmental Science, vol. 622, no. 1, p. 012019. IOP Publishing (2021)
16. Xiong, L., Yao, Y.: Study on an adaptive thermal comfort model with K-nearest-neighbors (KNN) algorithm. Build. Environ. **202**, 108026 (2021)
17. Chen, L.-C., Zhu, Y., Papandreou, G., Schroff, F., Adam, H.: Encoder-decoder with atrous separable convolution for semantic image segmentation. In: Ferrari, V., Hebert, M., Smin-chisescu, C., Weiss, Y. (eds.) ECCV 2018. LNCS, vol. 11211, pp. 833–851. Springer, Cham (2018). https://doi.org/10.1007/978-3-030-01234-2_49
18. Louche, A., Maurel, M., Simonnot, G., Peri, G., Iqbal, M.: Determination of Angstrom's turbidity coefficient from direct total solar irradiance measurements. Sol. Energy **38**(2), 89–96 (1987)
19. Woolley, H.: Urban Open Spaces. Taylor and Francis, Abingdon (2003)
20. 黄卓迪. 城市街道绿化对室外热舒适的影响研究. 华中农业大. (in Chinese)
21. Sarkar, C., Webster, C., Gallacher, J.: Healthy Cities–Public Health Through Urban Planning. Edward Elgar, Cheltenham (2014)
22. Takano, T., Nakamura, K., Watanabe, M.: Urban residential environments and senior citizens' longevity in megacity areas: the importance of walkable green spaces. J. Epidemiol. Commun. Health **56**(12), 913–918 (2002). https://doi.org/10.1136/jech.56.12.913
23. Maas, J., Van Dillen, S.M.E., Verheij, R.A., et al.: Social contacts as a possible mechanism behind the relation between green space and health. Health Place **15**(2), 586–595 (2009)
24. Bricker, K.S., Hendricks, W.W., Greenwood, J.B., Aschenbrenner, C.A.: Californians' per-ceptions of the influence of parks and recreation on quality of life. J. Park Recreat. Adm. **34**(3), 64–82 (2016). https://doi.org/10.18666/JPRA-2016-V34-I3-7441
25. Ekkel, E.D., de Vries, S.: Nearby green space and human health: evaluating accessibility metrics. Landsc. Urban Plan. **157**, 214–220 (2017)
26. Xu, K., Tartakovsky, A.M., Burghardt, J., et al.: Learning viscoelasticity models from indirect data using deep neural networks. Comput. Methods Appl. Mech. Eng. **387**, 114124 (2021)
27. Climate Bulletin of Fujian Province in 2020. https://weibo.com/ttarticle/p/show?id=230940 4614706022449491

A Composite Grid Clustering Algorithm Based on Density and Balance Degree

Limin Guo, Dongze Li, and Zhi Cai$^{(\boxtimes)}$

Beijing University of Technology, Beijing, China
{guolimin,lidongze,caiz}@bjut.edu.cn

Abstract. With the rapid growth of bike-sharing comes the challenge of unregulated bike-sharing parking in cities, which can lead to an unbalanced distribution of bikes and negatively impact the user experience and the operating costs of bike-sharing companies. To address these challenges, bike-sharing companies can create temporary parking stations or electronic fencing and implement bicycle rebalancing strategies across districts. However, these strategies require real-time data analysis and should take into account other factors, such as the inflow and outflow of bikes in each zone. To solve this problem, we proposes a composite clustering algorithm based on density and inflow-outflow balance to divide the city into a grid and extract hotspots as suitable areas for bicycle docking stations. Comparative experiments on common clustering algorithms for shared bicycles demonstrate the reasonableness and high precision of our method.

Keywords: Grid Clustering · Local Density · Inflow Outflow Balance

1 Introduction

With rapid economic growth and accelerated urban modernization, motor vehicle travel has soared and bicycle travel has plummeted, causing urban traffic congestion, air pollution and traffic safety issues. As a result, transportation reform methods with the concept of sharing have emerged to alleviate this situation, and new models of online car travel have achieved unprecedented success and have been inspired by this model, resulting in the emergence of shared bicycles. As an increasingly popular mode of transportation, the bike-sharing system is designed for short trips, not only improving the efficiency of short trips, but also alleviating traffic congestion and air pollution. However, this has caused some trouble for traffic management, as people flexibly choose to travel with shared bikes and park them anywhere they want. This has led to an imbalance of shared bicycles in many places. This has led to a redundancy of bicycles in some areas and a lack of bicycles in others. This phenomenon not only makes it difficult to find bikes in places where there is a shortage of bikes, but also affects the state of traffic in places where bikes are piled up. This situation not only greatly affects the travel experience of users, but also greatly increases the daily management costs of bicycle operating companies.

X. Meng et al. (Eds.): SpatialDI 2023, LNCS 13887, pp. 55–69, 2023.
https://doi.org/10.1007/978-3-031-32910-4_4

To address these challenges, bicycle sharing companies need to take measures, such as by establishing temporary parking sites or electronic fences for shared bicycles, and by implementing bicycle rebalancing methods between different areas. These measures can address such problems to some extent. However, these strategies rely on real-time data analysis and do not address the needs of users in a timely manner. The heat map of bike-sharing orders in Shanghai is shown in the figure. It can be seen that the closer to the city center, the more densely distributed the orders are. Heat map of bicycle orders in Shanghai as Fig. 1.

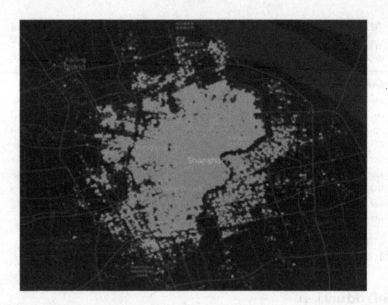

Fig. 1. Heat map of bicycle orders in Shanghai.

The current research on this aspect mainly focuses on density clustering. Wang et al. [1] proposed a method based on urban cab data, gridding the city and filtering the grid according to the threshold of the number of passengers in the grid, and considering the calculation of local density to extract clusters of hotspot area grids to establish urban cab stations.

However, the station setting problem should not only consider the density of vehicles, but also the balance degree of inflow and outflow of single vehicles in the area. When the balance degree is stable within a range, it means that the pickup and parking in the area are in line with the user's demand, and the balance degree actually represents the demand of the area. Therefore, this paper proposes a compound clustering algorithm based on density and inflow and outflow balance, divides the city into grids, extracts hotspot areas according to the density of bicycles and the balance of inflow and outflow in each grid area, and uses them as suitable site areas for bicycle parking stations, because the grid size, density threshold and balance value threshold can be customized with certain flexibility.

The algorithm proposed in this paper has a better clustering effect as well as clearer boundary delineation, based on the grid division, which can fit the road boundary of the urban domain, and provides a planning strategy for setting shared bicycle parking sites or even other transportation sites in the future with density and balance degree as the compound clustering conditions.

2 Related Work

In recent years, the rapid development of wireless sensors as well as communication technologies has facilitated the collection of traffic data, making it possible to use the data to improve traffic services. Many studies have explored the hotspot areas of bike-sharing based on different clustering approaches. Most of the hotspot areas are explored by clustering methods, and the common clustering methods are divided into divisive clustering methods, density-based clustering methods, hierarchical clustering methods, and new methods.

Delimited clustering methods, the clustering goal is to make the points within a class close enough and the points between classes far enough. MacQueenJ [2] proposed the K-means algorithm, which requires the user to randomly select an object as the initial center, use the mean of the objects within the class as the center of the class cluster, and sequentially group the samples into the class in which the nearest center is located until the clustering results converge.

Density-based clustering methods, when the density of neighboring regions exceeds a certain threshold, the clustering continues. Ester et al. [3] and others proposed the DBSCAN algorithm, which is a representative density-based clustering algorithm. Compared with the traditional K-means algorithm, which can only be used for clustering convex sample sets, the DBSCAN algorithm is applicable to both convex and non-convex sample sets, and it works better for noisy data sets. The algorithm clusters the set of densely connected samples through the related concept of density reachable, and this sample set is a cluster of the final clustering result. The OPTICS algorithm proposed by Ankerst M et al. [4] solves the problem of parameter selection, and its core idea is to output an ordered list of objects that contains enough information for extracting clusters.

Connection-based clustering methods, also called hierarchical clustering methods. Hierarchical clustering methods are generally divided into two categories: top-down and bottom-up. Campello [5] proposed an HDBSCAN algorithm, which is a combination of DBSCAN algorithm and hierarchical clustering based algorithm, and is an improvement of OPTICS algorithm, but the effect is not ideal for the processing of boundary points; Dockhorn [6] proposed the *mpts*-HDBSCAN algorithm for the shortcomings of the HDBSCAN algorithm, which overcomes the poor clustering effect of the boundary points of the HDBSCAN algorithm, but because the number of core points *mpts* is used as a global parameter, the effect of clustering is not satisfactory when the data density distribution differs greatly.

Grid-based clustering methods. Wang [7] et al. proposed the grid-based spatial clustering algorithm STING, which uses a multi-resolution technique to divide the spatial data region into rectangular cells. The processing method is similar, the difference is that the former processes the object as a grid while the object processed is points. The algorithm has fast processing speed, parallel processing and incremental updates, but reduces the clustering quality and accuracy. Two typical clustering algorithms proposed in 1999, WaveCluster [8] and clique [9], both combine density and grid-based ideas. The former uses wavelet transformation of the original data feature space on the basis of data gridding and finds high-density regions in the transformed new space. The latter divides the data space into several rectangular grid cells, and the number of points falling into each cell grid is the data density of that cell, and the cells exceeding a certain threshold are regarded as dense, and the process of clustering is to find the maximum set of connected dense cells, although it is more efficient, the determination of the grid step value, density threshold both and the control of the precision value of the clustering boundary are not ideal. Many scholars have improved on the basis of CLIQUE algorithm, such as CAG-CLIQUE algorithm [10] uses the dynamic adjustment technique of boundary to constantly modify the grid step to control the boundary accuracy, GDCAP algorithm [11] selects the density threshold by the product difference of grid density expectation, A-Stream algorithm [12] uses the sum of average density and standard deviation of data to select the density threshold The above algorithms reduce the difficulty of parameter setting and improve the accuracy of the clustering boundary; however, the outliers in the real data will affect the mathematical expectation and standard deviation, which will reduce the adaptive effect of the above algorithms [13]. Cai et al. [14] proposed a dynamic grid-based density visualization method, which visualizes the access point density in areas not covered by rail stations and clusters the access point density in these uncovered areas to predict the location of new rail stations.

In addition to the above clustering approaches, there are many new clustering methods as well as derived methods. Chakraborty et al. [15] proposed an incremental clustering algorithm. This algorithm is used for clustering dynamic databases where data is frequently updated, by directly projecting new data to existing class clusters instead of performing the entire clustering algorithm all over again. The algorithm is good at discovering new class clusters as well as new outliers in the database.Liu et al. [16] proposed an adaptive clustering algorithm ADPC-KNN by introducing the idea of K-nearest neighbor method to calculate the truncation distance and local density of each data point, which allows the algorithm to automatically select the initial clustering centers and aggregate clusters with reachable density. Cai et al. [17]used the method of selecting the best clustering parameters to predict candidate transit stations, and LeaderRank and Gaussian Mixed models for subway station location studies.

3   Preliminaries

3.1   Problem Definition

The given data is divided in the form of a grid and each grid is considered as a data point. A graph $G = (V, E)$ is obtained and we take the node V by executing a clustering algorithm in terms of density as well as balance to obtain a set of clusters that conforms to a clustering result that is dense and the balance degrees is limited by a threshold, The balance degrees means the absolute value of the inflow into and out of single grid $|flowin - flowout|$.

3.2   Mathematics Formulation

We consider an undirected and unweighted graph $G = (V, E)$, with V and E denoting the set of nodes and edges, respectively,N denoting the number of nodes in the complex network graph, M denoting the number of elements in the attribute set associated with a node in the complex network, and K denoting the number of clusters in the network with a single node as a single lattice. The whole problem is modeled as solving for how many clique communities C within graph $G = (V, E)$ for which the valid condition Q is true.

Validity of Nodes: Nodes are represented by v_i. If we make g_i denote the validity of v_i, g_i is valid, $v_i = 1$; otherwise invalid, $v_i = 0$.

Clique Community: Given a graph G, a clique C in G is a set of nodes for which there exists an edge $(u, v) \in E$ for any node $u \in C, v \in C, (u \neq v)$. A clique community C is said to be an extremely large clique community C in graph G if there does not exist a clique community C' such that $C \subset C'$. Clique community C in graph G.

The Clique Community Search Problem Under Complex Attributes: Given a network graph $G = (V, E)$, where: V is the set of nodes; the number of nodes $n = V(G)$; E is the set of edges; and the number of edges $m = E(G)$. Denote by Q the conditions for satisfying the validity of nodes, for the graph we perform the search for a community C that satisfies the following conditions: 1) $C \subset V$; 2) C is connected and is a greatly clique community; 3) the complex property condition Q is true for a given community $C(Q$ is whether g_i is valid or not).

4   Methodology

4.1   Local Density

BLA-CLIQUE defines a new way of calculating the local density with respect to the Clique algorithm. For new grids merged into clustered clusters, the local density needs to be recalculated from the density of the original cluster as follows. For each grid cell there is its own local density derived from the nearby grid, to indicates the number of data objects in the grid cell. The local density of the grid can be obtained by summing the Gaussian kernel functions of the grid and its neighboring points, and the smaller the distance between the point and its neighboring points, the larger the local density. The formula for calculating the local density is as follows:

$$\rho_i = \sum e^{-\left(\frac{d_{ij}}{d_c}\right)} \tag{1}$$

For point i, simply calculate its Gaussian kernel function to the neighboring grid and sum up, then the local density of the grid can be obtained, and the smaller the distance between the point and its immediate neighbors, the larger its local density will be. Local density diagram as Fig. 2.

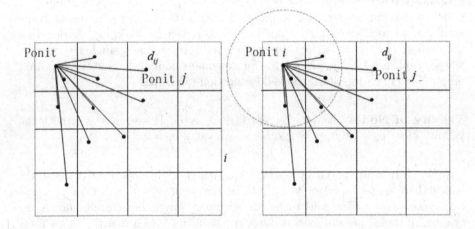

Fig. 2. Local density diagram.

4.2   Distance Metric

Clustering is the process of dividing a dataset into classes such that data objects in this class have high similarity to each other and data objects in different classes have low similarity to each other. The study needs to use distance as its metric, so two common distance metrics are introduced.

Euclidean Metric. Suppose there exist two points A and B in two-dimensional space with coordinates $A(x_1, y_1)$, $B(x_2, y_2)$,respectively, then the Manhattan distance D between A and B is the sum of the straight-line distances between the two points in the east-west and north-south directions, which is calculated as:

$$D = \sqrt{(x_1 - x_2)^2 + (y_1 - y_2)^2} \tag{2}$$

Manhattan Metric. Suppose there exist two points A and B in two-dimensional space with coordinates $A(x_1, y_1)$, $B(x_2, y_2)$, respectively, then the Manhattan distance D between A and B is the sum of the straight-line distances between the two points in the east-west and north-south directions, which is calculated as:

$$D = |x_1 - x_2| + |y_1 - y_2| \tag{3}$$

In the used algorithm, the distance metric we use Manhattan distance, mainly because of the following two reasons.

i. The clustering is performed by grid division, and the distance metric is performed by east-west and north-south directions, which fits the grid boundary, so it is more appropriate to use Manhattan distance to calculate the distance describing the shared bike shop.

ii. The data volume of shared bicycle is huge, although after data pre-processing, part of the noise points are erased, but the data volume is still huge, because it can be regarded as OD data, the statistical data volume of one day is nearly 200,000 items. The Manhattan distance metric is calculated using only addition and subtraction, which is faster compared to the Euler distance metric.

4.3 BLA-Clique Clustering

BLA-Clique algorithm is a clustering algorithm based on grid division, and it is worth mentioning that because the step size of grid division is small, the behavior of switching locks in the grid is expressed as the inflow and outflow of the region in this paper. BLA-CLIQUE grid clustering algorithm will project the data objects directly into the grid space according to the given grid step gs and calculate the grid density and balance value, if the grid density and balance value is greater than the given density threshold τ, then determine the grid is dense and balanced grid, join the current clusters and search the grid until all the neighboring grids are non-dense and non-balanced grid, end the cycle; Repeat the above operation until all clusters are found. Considering the clustering approach is to use a grid division, we solve the algorithm before making the following definition:

Grid Cells

$DS = D_1, D_2, D_3, ..., D_n$ is an n-dimensional data set, the subspace D_i is expanded to be equal to the largest subspace D_{max}, and D_i is divided into m equal intervals according to the grid step gs, thus dividing D_i into m disjoint rectangular cells, i.e. grid cells g.

Dense Cells

Given a density threshold θ_d, g is a dense cell g_d when the number of data objects $x > \varepsilon$ projected by DS into the range g; and vice versa for a non-dense cell $\overline{g_d}$.

Balancing Cells

Given a balance threshold θ_b, g is a balance cell g_b when the number of data objects $x > \varepsilon$ projected by DS into the range g; and vice versa for a non-balance cell $\overline{g_b}$.

Boundary Grid

Given a threshold θ, in D_i, $\forall g \neq g_d$, $g \neq g_b$ and $\exists g_d \in \{adjacent\ cells\ of\ g\}$, $g_b \in \{adjacent\ cells\ of\ g\}$, if $\rho_g > \theta$, then g is a boundary grid.

Distance Between Cluster Centers of Mass

The distance from the cluster cluster to the center of mass of the neighboring grid, denoted by ds.

Algorithm

The BLA-CLIQUE algorithm is based on CLIQUE, and the density threshold ϵ is passed in advance, and the boundary grid density threshold θ is used to determine the boundary grid to improve the cluster boundary accuracy, The CLIQUE algorithm uses the DFS depth search algorithm to calculate the k-1 dimensional subspace under the k-dimensional space, and its time complexity is $O\left(nd\right)$ (d is the dimension of the data set); the BLA-CLIQUE algorithm initializes the data information of the grid cells, and its time complexity is $O\left(n\right)$ (n is the number of data points after mapping) when calculated by the adaptive generation strategy. The time complexity is $O\left(2n + nd\right)$, and the time complexity of the whole algorithm is $O\left(nd\right)$ because the empty cells with weight 0 have been removed. The algorithm is as follow Algorithm 1:

Algorithm 1. BLA-CLIQUE.

Input:
$\quad DS, gs, \theta_d, \theta_b$;
Output:
$\quad$ BLA-CLIQUE algorithm results $clusters$
1: $g = divideGrids\left(DS, gs\right)$;
2: Generate Initial $clusters$ and search all grids: setting the densest grid as the initial
$\quad$ cluster $clusterNo = 0$;
3: **for** $i = 1$ to $g.length$ **do**
4: $\quad$ $clusterNo + +$;
5: $\quad$ **if** $g\left[i\right] == 0$ **then**
6: $\quad\quad$ **if** $\rho_i > \theta_d$ and $\tau_i > \theta_b$ and $ds < 2gs$ **then**
7: $\quad\quad\quad$ $cluster.add\left(g\left[i\right]\right)$;
8: $\quad\quad\quad$ $Recursively\ searching\ g\left[i\right]$;
9: $\quad\quad$ **else if** $density\left(\rho_i\right) < \theta_d$ **then**
10: $\quad\quad\quad$ $Recursively\ searching\ g\left[--i\right]$;
11: $\quad\quad$ **end if**
12: $\quad\quad$ $g\left[i\right] = 1$;
13: $\quad$ **end if**
14: $\quad$ $clusters.add\left(g\left[i\right]\right)$;
15: **end for**
16: **return** $clusters$

In Algorithm 1, first, the full domain data is divided according to gs to obtain the grid set g. Treating each grid as a data point (row 1), for each data point, calculate its local density and natural neighbors, the set containing its own data points, locate the densest grid with initial clusters and number 0, and arrange the grid in descending order (row 2), traverse the entire set, count each data point's own density, calculate to find the set of densities larger than the current data points (row 3), cluster numbering increment (row 4), then, the algorithm repeats the following process to determine if the data points are visited until they are all marked: the data points are qualified according to the local density and the truncated distance between the equilibrium value and the center of mass between the data points (row 6), and then this paper based on the local density and the distance between the high density and the centroid distance selects candidate centroids and adds them to the cluster, and recalculates the local density, balance value and center of mass of the cluster (row 7), recursively searches for the cluster with the next lowest density (rows 8-row 9), and clusters the points with direct density reachable with natural neighbors to the cluster using the truncation distance as the threshold, and marks the visited data points as 1 (rows 10-row 13). Finally, the clustering cluster results are output (row 14).

5   Experiment Results and Analysis

In order to test the clustering effect of BLA-CLIQUE algorithm and its performance in the application detection of residential hot zone distribution, the experimental benchmark database is selected from the GPS dataset of shared bikes in Shanghai (referred to as dataset bike) for the experiment. The GPS point dataset is about 100,000 data collected by Shanghai Mobiles in August 2016 within one month. Where the source text is stored in CSV format and each row of records represents the order data of the shared bicycle, the source data format ad declared as Table 1, and the sample of source data as follows Table 2:

The computer used for the experiments is Intel (R) Core (TM) i5-1050Ti CPU @ 2.40 GHz, Windows 10 64-bit operating system with 12.0 GB of memory and python language for algorithm implementation and Python language for data visualization.

5.1   Data Preprocessing

Due to the errors of Bluetooth devices, GPS positioning modules and other devices, as well as the abnormalities of data communication, database storage and other technologies, there are a certain number of errors in the shared bicycle data and shared bicycle GPS positioning data. Data pre-processing is the conversion of raw real data into experimental data suitable for data mining in a specific domain, providing a good basis for better implementation of mining

Table 1. August 2016 Shanghai Mobikes Source Data Set Data Format.

number	name	Comments
1	Order ID	7 characters
2	Bike ID	6 characters
3	User ID	5 characters
4	Start time	Format:yyyy/MM/dd/hh:mm,Beijing time
5	Start longitude	Format:ddd.ddd,in degrees
6	Start latitude	Format:ddd.ddd,in degrees
7	End time	Format:yyyy/MM/dd/hh:mm,Beijing time
8	End longitude	Format:ddd.ddd,in degrees
9	End latitude	Format:ddd.ddd,in degrees
10	Track	Format:(ddd.ddd,ddd.ddd)#(ddd.ddd,ddd.ddd)#..., in degrees,separated by #,sequence of track points in latitude and longitude

Table 2. Sample source data.

Order ID	Bike ID	User ID	Start time	Start longitude
78387	158357	10080	2016/8/20/ 6:57	121.348
891333	92776	6605	2016/8/29/ 19:09	121.508

Start latitude	End time	End longitude	End latitude	Track
31.389	2016/8/20/ 7:04	121.357	31.388	"121.347,31.392#121.348,31.389# 121.349,31.390#121.350,31.390#..."
31.279	2016/8/29/ 19:31	121.489	31.271	"121.489,31.270#121.489,31.271# 121.490,31.270#121.490,31.271#..."

algorithms and for deriving mining results. These data anomalies usually include data redundancy, missing data and data errors, etc. Some pre-processing of these anomalies is needed to avoid affecting the clustering results of shared bikes. The anomalies of shared bicycle passenger swipe card data and shared bicycle GPS positioning data and the corresponding processing measures are described as follows: 1) Data redundancy First, if there are 2 or more identical data entries in the data table, only the first data that appears in the data table is retained, and the rest of the data are deleted. Secondly, if there are 2 or more identical data entries in the data table for the vehicle number Bike_ID, only the first data that appears in the data table is retained and the rest of the data is deleted. (2) Missing data In the data table, if the value of a field attribute of a data entry is empty, the data will be deleted. (3) Wrong data In the data table of shared bicycle, the attribute value of the vehicle number Bike_ID field has a fixed format and length. (2) GPS location data of shared bicycle 1) Data redundancy Firstly, if there are 2 or more identical data entries in the data table, only the first data that appears in the data table will be retained and the rest of the data will be deleted. (2) Missing data In the data table, if the value of a field attribute of a data entry is empty, the data will be deleted. (3) Data error In the GPS positioning data table of shared bicycle, the attribute value of the vehicle number

Table 3. The environment configuration used for the experiment.

CPU	AMD Ryzen 5 5600X @ 3.70 GHz
Operating System	Windows10 64-bit
Memory	12.0GB
GPU	GTX1050Ti
Programming Languages	Python 3.8

Bike_ID field has a fixed format and length, and the data entry that does not conform to these formats and lengths will be deleted; the attribute value of the latitude and longitude fields (LONGITUDE, LATITUDE) should be within the range of Shanghai (*longitude* : $[120.52, 122.12]$, *latitude* : $[30.40, 31.53]$)), delete the data in the table that exceed this value range (Tables 3 and 4).

5.2   Experiment

First of all, we use DBSCAN algorithm for clustering, considering that bicycle travel users use bicycle travel range in 1–3 km as the most short-distance travel to meet the phenomenon of solving the last mile of urban commuting. Therefore, the eps of DBSCAN algorithm can be set as 1 km, 2 km and 3 km. The distance users ride one way using shared bicycles as shown in the Fig. 3. Its clustering image is shown in Fig. 4. It can be found that the current clustering algorithm has the best clustering effect when eps is set to 1 km.

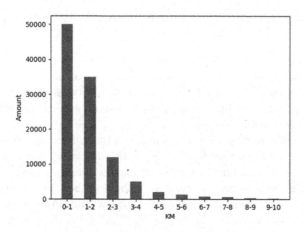

Fig. 3. The distance users ride one way using shared bicycles.

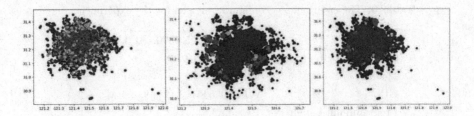

Fig. 4. Clustering results of DBSCAN at eps=1 km, 2 km, 3 km.

Secondly, we use the K-mean algorithm to cluster the hotspot areas of shared bicycles. When the number of clusters is assumed to be 100, 200, 500. The results are shown in the figure. It can be found that when the number of clusters is higher, the boundary of the clustering area is not clear and its clustering distribution is not obvious. Clustering results of K-means as shown in Fig. 5.

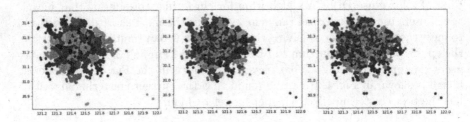

Fig. 5. Clustering results of K-means at k=100,200,500.

We then use the BLA-CLIQUE algorithm for clustering. It can be found that the clusters show regional type distribution and present different size differences. The clusters are more dispersed than the first two types of clusters, which is conducive to the siting of bicycle stations in a small area. Clustering results of BLA-CLIQUE as shown in Fig. 6.

In order to evaluate the effectiveness and precision of the clustering algorithm, the *Dunn* index is used as the effectiveness evaluation index, which is a nonlinear combination of inter-cluster distance and cluster diameter. In clustering, the larger the minimum distance between any clusters, the higher the inter-cluster separation; the smaller the maximum distance within any cluster, the higher the intra-cluster compactness; therefore, the better the clustering pattern, the larger the *Dunn* value. Therefore, the better the clustering pattern, the greater the *Dunn* value. Three sets of algorithm comparison experiments were conducted on the mobike dataset, in which the first set of experiments were conducted to manually adjust the grid step parameters and density threshold parameters of the CLIQUE algorithm to obtain the parameter set with the best *Dunn* index. In the second group, the optimal values of the grid step are obtained in the first

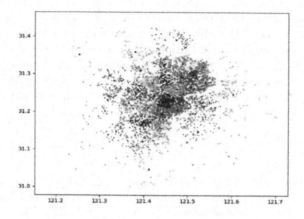

Fig. 6. Clustering results of BLA-CLIQUE

group and passed into the CLIQUE algorithm for clustering analysis. The third group of experiments uses the BLA-CLIQUE algorithm to generate six clusters. The *Dunn* indices of the three groups of seven experiments were calculated separately and the parameters and clustering effects were compared. The results are shown in the table.

Table 4. Three sets of experimental clustering results analysis table.

Algorithm	Density Threshold	Cluster Number	Mesh tep	Dunn Validity Index
Classical CLIQUE Algorithm	1.8	121	0.25	0.105
	2.1	116	0.50	0.091
	2.1	117	0.25	0.097
	2.1	126	0.10	0.087
	2.2	122	0.25	0.082
Algorithm with Adaptive Parameters	2.01	131	0.25	0.111
BLA-CLIQUE	2.01	133	0.25	0.121

The data show that the BLA-CLIQUE algorithm proposed in this paper can accurately identify clusters and improve the accuracy of cluster boundaries compared with the traditional CLIQUE.

6   Conclusion

The BLA-CLIQUE algorithm can effectively identify dense cells by calculating the density threshold and the equilibrium amount threshold of the shared bicycle access area, and dividing the data space according to the given division parameters; by calculating the boundary grid density and the equilibrium threshold, the clustering edge identification algorithm is optimized to improve the clustering accuracy and find the equilibrium and dense areas of shared bicycles.

The experiments use the Shanghai Mobiles data set, and verify the engineering applicability of the algorithm through a large number of algorithm experiments and application experiments, and compare the algorithm with the conventional clique algorithm. If we can obtain more data sets and add more attributes such as age, occupation and income of residents, and mine more geolocation-related data features from the high-dimensional data, we can provide better intelligent decision making.

References

1. Wang, H., Chen, X.J., Wang, Y., et al.: Local maximum density approach for small-scale clustering of urban taxi stops. International Archives of the Photogrammetry, Remote Sensing and Spatial Information Sciences, vol. 42(2/W13) (2019)
2. MacQueen, J.: Classification and analysis of multivariate observations. In: 5th Berkeley Symposium on Mathematical Statistics and Probability. Los Angeles LA USA: University of California, pp. 281–297 (1967)
3. Ester, M., Kriegel, H.P., Sander, J., et al.: A density-based algorithm for discovering clusters in large spatial databases with noise. KDD **96**(34), 226–231 (1996)
4. Ankerst, M., Breunig, M.M., Kriegel, H.P., et al.: OPTICS: ordering points to identify the clustering structure. ACM SIGMOD Rec. **28**(2), 49–60 (1999)
5. Campello, R.J.G.B., Moulavi, D., Sander, J.: Density-based clustering based on hierarchical density estimates. In: Pei, J., Tseng, V.S., Cao, L., Motoda, H., Xu, G. (eds.) PAKDD 2013. LNCS (LNAI), vol. 7819, pp. 160–172. Springer, Heidelberg (2013). https://doi.org/10.1007/978-3-642-37456-2_14
6. Dockhorn, A., Braune, C., Kruse, R.: An alternating optimization approach based on hierarchical adaptations of DBSCAN. In: 2015 IEEE Symposium Series on Computational Intelligence, pp. 749–755. IEEE (2015)
7. Wang, W., Yang, J., Muntz, R.: STING: a statistical information grid approach to spatial data mining. VLDB **97**, 186–195 (1997)
8. Sheikholeslami, G., Chatterjee, S., Zhang, A.: WaveCluster: a multi-resolution clustering approach for very large spatial databases. VLDB **98**, 428–439 (1998)
9. Agrawal, R., Gehrke, J., Gunopulos, D., et al.: Automatic subspace clustering of high dimensional data for data mining applications. Proceed. ACM SIGMOD Int. Conf. Manag. Data **1998**, 94–105 (1998)
10. Zhaohua, C.: Improvement and application of cluster analysis algorithm CLIQUE. Central South University, Changsha (2009)
11. Wu, X., Zurita-Milla, R., Kraak, M.J., et al.: Clustering-based approaches to the exploration of spatio-temporal data. Int. Arch. Photogramm. Remote Sens. Spatial Inf. Sci. **42**, 1387–1391 (2017)
12. Changzheng, X., Fei, W., Lili, W.: Density grid-based data stream clustering algorithm with parameter automatization. J. Front. Comput. Sci. Technol. **5**(10), 953 (2011)
13. Oleinikova, S.A., Kravets, O.J., Silnov, D.S.: Analytical estimates for the expectation of the beta distribution on the basis of the known values of the variance and mode. International Information Institute (Tokyo). Inf. **19**(2), 343 (2016)
14. Cai, Z., Ji, M., Mi, Q., et al.: Dynamic grid-based spatial density visualization and rail transit station prediction. ISPRS Int. J. Geo Inf. **10**(12), 804 (2021)
15. Ashbrook, D., Starner, T.: Using GPS to learn significant locations and predict movement across multiple users. Pers. Ubiquit. Comput. **7**, 275–286 (2003)

16. Yaohui, L., Zhengming, M., Fang, Y.: Adaptive density peak clustering based on K-nearest neighbors with aggregating strategy. Knowl.-Based Syst. **133**, 208–220 (2017)
17. Cai, Z., Wang, J., Li, T., et al.: A novel trajectory based prediction method for urban subway design. ISPRS Int. J. Geo-Inf. **11**(2), 126 (2022)

Visualization Analysis

Research on the Visualization Method of Weibo User Sentiment Analysis Based on IP Affiliation and Comment Content

Hao Geng[1], Xiang Li[1(✉)], Wenbing Liu[2], Wei Zhao[1], and Fang Ren[1]

[1] Information Engineering University, Zhengzhou 450001, Henan, China
ryolx13@126.com
[2] Army Logistics University of PLA, Chongqing 401311, China

Abstract. Aiming at the problems of huge number of comments in Weibo, complex data format, inconsistent emotion model, vague emotion identification and lack of effective spatial location expression, a visual research method of emotion analysis of Weibo users based on IP affiliation and comment content is proposed in combination with the open IP affiliation function of Weibo in 2022. The proposed method uses crawler to obtain Weibo comment data, and uses manual tagging and machine learning methods to segment words and analyze emotions of comment content; Finally, two methods are proposed to form maps by combining spatio-temporal data such as time and coordinates. Experimental results show that this method is feasible and effective for the visualization of emotion analysis of Weibo users, and can achieve better visualization results.

Keywords: Weibo · IP affiliation · comments · user emotion · visualization

1 Introduction

Weibo is one of the most influential social networking platforms in China at present. According to the financial report of the third quarter of 2022 released by Weibo, as of the end of the third quarter, the monthly active users of Weibo were 584 million, and the average daily active users were 253 million. Users express their views and opinions on Weibo, show their feelings and express their emotions. Obtaining these data to make them valuable information is the first big problem. Weibo is not only a platform for users to show their feelings, but also an important place for people to discuss social hot events. Comments on hot news contain netizens' attitudes, cognition and emotions. The diversity of Weibo comments represents the views and attitudes of different groups towards an event or problem. How to classify these emotions and express them through data model is the second biggest problem. With the opening of IP affiliation function on major social media platforms in April 2022, it puts more realistic geographical labels on users, which helps to show users' emotions and attitudes from geographical distribution. It is the third major problem to combine emotional attitude with IP affiliation and analyze emotional visualization with geographical characteristics. How to solve the above problems quickly and effectively has become a topic in related fields recently.

X. Meng et al. (Eds.): SpatialDI 2023, LNCS 13887, pp. 73–88, 2023.
https://doi.org/10.1007/978-3-031-32910-4_5

2   Related Work

The existing research methods can be divided into 3 parts.

(1) Web crawler technology. Web crawler (or spider) is a program or script that automatically crawls the information of the World Wide Web according to certain rules. The purpose of using web crawler technology in this study is to obtain the related content of Weibo comment area. Tian Yu used a crawler when collecting and preprocessing Weibo data: parsing the first URL to obtain its request and retrieving the callback function when it returned; Respond to parsing web page in callback function, return iteration of project object and request object, and include callback information in request, which is downloaded by Scrapy; Then the callback processing, in the callback function to the site content parsing, using Xpath selector to generate parsed data items. Sun designed an application program with four functional modules: configuration, crawling, storage and analysis on the basis of studying the basic concepts and principles of web crawler. The idea is: configure the Weibo users to be obtained, including Weibo UID, user name, etc., and configure other attributes; Web-side Weibo URL has certain rules, which contains JSON information, in which JSON data returns Weibo content, publishing time, page views, likes and other content; Using Python to parse JSON, you can get the information in it. Wang put forward the concept of "theme crawler" when studying the key technologies of network public opinion monitoring system, which consists of three key modules: web page analysis module, link analysis module and crawler module. The idea is as follows: crawl from the initial URL, search the web page according to the set search strategy, and analyze the relevance of the web page first, and remove the web page irrelevant to the theme; Then the extracted URL is analyzed by link correlation, and the priority of the URL is set and stored in the URL queue; When the stop condition is met, the crawling process ends.

To sum up, although the crawler algorithm is becoming more and more mature and can be well used for Weibo comment data comment, due to the opening of IP affiliation, the crawling data format is not specific enough to model and organize geospatial location information, and lacks specific and standard description methods.

(2) Weibo comment data modeling. In view of the need for structured processing of Weibo data, Zhao used octopus crawler software. After the crawling process, the original data is deduplicated and saved, and finally stored in the form of Excel table. The form mainly includes serial number, poster, blog post publishing time, commentator, evaluation content and comment time. Gu focused on the content of comments and designed a data table with serial numbers and samples as headers when studying the emotion classification of Chinese texts in Weibo comments. In the process of studying public opinion analysis and emotion analysis based on text mining, Wu determined the research target as the official Weibo of Leshan Normal University, and crawled the data for this object with web crawler technology. The collected fields include ID address, user ID, user nickname, publication time, number of likes and comment content. Through the above research, we can find that the author designed a certain data structure according to the purpose and direction of

his research, which is used to store the unstructured Weibo comment data obtained from the Internet. Structured data is beneficial to improve work efficiency in the subsequent data cleaning and processing, but on the other hand, the classification and modeling of newly opened IP territories are not involved much, especially for the data modeling of geospatial location, which lacks an effective spatial data model.

(3) Emotional annotation method of Weibo comment data. In view of the difficulty of manual tagging of large-scale Weibo corpus, Yang proposed a method of automatic tagging of emotional categories of Chinese Weibo corpus. The basic ideas are as follows: the collected Chinese corpus is preprocessed to obtain the corpus to be tagged; Then, the corpus to be tagged is automatically tagged by three methods and the results are produced respectively; Finally, the three labeling methods are integrated by voting to determine the final labeling results. In view of how to extract people's opinions and emotional tendencies from big data, Li proposed an automatic extraction algorithm of element words and emotional words combining automatic tagging algorithm and deep learning. The specific steps are as follows: constructing a candidate dictionary of element words; Constructing candidate dictionaries of emotional words; Filter a subset of rules; Automatic labeling. To solve the problem of insufficient emotion annotation data, Han proposed a Semi-Supervised Learning based on Dynamic Threshold and Multi-classifiers (SSDTM).

To sum up, researchers consider adopting different emotion labeling methods according to the accuracy, recognition efficiency and other aspects of emotion recognition. However, most emotion analysis is based on the content of corpus. Once some new network terms or other pronouns with abbreviations are encountered, their emotion recognition effect will decline, and they cannot be organically integrated into the dynamic changes of network context.

(4) Emotional Visualization Expression of Weibo Comment Data. Zhao used Auto-CAD drawing software to draw relevant scientific knowledge maps and topic keywords according to the previously calculated topic similarity and topic importance, combined with topic mining results. Taking the construction and analysis of the knowledge map of "Xinhuang Playground Burial Case" studied by the author as an example, the theme co-occurrence map, theme evolution map and keyword table are established, as shown in Fig. 1, Fig. 2.

In view of the design and implementation of Weibo analysis and visualization system, Ni pays attention to the transmission path of each blog post and the objects spread by each layer of communicators. From blogger posting to user forwarding step by step, the propagation path and users of each node are obtained, and the propagation network path tracking graph is formed (Fig. 3).

The above-mentioned visualization methods are mainly used in the current research. Knowledge map can reflect the deep relationship between events, and can combine emotional words to achieve better cognitive results. Word cloud can reflect the number of users with different emotions according to the frequency of keywords. Statistical charts can objectively and truly reflect the relationship between data. However, none of these methods can directly express the relationship between emotions and IP locality or geographical coordinates.

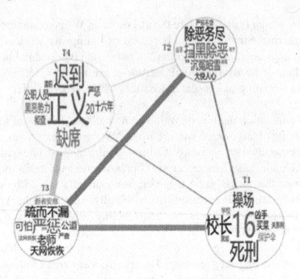

Fig. 1. Weibo word cloud visualization

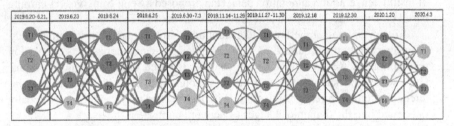

Fig. 2. Evolution map of Weibo theme

Fig. 3. The Propagation Network Path Tracking Graph

Based on this, this study is based on network big data, widely collects and analyzes Weibo data mainly based on IP attribution and comment data, and extracts the necessary information from these large-scale data for emotional classification or emotional cause pair extraction to assist in evaluating public opinion risks, so as to correctly guide public opinion, help predict and prevent emergencies in time, effectively reduce the negative impact caused by public opinion events, and have important practical significance for the control and management of netizens' emotions.

3 The Technical Route

In order to realize the visualization method of Weibo users' emotion analysis based on IP affiliation and comment content, this paper comprehensively studies the semantic modeling, extraction and analysis methods of Weibo comment data features, combines open IP affiliation and time information, and then finds the emotional changes and correlation rules hidden in massive comments, and visualizes them with spatio-temporal data to accurately and deeply grasp the public opinion orientation of related events. The specific design ideas are as follows (Fig. 4):

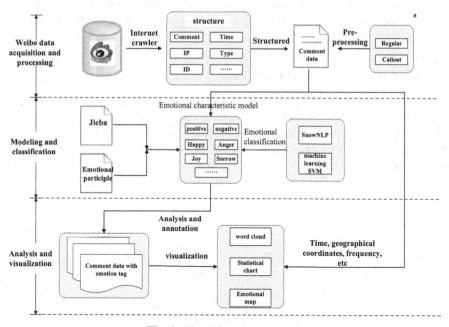

Fig. 4. The technology roadmap

In the process of emotion analysis of Weibo data, traditional emotion classification methods fail to make full use of the geographical spatial information and time information contained in it. Therefore, this paper proposes a visualization method of emotion analysis of Weibo users based on IP affiliation and comment content. The main contents include:

(1) Weibo data acquisition and processing. By applying for the Weibo open platform to obtain the official Weibo API, combined with the typical data structure of Weibo

comments, using web crawler technology to obtain a certain structured Weibo hot event comment data set, using regularization and manual annotation to screen the comment content to achieve data standardization preprocessing, designed a crawler data format suitable for the needs of this study.

(2) Modeling and classification of emotional characteristics. A preprocessing method of Weibo comment corpus based on crawler data format is proposed. Based on Jieba Thesaurus, a feature model with positive and negative emotions and various emotions such as joys, sorrows and sorrows is designed to form a dictionary with emotional identification; The natural language processing library and machine learning algorithm are used to analyze the emotion of the obtained Weibo comment data, so as to realize the emotion classification standard of comment data and form a comment data set with "emotion tag".

(3) Analysis and visualization of emotional characteristics. Combined with the attribute information such as time, IP attribution geographical coordinates and keyword frequency in Weibo comment data structure, the emotional temporal and spatial distribution map of Weibo hot events is constructed by using visual expression technologies such as keyword cloud, statistical chart and emotional map, and public opinion-oriented prediction and analysis are carried out according to the data visualization results.

3.1 Acquisition of Weibo Comment Data

There are two main methods to collect Weibo data, one is based on the open API interface of Weibo, and the other is to collect through web crawler. The method selected in this paper is based on web crawler. The crawler can send requests to the web page and convert the web page into JSON format with the help of the third-party library. The JSON format contains the required information. According to certain rules, the crawler can extract the relevant information of the comment area and save it in CSV table (Table 1).

Table 1. Data CSV table

User name	Time	IP	Comment
	2022/8/3	Hebei	
	2022/8/3	Guangdong	
	2022/8/3	Hebei	fabulous
	2022/8/3	Beijing	
	2022/8/3	Henan	fabulous

3.2 Weibo Corpus Preprocessing and Emotion Analysis Modeling

In this study, the modeling and classification of emotional characteristics of microblog comments is the core algorithm, and its specific process is shown in the Fig. 5. Firstly, the Weibo comment data obtained by the crawler is loaded, and regularized and marked with basic features; Secondly, a variety of emotional segmentation words constructed according to the emotional classification characteristics of Weibo comments are added to Jieba Word Segmentation Thesaurus; Read each emotion dictionary in turn, and read Weibo comments line by line, build a 1*5 emotion feature vector for each Weibo, and determine the emotion classification of Weibo according to the number size in the vector.

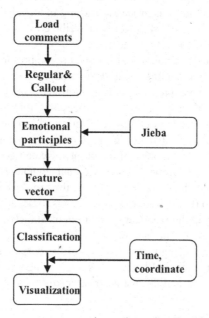

Fig. 5. Weibo corpus preprocessing and emotion classification process

(1) Weibo corpus preprocessing. Because the computer can not directly identify the unstructured text data, it is necessary to pre-process after obtaining the Weibo corpus, and transform the unstructured text data into recognizable structured data. The preprocessing methods are as follows: Firstly, the text data is segmented, followed by regularization, deletion of stop words and other operations, and finally a unified format of Weibo comment data set is formed. Most of the corpus in Weibo comments is mainly in Chinese. In terms of word segmentation, the difference between Chinese and English is that there is no natural discontinuity between English words in Chinese, so special word segmentation algorithms are needed for Chinese word segmentation. The method of word segmentation in this paper adopts the third-party Jieba library in Python, and uses the method of word segmentation based on statistics. It uses statistical machine learning model to train the rules of word segmentation for a large number of texts that have been segmented, that is, the library uses a large number of samples that have been segmented in the development process to train, so that it can find the rules of word segmentation, thus realizing the segmentation of unknown texts. At the same time, it supports adding new words

by itself, so as to achieve the purpose of optimizing word segmentation effect. It is mainly used to build an emotional dictionary. Regular expressions are expressions used to concisely express a set of string characteristics. It is mainly used to match strings in Weibo corpus. By using regular expressions, the regularization and standardization of Weibo comments are realized. Compared with other words, stop words have no actual meaning, such as interjections, punctuation marks, etc. This kind of string is not helpful for emotion analysis in this study, and will increase the amount of data in the analysis process, resulting in low analysis efficiency. Therefore, it is necessary to delete stop words in Weibo comment data, so as to improve the subsequent operation performance.

(2) Emotion analysis modeling of Weibo corpus. For the pre-processed Weibo corpus, two emotion analysis modeling methods are adopted, one is based on SnowNLP library in Python, and the other is based on emotion feature vector machine learning method. SnowNLP is a natural language processing library in Python, which supports the processing function of Chinese corpus, and can train new models according to actual needs without building or inputting emotional dictionaries. Using SnowNLP to analyze the emotion of the corpus, we can get the emotion tendency and score of the content. Among them, emotional tendencies include negative, neutral and positive; The closer the score is to 1, the more positive it tends to be, the closer the score is to 0, the more negative it tends to be, and the score close to 0.5 is neutral. However, in the practical application of SnowNLP, positive, neutral and negative tendencies do not include specific emotional categories. In order to reflect the specific emotional categories contained in the corpus, based on certain emotional keywords, an emotional keyword list containing five basic emotions: anger, sadness, fear, happiness and disgust is constructed (Table 2).

Table 2. Examples of Emotions and Corresponding Keywords

Emotion	Keywords
anger	Angry, anxious, complaining......
grief	Sad, deplorable, painful...
fear	In peril, panic, eerie......
delighted	Comfortable, auspicious, precious......
aversion	Abomination, contempt, conspiracy...

The paper of Long-Short Term Memory (LSTM) was first published in 1997. Because of its unique design structure, LSTM is suitable for processing and predicting important events with very long intervals and delays in time series. Because Weibo data has time attribute, it is more suitable for this neural network.

However, the number of output nodes and input features of traditional model is equal, but only one node can be taken in the final result, so other nodes must be discarded, and discarding nodes will lose information. It can be seen that the more input features, the more discarded nodes will lose information, and the discarded nodes actually participate in the calculation process, which will consume calculation resources, and eventually lead to poor classification effect and slow training speed of the model. That is, the more input features, the worse the training effect and the slower the training speed of the traditional model.

Therefore, an emotional feature vector matrix function is established for each corpus, and a 1*5 vector is used to represent the emotional features of the Weibo comment. For the pre-processed Weibo, by matching with the emotional keyword list, the 1*5 emotional vector of the Weibo comment is returned, and the numbers on each column represent the total number of emotional keywords appearing in this emotion. If there is only one column with the largest number, the emotion of this Weibo comment is the emotion of the corresponding column.

There is the possibility of complex emotions and no emotions in Weibo comments, so it is necessary to classify Weibo emotions. The classification results are presented in a nested list, where the first level is five emotions, and the second level is all Weibo comments contained by each emotion. If there is more than one non-zero maximum value in the column of a comment emotion vector, the Weibo comment is a complex emotion; If all five columns of emotion vector are 0, there is no emotion. Therefore, there are seven categories of emotion classification in Weibo, including five basic emotions, complex emotions and no emotions.

To solve the above problems, make some improvements to the traditional model, and the improved model structure is shown in Fig. 6.

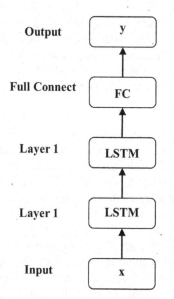

Fig. 6. The improvement structure of LSTM

3.3 Visual Expression of Emotional Characteristics of Weibo Comments

Using regular expression to extract the IP locality information and time information contained in the Weibo comment data set after emotion classification, and transform the Mars coordinate system at the same time. IP locality can be converted into latitude and longitude information for use. Then through the visualization method, we can draw the time and space distribution map, the individual distribution map of a certain emotion and the comprehensive distribution map of all emotions.

Visual expression of Weibo data is an effective means and method that can directly reflect the public opinion orientation of Weibo. Commonly used methods mainly include hot word cloud and statistical charts, and a few of these methods have certain geographical spatial positions. With the development of IP affiliation in Weibo, the geographical coordinates of users become a more accurate geographical data source. Combined with the comment timestamp attribute, the spatial and temporal visual expression of Weibo users' emotions can be well realized, and the trend and trend of emotional changes can be dynamically displayed from geographical dimension and time dimension.

There are three main visualization methods in this study: the first is emotional visualization combined with geographical coordinates corresponding to IP territories; The second is to make emotional statistical charts; The third is the word cloud showing the comment content under the Weibo.

A. Emotional visualization of geographic coordinates

The geographical coordinates of IP affiliation can be mapped from the field, and the emotional distribution map related to geographical space can be formed by combining with the analysis of emotions. Geopandas library is used, which extends the popular data science library pandas by increasing the support for geospatial data, and can store geometric columns and perform spatial operations, which is used to realize the organization and management of geospatial coordinate data.

B. Emotional statistical chart

The related information of emotion can be classified and counted according to time and space, and traditional statistical charts such as line chart, histogram and pie chart can be generated, and corresponding emotional heat map can also be generated according to the score of emotion. In this study, in order to achieve this function, we use Pyecharts library, which is a combination of Echarts and Python class library, which is convenient to connect with Python, and generate data statistical charts in Python, which can be used to make Weibo emotional statistical charts.

C. Word Cloud

Word cloud is a visualization tool of text data, which can visually highlight keywords that appear frequently in a large number of texts, thus filtering out a large number of text information, and viewers can appreciate the main idea of the text through Word cloud. By changing the font size and color of the text, the high-frequency words in the text can be effectively presented.

Word Cloud Library is a third-party library for word cloud display in Python, which can turn a text into a word cloud. Just put the original text or preprocessed text of Weibo comments into the library, and the corresponding word cloud can be obtained.

4 Experimental Design and Result Analysis

4.1 Construction of Feature Element Data Set

Using the Weibo comment area crawler based on IP locality, crawling the comment area content in the given Sina Weibo URL, including the commentator's user name, comment time, IP locality and comment content.

Through compiling and running, the data sets of several microblogs are obtained, including "30th Anniversary of a Brand Computer", "Public Opinion of a Commodity Market" and "Review of Cuiliu Street (Beijing)", etc.

Among them, there are 930 comments in the data of "30th Anniversary of a Brand Computer", including comment content, user name, time and IP affiliation. There are 17,177 comments in the data of "Public Opinion of a Commodity Market", including comment content, topic classification, evaluation and other information (Figs. 7 and 8).

Fig. 7. The general idea of the algorithm

Fig. 8. Review data set of "Public Opinion in a Commodity Market"

(1) Using the constraints of road environment, four types of feature elements, namely heading angle, velocity, acceleration and elevation, are extracted and calculated from the preprocessed original inertial navigation trajectory data, and combined with the idea of "trend feature", their segmented feature vectors are calculated.

(2) Combining the idea of "permutation entropy", the permutation entropy features of heading angle, velocity, acceleration and elevation are constructed, and the feature vectors are also constructed as corresponding feature elements;

(3) Inputting the combined feature vectors into the one-dimensional convolution neural network as input data, and outputting classification probabilities of different inertial navigation trajectory behavior features through deep learning and training;

(4) Using a data coding method to label the behavior feature labels of each inertial navigation trajectory entering the depth neural network;

(5) Outputting inertial navigation trajectory data set with behavior feature labeling.

4.2 Weibo Comment Emotion Classification

The emotional characteristic model of Weibo comments is constructed. Taking the Weibo comments of "a commodity market public opinion" as an example, combined with Jieba thesaurus and SnowNLP emotional analysis method, the traditional word cloud, heat map and statistical map are used to show the emotional classification.

Through compiling and running, the emotional characteristics of the data set are classified and analyzed, which shows the characteristics of the product under different user emotions. The heat map can show people's consistent understanding of the product.

In the word cloud map (Fig. 9), the size of the font represents the number of times the keyword appears, and the larger the font, the more times the keyword appears. At the same time, different colors are used to distinguish the emotional categories of different words.

In the emotional statistical chart (Fig. 10), the number of comments with different scores is mainly reflected, in which the horizontal axis is the score and the vertical axis is the number of times. The closer the score is to 1, the more positive the emotion is, and the closer the score is to 0, the more negative the emotion is.

Fig. 9. Emotional Word Cloud

The heat map (Fig. 11) can explore the correlation between different emotions, and the value is the correlation coefficient. The closer the coefficient is to 1, the stronger the positive (negative) correlation is, and the closer the coefficient is to 0, the weaker the correlation is. For example, the correlation coefficients of "difference" and "excellent" in the graph are extremely small, which shows that they are almost irrelevant.

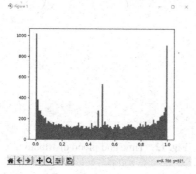

Fig. 10. Statistical Chart of Emotions

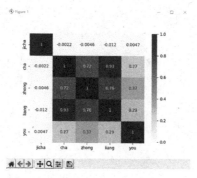

Fig. 11. Emotional heat map

4.3 Temporal and Spatial Visualization of Weibo Comment Emotion

Add time and space information such as longitude and latitude of Weibo comments, and then transform Mars coordinates. Taking the comment of Cuiliu Street (Beijing) as an example, show the spatial and temporal distribution of emotional characteristics of Weibo users visualized through maps.

Through the operation of the prototype system, the statistical map of time and emotion and the spatial distribution map are drawn respectively. There are two main ways to draw spatial distribution map, one is the geographical spatial emotion expression method based on SHP; The second is the geographical spatial emotion expression method based on GEO.

Through the results in the time emotion distribution map, we can see the change trend of Weibo users' comment emotion with time. The horizontal axis is time, the vertical axis is quantity, and curves of different colors represent different emotions. From the figure, the great changes are mainly concentrated in "happy" and "nonemotion".

In the SHP-based geographical spatial emotion expression method, SHP is used as the map base map, and emotions are expressed in the map with different color point symbols through coordinates and geodataframe library. The values of horizontal axis and vertical axis respectively represent the abscissa and ordinate in the transformed Mars coordinate system (Figs. 12 and 13).

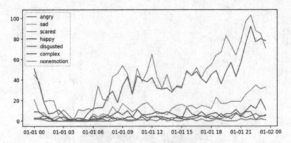

Fig. 12. Time and mood distribution

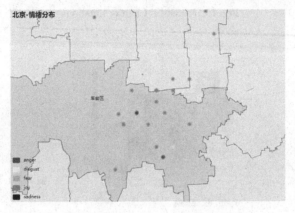

Fig. 13. Spatial Emotional Distribution Map

4.4 Analysis of Results

Through this experiment, the results of emotional analysis of Weibo comments are combined with geographic information. From the distribution of emotional points, it accords with the general cognitive law of population distribution: the population distribution in urban areas is denser than that in suburbs, and the denser places with dense roads are denser than those with sparse roads. After deleting the "no emotion" samples, some of them have negative emotions, but the density is lower than that of positive emotions.

Compared with the traditional emotion analysis method, this method adds IP affiliation and geographical coordinate information to expand the content of user comment data, and intuitively reflects the emotion distribution in the form of map expression, while retaining the statistical charts, heat maps and other methods in the traditional emotion analysis method. This method can effectively obtain Weibo comments, classify emotions and realize visualization.

5 Summary and Prospect

5.1 Summary

With the development of the Internet, there are more and more users of Weibo, which contains a lot of emotional information. However, due to the huge amount of data and complex format of Weibo comment data; Lack of emotion classification expression based on spatial data model; There are few outstanding problems such as visual analysis and expression methods integrated into time and space. In view of these problems, this paper puts forward a visualization method of emotional analysis of Weibo users based on IP affiliation and comment content, which has a certain positive effect on emotional analysis of netizens and consumer preferences analysis. The main research results are as follows:

(1) At the data level, taking the opening of IP affiliation as an opportunity, the geographical coordinate information is further integrated, enriching the data diversity of Weibo comments;
(2) At the method level, the traditional natural language processing method and machine learning method are combined to improve the efficiency and accuracy of emotion classification.
(3) In the visualization method, the map is used as the expression carrier, which reflects the user's emotion and public opinion orientation more intuitively and effectively.

5.2 Outlook

This paper studies the visualization method of Weibo users' emotion analysis based on IP affiliation and comment content, and has achieved some results and feedback, but there are still some shortcomings:

(1) There are still some deficiencies in the method of obtaining comment data, and the method of web crawler is only suitable for individual users who need less data. For users with large demand for data, they also need to design and call Weibo API interface and design database table structure to better meet their practical needs.
(2) There are still some shortcomings in the expression of complex emotions in the emotion classification model, and complex emotions are also diverse, so it is too simplistic to use only "complex emotions" for generalization. A more detailed emotion classification method needs to be added.
(3) The integration of the prototype system is still insufficient. The current prototype system code runs in functional modules, which is inefficient. In the future study, all functional modules will be integrated to realize the whole process of acquisition-processing-visualization.

References

1. Dai, D., Wang, Y., Wang, Y., et al.: Research on the construction of emotional map based on semantic analysis of big data in Weibo–taking Shenzhen as an example. In: Spatial Governance for High-quality Development–Proceedings of 2021 China Urban Planning Annual Conference (05 Application of New Technologies in Urban Planning), pp. 65–72 (2021)
2. Zhao, K.: Research on the Evolution of Weibo Public Opinion Based on Emotion Analysis. Guizhou University of Finance and Economics (2022)

3. Li, R., Wang, J., Shan, J., Wei, Z.: Analysis and visualization of emergency Weibo network public opinion-taking "Wuhan City Closure" as an example. Intell. Explor. **02**, 67–72 (2022)
4. Ni, J., Zhang, Q., Deng, M.: Design and implementation of microblog analysis and visualization system. Comput. Program. Skills Maint. (09), 15–16+33 (2021)
5. Wang, C., Zhang, H., Mo, X., Yang, W.: Summary of emotion analysis in Weibo. Comput. Eng. Sci. **44**(01), 165–175 (2022)
6. Pan, Y.: Research on word cloud generation based on Python-taking Chai Jing's Seeing as an example. Comput. Knowl. Technol. **15**(24), 8–10 (2019)
7. Raza, M.: Evaluation of public perception of vaccination in social media based on emotion analysis and topic modeling method. Beijing University of Chemical Technology (2021)
8. Luo, Q., Wu, N., Su, Y., Yu, T.: Investor surplus optimism and managers' catering--evidence based on social media emotional analysis. China Ind. Econ. (11), 135–154 (2021)
9. Wei, L., Wang, W.: Emotional analysis of video website barrage information based on interactive ritual chain theory-taking health science video as an example. Inf. Theory Pract. **45**(09), 119–126 (2022)
10. Zhang, C., Ma, X., Zhou, Y., et al.: Analysis on the evolution of public opinion of COVID-19 epidemic based on the change of users' emotions. J. Geo-Inf. Sci. **23**(02), 341–350 (2021)
11. Zhang, G., Bao, C., Wang, X., et al.: Text semantic mining and emotion analysis based on comment data. Inf. Sci. **39**(05), 53–61 (2021)
12. Tang, W., Ding, Z., Ma, J.: Public opinion analysis of traffic control under different types of major public events. J. Zhejiang Univ. (Eng. Ed.) **56**(11), 2271–2279 (2022)
13. Yang, L., Zeng, S., Huang, Y.: Combination prediction model of public opinion heat of major emergencies integrated with emotional analysis. Intell. Explor. **11**, 17–25 (2022)
14. Bai, J., Hong, X.: Text mining and emotion analysis of online public opinion based on barrage. Softw. Eng. **25**(11), 44–48 (2022)
15. Chen, X.: Research on overseas internet public opinion and emotion analysis based on the topic of public security events. Cyberspace Secur. **13**(04), 78–85 (2022)
16. Li, W., Yang, Q., Qin, Q.: Multi-feature mixed model text emotion analysis method. Comput. Eng. Appl. **57**(19), 205–213 (2021)
17. Wang, T., Yang, W.: Review of text sentiment analysis methods. Comput. Eng. Appl. **57**(12), 11–24 (2021)
18. Li, D., Li, L., Li, D.: Public opinion effect and enlightenment of the three-child policy-network big data analysis based on NLP. China Youth Res. **10**, 46–53 (2021)
19. Han, K., Xing, Z., Liu, Z., et al.: Study on public opinion analysis method in major public health events-taking Covid-19 epidemic as an example. J. Geo-Inf. Sci. **23**(02), 331–340 (2021)
20. Shi, W., Xue, G., He, S.: A summary of the research on online public opinion from the perspective of emotion. Libr. Inf. Knowl. **39**(01), 105–118 (2022)

Village Web 3D Visualization System Based on Cesium

Guoxing Qu, Jie He[✉], and Jiarong Wang

School of Geography and Planning, Ningxia University, Ningxia 750021, China
459195435@qq.com

Abstract. Cesium is currently the popular open source 3D map engine which widely used in 3D WebGIS and other fields. With the promotion of digital village development, the build of village network 3D information system is in full swing. In this paper, we apply 3D model data organization and load scheduling, single tilt photography 3D model and video stream and 3D scene fusion technology to develop a digital village 3D geographic information system based on Cesium open source 3D map engine. Taking Kangle Village, Shapotou District, Zhongwei City, Ningxia as an example, the results show that the real-time frame rate of system visualization is stable at about 35 FPS, which realizes the dynamic scheduling, real-time rendering, viewshed analysis and measurement of village 3D model and lays a foundation for the construction of digital and even smart village.

Keywords: Cesium · Oblique photography models · Visualization system · Digital village

1 Introduction

The arrival of the "big data era" will transform the construction of urban geographic information system (GIS) from a digital city to a more advanced smart city [1], and the construction of village GIS is also imperative. In the context of the information age, the construction of smart cities is in full swing. Relying on emerging technologies such as big data, cloud computing, artificial intelligence and three-dimensional visualization in smart cities [2], a digital village 3D GIS is constructed to improve the efficiency of village digital construction.

Governments have provided valuable experience for the construction of digital village areas by formulating relevant policies and regulations to continuously promote the innovation of agricultural village development model. In foreign countries, since the 1950s, the United States has started to implement the construction project of agricultural village information. With the help of the perfect infrastructure project of agricultural village information network, the agricultural information service system has been constructed, which promotes the process of village digitization in the United States [3]. The European Union actively promotes the project of "Building a Smart Village in the 21st Century", which greatly promotes the digitization, networking and intelligent development of the village [4]. Canada pays attention to the integration and sharing of

X. Meng et al. (Eds.): SpatialDI 2023, LNCS 13887, pp. 89–100, 2023.
https://doi.org/10.1007/978-3-031-32910-4_6

information resources in the construction of digital village and accelerates the construction of village information technology with the help of the Internet and digital media [5]. India's software industry promotes the development of agricultural information services and provides decision support for urban, village and agricultural development [6]. In china, digital village construction has achieved remarkable results. Domestic scholars have made in-depth research on village digitization and 3D visualization methods. Liu (2008) [7] uses Skyline as the secondary development platform, constructs a 3D visualization system of digital village, and achieves the basic 3D map operation function. Li (2010) [8] uses Skyline series software to build a 3D digital village system in Yunkangcun, which implements spatial analysis and other functions. Fu (2017) [9] built a beautiful village geographic information service system based on the WeChat public platform, which solved the inconvenience of village GIS in mobile devices and other issues. Tan (2018) [10] uses 3ds MAX software and ArcGIS software to realize 3D visualization of village landscape. Du (2021) [11] based on MVC system architecture and SuperMap platform, has designed and implemented a B/S mode digital Lianzhang 3D virtual GIS. The existing village digitization and 3D visualization methods provide a powerful reference for the construction of digital and even smart village. However, most of them are redeveloped based on Skyline, ArcGIS and other software. The client (C/S) mode or the mode of installing plug-ins on the browser for browsing are mainly used, which can not meet the current requirements of village GIS construction. At the same time, 3D village visualization based on open source GIS platform needs further study.

Compared with commercial GIS software, open source GIS software has the characteristics of flexibility and economy, and plays an important role in the field of GIS [12]. As a popular open source 3D map engine, Cesium can integrate multi-source and heterogeneous spatial data on the digital earth and has the ability to interact with the server asynchronously [13]. Based on the Cesium open source 3D map engine, take Kangle Village, Changle Town, Shapotou District, Zhongwei City, Ningxia as an example to construct a digital village 3D GIS and express the comprehensive multi-source geographic information of Kangle village.

2   System Architecture

The digital village 3D GIS adopts B/S architecture, which is divided into three layers: data layer, service layer and presentation layer. The data layer includes basic geographic data, real-time/local video files, 3D tiles model resources, etc. It is mainly responsible for maintaining spatial data and attribute data to provide data support for the system. The core of the system is the service layer composed of Web server, GIS server and streaming media server. The Web server is responsible for the deployment of Web applications, the GIS server is in charge of the release of geographic data services, and the streaming media server is applied for the storage, coding and transmission of video streaming data. As the liaison layer between presentation layer and data layer, service layer is mainly responsible for the data interaction between front and back end. The presentation layer is the part of users' intuitive perception, which mainly realizes the coordination operation between users and the system. The overall structure is shown in Fig. 1.

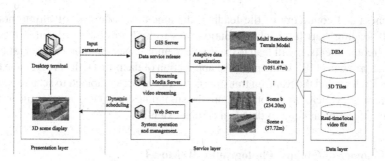

Fig. 1. System architecture

3 The System Design

3.1 Data Organization and Loading Scheduling of 3D Model

In order to present the structure and texture features of massive 3D models to the maximum extent and restore the details of buildings, 3D tiles are used for the organization of village 3D real scene data by analyzing the data format of Cesium 3D real scene model. 3D tiles are based on GL transmission format and combined with LOD technology to improve the rendering efficiency of 3D geographic information data in the 3D Web-GIS framework [14]. The tile set data is stored by a file in tileset.json format, and the tile data is responsible for storing geometric and attribute data. The loading efficiency of 3D tiles depends on the spatial index structure of tiles, which typically includes quadtree, octree, k-d tree, grid structure, etc. [15]. The browser side has certain limitations in rendering massive 3D real data. When users browse massive village 3D real data, the objects observed are only part of them. By eliminating the view field, the amount of data for rendering massive 3D model by the browser is reduced, so as to improve the efficiency of data scheduling. The rendering accuracy of the 3D model is determined by the screen space error (SSE), and the current SSE ρ is calculated by formula (1) [16, 17]. Compared with the given threshold ε, if $\rho > \varepsilon$, the node of the next level is continued to be loaded, and if $\rho < \varepsilon$, the tiles of the current level are used for scene visualization.

$$\rho = \frac{H}{2tan(\alpha/2)} \times \frac{\delta}{D} \tag{1}$$

where, ρ is the SSE; δ is the static error of the node; α is the field of view angle; H is the screen height; D is the distance from the viewpoint to the node.

The study area is located in a village area, and the density of buildings is inconsistent and uneven. According to the characteristics of spatial data, a continuous Hierarchical Level of Detail (HLOD) model is generated by the corresponding spatial partition method. The leapfrog transmission strategy [18] is adopted to schedule the scene HLOD. When the viewpoint parameters change, if the SSE of the tile is greater than the threshold, it is necessary to recursively traverse the sub tiles of the current tile until a tile with a resolution meeting the refinement conditions is found for rendering. This scheduling strategy will cause problems such as unreasonable tile detail level filtering, and the scene loading is not smooth. Although the progressive transmission strategy can ensure the smoothness and continuity of tile loading, the amount of tile data of tilting model is large. If loading start from low resolution tiles to high resolution tiles that meet the refining requirements, it will lead to excessive memory consumption, browser stuttering and other problems [19]. In the practical application of the project, the progressive transmission strategy and the leapfrog transmission strategy are combined to set a reasonable SSE threshold, which can not only ensure the smoothness and continuity of tile loading, but also reduce the amount of data to a certain extent.

3.2 Monomer of Oblique Photography 3D Model

The 3D model produced by the oblique photography technology is a continuous triangulated irregular network (TIN), which cannot realize the functions of independent selection, query and attribute assignment of the target object. On the basis of not destroying the continuity of the physical layer of the 3D model, dynamic rendering is used to realize the monomer of the 3D model [20]. The implementation principle is to superimpose the vector base map on the object that needs to be monomer, and dynamically render the monomer effect of the ground object. Cesium's process of realizing 3D model monomer is essentially a process of dynamic rendering monomer. The key is the generation of bounding box, through the terrain contour vector data, and the bounding box is superimposed with the tilt photography model to achieve model segmentation visually. Since the physical structure of the 3D model is not damaged, the rendering efficiency of the 3D model will not be affected.

The monomer of 3D model is an urgent problem to be solved when the 3D model of oblique photography is applied to GIS. The monomer of model is the prerequisite for the realization of spatial analysis and attribute query. The non-offset image map was obtained according to the spatial position of the 3D model of oblique photography, which was imported into ArcGIS software to vectorize objects to be monomer and add attribute information such as name, address and height. The vector plane was imported into CesiumLab data processing system. The shape file is converted into bounding box 3D tiles by the vector block slicing tool, which is superposition with the tilted 3D model to achieve monomer.

3.3 Video Streaming and 3D Scene Fusion

Video stream and 3D scene fusion technology can generate dynamic virtual scenes on static 3D models, and integrate the monitoring video with the corresponding 3D scene to achieve the effect of virtual reality fusion [21]. In this paper, the projection texture mapping [22] method is used to render the monitoring picture as a dynamic texture in real time, realizing the close integration of monitoring video and 3D scene. The key to achieve the video fusion effect is video projection. The model view matrix M_{mv} and projection matrix M_p are calculated by camera position and orientation information, and the pixel texture coordinates s corresponding to the vertex coordinates p of the model surface are calculated by formula (2), then the occluded part of the model is clipped to improve the fusion efficiency. After the pixel texture grating, the video fusion effect is finally achieved. The texture of the video model is obtained from the streaming media server by the <video> tag on the browser side.

$$S = M_p \cdot M_{mv} \cdot P \qquad (2)$$

The texture of the video model is provided by the streaming media server, which obtains real-time video data from the webcam through the Real Time Messaging Protocol (RTMP) and sends it to the user's browser after encoding. The transmission of video stream to the browser is realized through HTTP Live Streaming (HLS) protocol. The Streaming media server fragments the surveillance video according to HLS protocol and sends it to the browser through HTTP. The <video> tag on the browser side can obtain real-time video streams by requesting configuration files and video shards of real-time streams. If the browser requests a locally cached video, the streaming media server directly finds the corresponding cache file and sends it to the requesting browser.

4 Experiment

In order to verify the practicability and feasibility of the design scheme and implementation technology, a digital village 3D GIS was built in Kangle Village, Changle Town, Shapotou District, Zhongwei City, Ningxia, for experimental verification and analysis.

4.1 Experimental Environment and Data

The experimental hardware environment is as follows: Intel(R) Xeon(R) CPU E3-1225 V5@3.30 ghz, 16 GB memory, NVIDIA GeForce GTX 1060 6 GB graphics card. The software environment is Windows7 64-bit operating system and Google Chrome browser.

The data used are the oblique photography data of the experimental area which is about 1.1 km². The source data format of the oblique photography model is OSGB, and the data volume is 4.45 GB, and the data volume after format conversion is 1.73 GB. Experiment 1 explores the changes of visualization efficiency under different view heights, only change the view heights, intercept the 3D visualization scene of Kangle Village under different view heights, and record the changes of visual frame rate during the change of view heights in real time. The experiment is tested in LAN environment. Experiment 2 explores the differences in visualization efficiency during scene interaction under different network environments, and records the changes of visual frame rate under wireless network and broadband network in real time. The experiment is tested under wireless network and broadband network respectively.

4.2 Results

In Experiment 1, the 3D visualization scene of Kangle Village is shown in Fig. 2, and the effect of view height on frame rate is shown in scene d. The initial loading adopts a large-scale macro perspective, with a height of 1051.67 m (scene a). In the process of 3D scene visualization rendering, tiles of different fineness are dynamically loaded with the change of the perspective. When the viewpoint height is high, low resolution tiles are loaded. At this time, the bounding box of tiles is large. As can be seen from the real-time frame rate graph (real-time frame rate d), there are many tiles at the beginning of scene loading, and the frame rate is low. When the height drops to 234.20 m (scene b), the visual range of the scene decreases, the number of tiles loaded decreases, and the frame rate will gradually increase and remain stable. When the height is reduced to 57.72 m (scene c), tiles with different resolution levels of detail are dynamically loaded. At this time, the tile bounding box is small, and the frame rate is further increased and remains stable. During the whole scene loading process, the number of tiles loaded is reduced while satisfying the visual effect.

In Experiment 2, the visual real-time rendering frame rate under broadband network and wireless network environment is shown in Fig. 3. The visualization frame rate is stable at about 35 FPS in both broadband network and wireless network environments, which proves that the proposed method can meet the requirements of 3D visualization of Kangle village under different network environments.

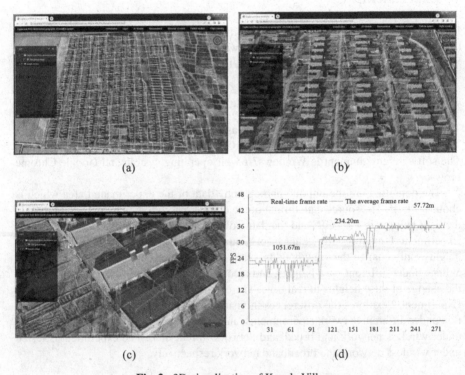

(a)   (b)

(c)   (d)

Fig. 2. 3D visualization of Kangle Village

4.3 System

This paper mainly realize the functions of monomer, plotting measurement, the viewshed analysis, particle system, real-time dynamic information release and so on.

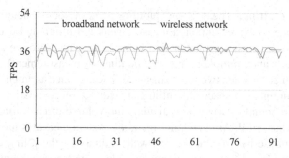

Fig. 3. Visualized frame rates under different network environments

Monomer of Oblique Photography 3D Model. The key to realize the monomer function of dynamic rendering of tilting photography 3D model lies in the conversion of data format and the acquisition of bounding box 3D tiles. In this paper, CesiumLab Data processing system was used for Data format conversion. Metadata.xml file and Data file were input and parameters were set according to the conversion requirements to realize the conversion between OSGB and 3D tiles. Shape file was converted into bounding box 3D tiles by vector block slicing tool. The 3D tiles of the bounding box are superimposed with the tilted photographic model to realize dynamic monomer. Finally, the mouse click event is set to query the location and ownership of the house and highlight the monomer object when the monomer model is clicked. The effect is shown in Fig. 4, which can query the location of the house and other information in real time and highlight the monomeric object.

Fig. 4. Monomer of the 3D model

Measuring and Plotting. The system plotting measurement includes three sub-functions: distance measurement, area measurement and filling and excavation calculation. The distance measurement function can not only measure the spatial distance between two points and multiple points (e.g. continuous measurement), but also obtain the height difference between two points in space. The area measurement function refers to the area measurement of space. The filling and excavation calculation is to divide the selected area into countless triangles, calculate the volume of each triangle and judge whether to excavate or fill. As shown in Fig. 5, the system measures the space distance and area of the house in a digital way, as well as analyzes the filling and excavation based on a datum plane, which can effectively reduce the labor and material input and improve the measurement efficiency.

Fig. 5. Plotting measurement

The Viewshed Analysis. The viewshed analysis is widely used in village planning, sunshine analysis, shading of road features (traffic signs, signal lights, etc.), location selection of surveillance cameras, etc. [23]. In this paper, the viewshed analysis is applied to the location selection of surveillance cameras in village areas. After the observation points and viewing angles are determined, the viewshed analysis is carried out on the village 3D scenes. The viewshed analysis results are shown in Fig. 6, in which green represents the visible area and red represents the invisible area. The system can simulate the visual monitoring effect of different observation points and viewing angles in real time to determine the best deployment mode of the camera.

Particle System. Particle system is a graphics technology used to simulate complex physical effects [24]. It describes the changes of irregular objects by setting the position, shape, moving speed, moving direction, life cycle and other attributes of particles. The particle system can simulate irregular objects such as rain, snow and flame in real time,

Fig. 6. Viewable analysis

and effectively enhance the realism of 3D scenes. As shown in Fig. 7, the rainfall scenario of Kangle Village is simulated.

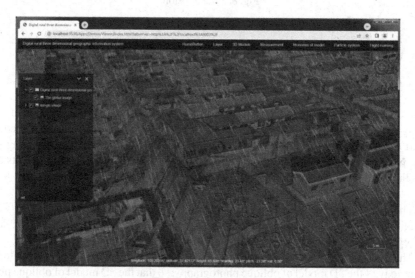

Fig. 7. Particle system

Real-time Dynamic Information Release. Real-time dynamic information in the village, such as electronic announcement service and real-time monitoring video, are indispensable information sources to reflect the village dynamics. In this paper, the projection texture mapping method is used to integrate the dynamic information and monitoring video of village revitalization with 3D scenes, so as to realize the real-time dynamic information release and online viewing of surveillance video. As shown in Fig. 8, the dynamic information of village revitalization is integrated with the 3D scene.

Fig. 8. Video fusion

5 Conclusions

This paper adopts B/S architecture, based on Cesium open source 3D map engine, relying on big data, virtual reality, 3D visualization and other emerging technologies owned by smart cities, and takes Kangle Village, Changle Town, Shapotou District, Zhongwei City, Ningxia as an example to build a digital village 3D GIS. The research results are as follows:

1. The construction and efficient visualization of village 3D scenes are realized with oblique photography data as the basic support, combined with 3D model data organization and loading scheduling technology.
2. The dynamic monomer of village landscape is realized by using the monomer technology of the 3D model of oblique photography, so that the 3D model of oblique photography has the characteristics of vector data. On this basis, the attribute information query of geographical elements of Kangle Village in Changle Town is realized.
3. The system realizes the spatial analysis of the 3D scene of Kangle Village, and carries out plotting measurement and visibility analysis of the geographical elements of Kangle Village in a digital way. The rainfall scene of Kangle Village is simulated by particle system to improve the interactivity of scene simulation and enhance the reality of 3D scene.

4. The system integrates real-time dynamic information, terrain data, video data, panorama data and other multi-source information. On the basis of solving the key technologies such as the organization and transmission of multivariate data, it realizes the visualization of village 3D scene, and carries out all-round multi-source geographic information expression for the village, making the static village data "fresh" and "rich".

Digital village 3D GIS is developed based on open source platform, which has certain requirements for spatial data format. Different types of spatial data need format conversion, so it is necessary to conduct in-depth research on data sources and data interfaces, reduce the dependence of the platform on the data format, and improve the development efficiency of the system. The digital village 3D GIS can be used as the basic information platform of Kangle Village to further integrate village announcement, asset management, construction planning and other businesses and functions into it, providing a technical basis for the construction of smart villages.

Acknowledgements. This work was supported by the Ningxia Natural Science Foundation under Grant 2022AAC03054 and National Natural Science Foundation of China under Grant 42061062. The authors would like to thank the anonymous reviewers for their valuable comments and insightful ideas.

References

1. Wang, J.Y.: Smart city in big data era. Sci. Surv. Mapp. **39**(05), 3–7 (2014)
2. Zhu, Q.: Full three-dimensional GIS and its key roles in smart city. J. Geo-Inf. Sci. **16**(02), 151–157 (2014)
3. Eanes, F.R., Singh, A.S., Bulla, B.R., et al.: Midwestern US farmers perceive crop advisers as conduits of information on agricultural conservation practices. Environ. Manag. **60**, 974–988 (2017)
4. Harakaľová, Ľ.: Smart villages–new concept of rural development of the EU. In: Proceedings of the 4th International Conference on European Integration 2018, pp. 413–421 (2018)
5. Trendov, M., Varas, S., Zeng, M.: Digital Technologies in Agriculture and Rural Areas: Status Report (2019)
6. Kalmegh, S.R., Joshi, D.: Community information center for Indian agriculture. IETE Tech. Rev. **20**(3), 261–264 (2003)
7. Liu, X.J.: Design and Implementation of 3D Visualization System for Digital Countryside. Kunming University of Science and Technology (2009)
8. Li, D.: The application of 3D GIS in the construction of digital village based on skyline. Yunnan Geogr. Environ. Res. **22**(02), 5–8 (2010)
9. Fu, Z.L., Zheng, H.Q.: Design and implementation of beautiful village GIS based on WeChat public platform. J. Geomat. **42**(06), 82–84 (2017)
10. Tan, Z.: Design of rural landscape design system based on 3D virtualization. Mod. Electron. Tech. **41**(22), 38–41 (2018)
11. Du, P.F.: Design and Implementation of 3D Virtual GIS for Digital Village. North China Institute of Aerospace Engineering (2021)
12. Fan, J.F., Hu, T.Y., He, H.X., et al.: Multi-source digital map tile data mashup scheme design based on Cesium. Natl. Remote Sens. Bull. **23**(04), 695–705 (2019)

13. Cao, Y.N., Wang, J., Gu, D.P.: Digital highway method for multi-source data integration. Sci. Technol. Eng. **19**(19), 214–221 (2019)
14. Xu, Z., Zhang, L., Suo, H., et al.: IFC-based data visualization of 3D tiles for buildings. J. Zhejiang Univ. (Eng. Sci.) **53**(06), 1047–1056 (2019)
15. Cao, H.Z.: Analysis for 3D Tiles Definition and Design for Production Standard. Wuhan University (2018)
16. Zhang, Y.H., Zhu, Q., Zhu, J., et al.: Lightweight web visualization of massive DSM data. J. Geomat. Sci. Technol. **34**(06), 649–653 (2017)
17. Cozzi, P., Ring, K.: 3D Engine Design for virtual globes. AK Peters/CRC Press, (2011)
18. Wang, R., Huo, L., Bao, P., et al.: Rapid visualization method of oblique airborne photogrammetry model based on skipping HLOD. J. Beijing Univ. Civ. Eng. Archit. **33**(04), 27–32 (2017)
19. Song, Z., Li, J.: A dynamic tiles loading and scheduling strategy for massive oblique photogrammetry models. In: 2018 IEEE 3rd International Conference on Image, Vision and Computing, pp. 648–652 (2018)
20. Sun, S.M., Huang, T.J., Sun, Y.: Construction and application of high-precision three-dimensional monomerization model for urban scenes. Bull. Surv. Mapp. **01**, 108–111 (2021)
21. Bai, H.R.: Design and implementation of 3D GIS intelligent monitoring system based on multi-scene fusion. Beijing University of Posts and Telecommunications (2020)
22. Zhou, Y., Meng, M., Wu, W., et al.: Virtual-reality video fusion system based on video model. J. Syst. Simul. **30**(07), 2550–2557 (2018)
23. Mi, X.X., Yang, B.S., Dong, Z.: Fast visibility analysis and application in road environment with mobile laser scanning data. Geomat. Inf. Sci. Wuhan Univ. **45**(02), 258–264 (2020)
24. Wang, R.J., Tian, J.Q., Ni, Z.G.: Realtime simulation of rain and snow based on particle system. J. Syst. Simul. (04), 495–496+501 (2003)

Spatial Big Data Analysis

Spatial-Aware Community Search Over Heterogeneous Information Networks

Yi Zhou$^{(\boxtimes)}$, Lihua Zhou, Jialong Wang, Lizhen Wang, and Bing Kong

School of Information Science and Engineering, Yunnan University, Kunming 650091, Yunnan,
People's Republic of China
zhyi4635@163.com

Abstract. The prosperity of smart mobile devices and the popularity of social
networks have led to the rapid growth of spatial social networks. Spatial-aware
community search aims to look for a cohesive subgraph that contains a query vertex in spatial social networks, whose vertices are close structurally and spatially.
However, existing studies only focus on homogeneous graphs, and ignore the heterogeneity of the networks, which results in the searched community is not refined
enough to meet the specific applications of scenarios. In this paper, we propose
a novel problem, named *spatial-aware community search over a heterogeneous
information network* (SACS-HIN), which retrieves a refined community by capturing rich semantics in the network, taking into account spatial proximity and
social relevance. To solve this problem, we develop three algorithms based on the
structure-first strategy and distance-first strategy. Finally, extensive experiments
are conducted on four datasets to evaluate both the effectiveness and efficiency
of our proposed algorithms. The community size analysis and case study verify
that the proposed algorithms can obtain a refined community that satisfies query
conditions. The efficiency evaluation explores the effect of different parameters
on the efficiency of the algorithms.

Keywords: Heterogeneous Information Network · Community Search ·
Spatial-Aware · Search Strategy

1 Introduction

Community search [1], as an important research problem in social network analysis,
aims to search for a cohesive subgraph that contains a query vertex, while spatial-aware
community search additionally considers the actual distance between vertices based on
community search, requiring the target community not only needs to be structurally
cohesive but also expects the spatial positions of the vertices to be close to each other.
A large amount of location information contained in spatial social networks reveals
people's various life patterns, laws, and preferences, which can be used to find a more
refined community and to provide users with location-based activity planning and new
applications [2], bringing convenience to life.

X. Meng et al. (Eds.): SpatialDI 2023, LNCS 13887, pp. 103–114, 2023.
https://doi.org/10.1007/978-3-031-32910-4_7

Spatial community search [3–5] has been studied by many researchers, but all these studies focused on homogeneous information networks with one type of vertices. Compared with homogeneous information networks, heterogeneous information networks (HINs) express richer semantic information and provide a more complete, natural, accurate, as well as detailed description of complex networks.

Figure 1(a) illustrates a homogeneous network consisting of authors with locations, extracted from DBLP, and Fig. 1(b) is a spatial HIN with three types of vertices, extracted from DBLP, namely, author (A), paper (P), and topic (T), which contains the semantic relationships among vertices of different types. For example, the authors a_1, a_2, and a_3 have written a paper p_3, which mentions the topic t_1.

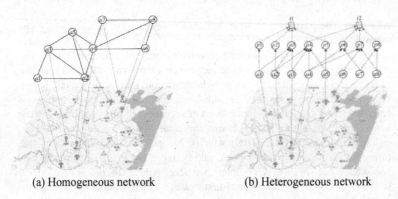

(a) Homogeneous network   (b) Heterogeneous network

Fig. 1. The network instance of DBLP

Spatial community search over HINs can have many applications in real life. For example, suppose authors a_1a_1 want to organize a local workshop, we use the model $k-$core with $k = 2$ to ensure participants are required to be acquainted with at least two people in the community, the three authors $\{a_1, a_2, a_3\}$ is a good result since their research expertise is relevant and their locations are close, the relationship between them is defined by the meta-path a_1pt_1pa. However, in Fig. 1(a), the result set will be $\{a_1, a_2, a_3, a_4\}$, although author a_4 isn't the researcher of topic t_1 as other authors. From the above example, we can see that the community of $\{a_1, a_2, a_3\}$ is more refined than $\{a_1, a_2, a_3, a_4\}$ and will better meet the requirements of users.

In this paper, we study the problem of spatial-aware community search over heterogeneous information network, aims to search for a community that is both structurally cohesive and spatially adjacent in networks that contains multi-type objects and complex relationships, which can provide a feasible solution for offline social activities such as academic seminars and team collaboration. To achieve this purpose, we present a structure-first strategy and a distance-first strategy, and develop an algorithm named ReaFirst based on the structure-first strategy, and two algorithm called DistFirst and FastDist based on the distance-first search strategy, and in FastDist, a labeled batch search in introduced to optimize the search efficiency further.

The main contributions of this paper are as follows: (1) A spatial-aware community search problem SACS-HIN in heterogeneous information networks is proposed, and a formal definition is given for the proposed problem. (2) For the SACS-HIN problem, two search strategies, structure-first and distance-first, were designed respectively. In each strategy, the search was from the two stages of structurally cohesive and spatial proximity, and we propose the ReaFirst algorithm, the DistFirst algorithm, and the Fast-Dist algorithm. (3) We conduct extensive experiments on four datasets to evaluate the effectiveness and efficiency of our algorithms.

The remained paper is organized as follows: Sect. 2 introduces the related work; Sect. 3 elaborates some basic concepts and gives a formal problem definition; Sect. 4 presents three algorithms proposed based on two strategies; Sect. 5 describes the experimental preparation and settings, and reports the experimental results; Sect. 6 summarizes the paper.

2 Related Work

Existing community search methods focus on different types of networks and find communities in different ways. Fang et al. [6] gave a comprehensive overview of relevant community search work in homogeneous information networks, including spatial-aware community search [4], and temporal network community search [7] and influential community search [8]. We mainly introduce the research work related to this paper from two aspects: spatial-aware community search over homogeneous information networks and community search over HINs.

A large number of spatial-aware community search studies exist in homogeneous information networks. David et al. [9] showed that users' social network relationships are influenced by spatial location information through numerous experiments. Sozio [10] who proposed a community search problem around the scenario of how to plan a successful cocktail party. Zhu et al. [11] considered rectangular spatial window, relaxed nearest neighbor, and strict nearest neighbor constraint to solve the problem of GSGQ. Wang et al. [12] used a radius-bounded circle to limit the user's position in the spatial social network. Fang et al. [4] searched for a spatial-aware community (SAC) in a large spatial network, determined a minimum covering circle (MCC) through three points on the boundary. Although these researches achieved many results, whether it is based on a rectangle, based on a bounded circle, or based on a minimum coverage circle, which are essentially spatial community search based on the homogeneous information network.

HINs can fit better with real-life complex networks, so relevant research in recent years has begun to extend to HINs [13]. Wang et al. [14] investigated an online technique that can match user pairs in different social networks in a short time. Fang et al. [15] used meta-paths to define a series of relationships between different types of vertices in HINs, proposed the concept of $(k, \mathcal{P})$-core, and designed the FastBCore algorithm with good search performance. Qiao et al. [16] conducted research on keyword-centric community search in large HINs. Jiang et al. [17] performed an effective community search in a star-schema HIN, solved the limitation of requiring users to specify meta-paths and relational constraints for users unfamiliar with HINs. These community search methods all capture the rich semantics embedded among multiple types of objects in HINs, but they all do not take into account the actual spatial distance of the objects and still have a large gap with the real world.

Synthesizing the above analysis, most of the methods either ignore the heterogeneity of the network or the spatial distance between community members, and such community search results have limitations for many scenarios. To this end, we proposed a study of spatial-aware community search in HINs to mine the cohesive structural groups and spatial proximity groups in user groups and location circles, respectively, which can obtain the best community that meets the query requirements.

3 Basic Concepts and Problem Definition

In this paper, we introduce some concepts of HINs and community search and then give a specific definition for the problem of spatial-aware community search over the heterogeneous information network.

3.1 Basic Concepts

Definition 1: Heterogeneous Information Networks (HIN) [18]. An HIN is a directed graph $G = (V, E)$ composing of a vertex set V and an edge set E, the vertex type mapping function is $\varphi : V \rightarrow \mathcal{A}$ and the edge type mapping function is $\phi : E \rightarrow \mathcal{R}$. Where each vertex $v \in V$ belongs to a vertex type $\varphi(v) \in \mathcal{A}$, and each edge $e \in E$ belongs to an edge type (also known as a relation) $\phi(e) \in \mathcal{R}$. A network is called an HIN if $|\mathcal{A}| + |\mathcal{R}| > 1$.

Definition 2: Network Schema [18]. Given a HIN $G = (V, E)$ with vertex-type mapping $\varphi : V \rightarrow \mathcal{A}$ and edge-type mapping $\phi : E \rightarrow \mathcal{R}$, its schema T_G is a directed graph defined over vertex types $\mathcal{A}$ and edge types (relations) $\mathcal{R}$, namely $T_G = (\mathcal{A}, \mathcal{R})$.

Definition 3: Meta-path [18]. A meta-path $\mathcal{P}$ is a path defined on a heterogeneous information network schema $T_G = (\mathcal{A}, \mathcal{R})$ and represented as $A_1 \xrightarrow{R_1} A_2 \xrightarrow{R_2} \cdots \xrightarrow{R_l} A_{l+1}$, where $L = |\mathcal{P}|$ denotes the length of meta-path $\mathcal{P}, A_i \in \mathcal{A}(1 \leq i \leq L+1), \mathcal{R}_j \in \mathcal{R}(1 \leq j \leq L)$.

Definition 4: k-core [19]. Given an integer $k(k > 0)$, the $k-$core of G is the largest subgraph of G, in which the degree of each vertex v is no less than k.

3.2 Problem Statement

Given a HIN $G = (V, E)$, a non-negative integer k, a query vertex q and a maximum user spatial distance constraint d, the SACS-HIN returns a community $C \subseteq V$ satisfying the following constraints: (1) Connectivity: C is connected and needs to contain q; (2) Structure cohesiveness: The minimum degree of nodes in C is no less than k; (3) Spatial proximity: $\forall v \in C, d(v, q) \leq d$; Note that a vertex $v \in V$ of the user type in the network has a location $(v.x, v.y)$, where $v.x$ and $v.y$ represent its position along the x-axis and y-axis in two-dimensional space.

4 SACS-HIN Search Algorithms

According to the definition of the SACS-HIN problem, two effective algorithms (ReaFirst, DistFirst) and one efficient algorithm (FastDist) are designed in this section based on the structure-first strategy and the distance-first strategy, respectively.

4.1 The ReaFirst Algorithm

Based on the structure-first search strategy, this section proposes the ReaFirst algorithm as shown in Algorithm 1. The main idea of this algorithm is: we start with a query vertex, search for a maximum subgraph that satisfies $(k, \mathcal{P})$−core as a candidate subgraph. Then search the subgraph with the spatial location in the range of d from the candidate subgraph. Finally, the set of vertices will be returned as the resultant community.

Algorithm 1: ReaFirst

Input: G, q, $\mathcal{P}$, k, d;
Output: C;
1   Initialize $C \leftarrow \varnothing$, $S \leftarrow \{q\}$;
2   add all the vertices with the same type as q to S;
3   **foreach** vertex $v \in S$ **do**
4   delete the vertices in S whose $\deg(v) < k$;
5   if $d(v,q) > d$ **then** remove v from S;
6   **foreach** $u \in S$ **do**
7   **if** u is the $\mathcal{P}$-neighbor of v **then** remove v from $\mathcal{P}$-neighbor[u];
8   update $\deg(v)$;
9        $C \leftarrow$ remove all the vertices that are not $\mathcal{P}$-connected with q from S;
10   return C;

The time complexity of Algorithm 1 is $\mathcal{O}(n_1 \times d_{1,2} + n_1 \sum_{i=1}^{L} n_i \times d_{i,i+1})$, where n_i represents the number of vertices corresponding to the i-th vertex type of the meta-path $\mathcal{P}$, and $d_{i,i+1}$ denotes the maximum number of vertices corresponding to the $(i + 1)$-th vertex type of the meta-path $\mathcal{P}$, which are connected to the vertices corresponding to the i-th vertex type.

4.2 The DistFirst Algorithm

Algorithm 1 considers the structural cohesiveness of the community in the first stage, in which there exist a part of distant vertices. After removing these over-range distant vertices in the second stage, their degrees of these vertices will be affected and become no longer satisfied with k, so it is necessary to recalculate k−core. To optimize this step, this section considers dealing with the distant vertices first and proposes the DistFirst algorithm shown in Algorithm 2.

Algorithm 2: DistFirst

Input: G, q, $\mathcal{P}$, k, d;

Output: C;

1   Initialize $C \leftarrow \varnothing$, $S \leftarrow \{q\}$;
2   add all the vertices with the same type as q to S;
3   **foreach** vertex $v \in S$ **do**
4   if $d(v,q) > d$ **then** remove v from S;
5   **foreach** $u \in S$ **do**
6   **if** u is the $\mathcal{P}$-neighbor of v **then** remove v from $\mathcal{P}$-neighbor[u];
7   update $\deg(v)$;
8   delete the vertices in S whose $\deg(v) < k$;
9   $C \leftarrow$ remove all the vertices that are not $\mathcal{P}$-connected with q from S;
10 return C;

First, initialize the target community C, and the vertex set S containing the query vertex (line 1). Then, in the first stage, all vertices with the target type are added to the set of vertices S. Vertices outside the specified range d are iteratively removed, and these vertices are removed from the set of their neighbors (lines 2–6); based on this, the second stage is performed, where the degree of each vertex is updated, and vertices not satisfying k are removed under the condition that the spatial proximity constraint is satisfied (lines 7–8), and the final S is the community searched by the algorithm (lines 9–10). The time cost of Algorithm 2 is $\mathcal{O}(n_1 \times d_{1,2} + n_1 \sum_{i=1}^{L} n_i \times d_{i,i+1})$.

4.3   The FastDist Algorithm

Inspired by Algorithm 2, we incorporate the labeled batch search strategy (BSL) based on the distance-first approach and propose a fast search algorithm FastDist as shown in Algorithm 3.

Algorithm 3: FastDist

Input: G, q, $\mathcal{P}$, k, d;

Output: C;

1   Initialize $C \leftarrow \varnothing$, $S \leftarrow \{q\}$;
2   **for** $i \leftarrow 1$ to L **do**;
3     $Y \leftarrow \varnothing$;
4   **for** each vertex $v \in S$ **do**
5   **for** each neighbor u of v **do**
6   **if** (v,u) matches with i-th edge of $\mathcal{P}$ **then**
7   **if** (v,u) does not have a lable i **then**
8             $Y.\text{add}(v)$ and attach a lable i to (v,u);
9     $S \leftarrow Y$;
10 **foreach** vertex $v \in S$ **do**
11   if $d(v,q) > d$ **then** remove v from S;
12   **foreach** $u \in S$ **do**
13   **if** u is the $\mathcal{P}$-neighbor of v **then** remove v from $\mathcal{P}$-neighbor[u];
14   update $\deg(v)$;
15   delete the vertices in S whose $\deg(v) < k$;
16 $C \leftarrow$ remove all the vertices that are not $\mathcal{P}$-connected with q from S;
17 return C;

Similarly, first, initialize the target community C, and the vertex set S containing the query vertices (line 1). Use the BSL strategy to search for all $\mathcal{P}-$neighbor vertices of the query vertex q and assign them to S (lines 2–9); in the first stage, vertices outside the specified range d are iteratively deleted, and these vertices are removed from their neighbor vertex sets (lines 10–13). Then, the second stage is performed by updating the degree of each vertex and removing the vertices that do not satisfy k under the condition that the spatial proximity constraint is satisfied (lines 14–15), and the remaining S is the community searched by the algorithm (lines 16–17). The total time cost of Algorithm 3 is $\mathcal{O}(d_{1,2} + \sum_{i=2}^{L} n_i \times d_{i,i+1})$.

5 Experiments

5.1 Experiment Settings

Datasets. In this paper, experiments are conducted on four datasets of HINs, and the details of the datasets are shown in Table 1. Among them, DBLP [20] is a co-author network constructed by research papers published in the field of computer science. SDBLP contains real communities and is a small dataset extracted from DBLP for the case study in Sect. 5.2. The Foursquare [21], containing check-in records of U.S. cities, is extracted from a service website based on user's location information. IMDB [22] contains rating records of 1,648,434 movies.

In addition, since users in DBLP, Foursquare, and IMDB are without specific location information, this paper uses a random number generated within a specified interval as the spatial location information of each user.

Table 1. Statistical information about the dataset

Dataset	Vertices	Edges	Vertex Type	Edge Type	Meta-paths
SDBLP	37791	170794	4	3	12
DBLP	682819	1951209	4	3	12
Foursquare	43199	405476	5	4	20
IMDB	2467806	7597591	4	3	12

Evaluation Indicators and Parameters. The ranges of the parameters involved in the experiments and their default values are shown in Table 2. k denotes the minimum degree required to be satisfied by a vertex, d is the minimum distance between two objects, c is the maximum number of core, and n represents the percentage size of the subgraph drawn from the original dataset. When a parameter is changed, the rest of the parameters are set to their default values. When testing the scalability, the percentage size from 20% to 100% of the original dataset are randomly selected by varying n, with the default value fixed at 100%. Note that to avoid accidental extreme values affecting the accuracy of the experimental results, the data are the average results after 100 tests.

Table 2. Summary of Parameters

Parameter	Range	Default
c	4, 8, 12, 16, 20	4
k	4, 8, 12, 16, 20	4
d	50, 150, 250, 350, 450	350
n	20%, 40%, 60%, 80%, 100%	100%

5.2 Effectiveness Evaluation

In order to evaluate the effectiveness of the SACS-HIN problem, this section compares the proposed algorithm with the HomeBCore [15] algorithm that does not consider user's location information and then presents a case study on SDBLP.

Community Size Analysis. Figure 2 reports the experimental results compared with the HomeBCore algorithm that does not consider the user's geographic location information. Note that since the community results calculated by our proposed three algorithms are as same, in this paper, we only show one result computed by the ReaFirst algorithm to compare with HomeBCore. From the experimental results, we can see that under the same parameter settings, the community results obtained by considering user locations are all smaller in size than the community results that do not involve user locations. It's meaningful to explore the impact of the user's spatial location on the resultant community in community search, which will find scenario-appropriate and more accurate communities for the query.

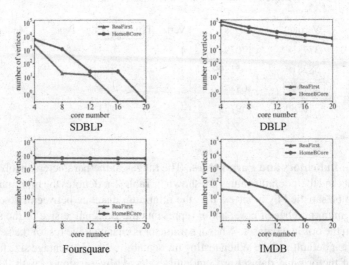

Fig. 2. Core size distributions

Case Study. Suppose a famous scholar plans to organize a local offline workshop. He hopes that the participants will have a certain social connection with him and be close to the area where he is located. Based on the description of the case, the search for eligible participants with Chao Li as the organizer is reported in Fig. 3 for the unspecified range (Fig. 3(a)), the specified range of 50 km (Fig. 3(b)), and 200 km (Fig. 3(c)) settings, respectively.

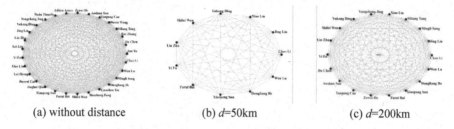

(a) without distance   (b) d=50km   (c) d=200km

Fig. 3. Case study on SDBLP with distance (q = ChaoLi, k = 4)

It is observed that without considering the spatial proximity of users, 29 scholars will be invited to the conference. When the distance range is specified as 50 km, 11 scholars are found by the organizer. When the distance range was expanded four times to 200 km, the number of eligible participants found increased to 18. As can be seen, considering the spatial proximity of users in a specific scenario is beneficial for identifying more accurate communities.

5.3   Efficiency Evaluation

The three algorithms proposed in this paper, ReaFirst, DistFirst, and FastDist, all involve parameters k, d, and n, therefore, this section conducts the following three sets of experiments on the four data sets mentioned above to test the effect of several parameters on the efficiency of the algorithms.

The Influence of Parameter k on the Efficiency of the Algorithm. The variation of the running time with k for the three algorithms on different datasets is reported in Fig. 4. It can be seen that the runtime of the ReaFirst algorithm is consistently higher than the other two algorithms on all datasets, which is due to a lot of time consumed in constructing an induced homogeneous graph for all vertices matching the target type.

The Influence of Parameter d on the Efficiency of the Algorithm. The variation of the running time with d for the three algorithms on different datasets is reported in Fig. 5. It can be seen from the results that the running time of the FastDist algorithm is always the least, the performance of the DistFirst algorithm is second, and the time required for the ReaFirst algorithm is the most. To a certain extent, the running time consumption of the algorithm mostly shows an increasing trend as the parameter d rising on different data sets. This is because under the relaxed distance constraint, the range of query object-based lookups is consequently expanded, and thus the required running time increases.

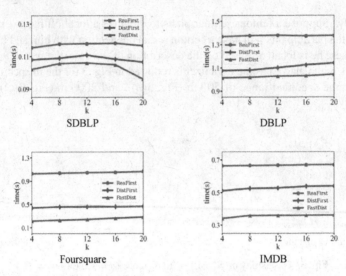

Fig. 4. The effect of varying k

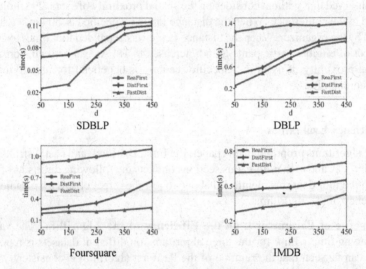

Fig. 5. The effect of varying d

The Influence of Parameter n on the Efficiency of the Algorithm. The variation of the running time with n for the three algorithms on different datasets is reported in Fig. 6. It can be seen that all algorithms scale well with the number of vertices. Among algorithms based on priority judgment distance, FastDist is always the best. In particular, the FastDist algorithm performs better when the dataset is larger. Even in the million-scale dataset IMDB, FastDist can complete in a very short time.

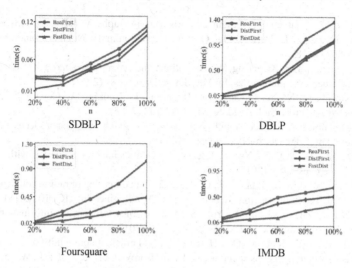

Fig. 6. The effect of varying n

6 Conclusion

In this paper, we study the problem of SACS-HIN and proposed two search strategies, structure-first and distance-first, which are designed for three algorithms. The experimental results on four HINs show that the proposed solutions are effective and efficient for searching communities on HINs, and a real application case is given. In the future, we will study how to conduct a more efficient heterogeneous information network community search while incorporating time.

Acknowledgments. This work was supported by the National Natural Science Foundation of China (62062066, 61762090, 61966036), Yunnan Fundamental Research Projects (202201AS070015), the Scientific Research Fund Project of Yunnan Provincial Education Department (2023Y0249), and the Postgraduate Research and Innovation Foundation of Yunnan University (2021Y024).

References

1. Huang, X., Lakshmanan, L., Xu, J.: Community Search over Big Graphs, vol. 14, pp. 1–206 (2019)
2. Ghosh, B., Ali, M.E., Choudhury, F.M., Apon, S.H., Sellis, T., Li, J.: The flexible socio spatial group queries. Proc. VLDB Endow. **12**, 99–111 (2018)
3. Al-Baghdadi, A., Lian, X.: Topic-based community search over spatial-social networks. Proc. VLDB Endow. **13**, 2104–2117 (2020)
4. Fang, Y., Cheng, R., Li, X., Luo, S., Hu, J.: Effective community search over large spatial graphs. Proc. VLDB Endow. **10**, 709–720 (2017)
5. Guo, F., Yuan, Y., Wang, G., Zhao, X., Sun, H.: Multi-attributed community search in road-social networks. In: 2021 IEEE 37th International Conference on Data Engineering (ICDE), pp. 109–120 (2021)

6. Fang, Y., et al.: A survey of community search over big graphs. VLDB J. **29**, 353–392 (2019)
7. Li, R.H., Su, J., Qin, L., Yu, J.X., Dai, Q.: Persistent community search in temporal networks, pp. 797–808 (2018)
8. Bi, F., Chang, L., Lin, X., Zhang, W.: An optimal and progressive approach to online search of top-k influential communities. In: Very Large Data Bases (2017)
9. Liben-Nowell, D., Novak, J., Kumar, R., Raghavan, P., Tomkins, A.: Geographic routing in social networks. Proc. Natl. Acad. Sci. U. S. A. **102** (2005)
10. Sozio, M., Gionis, A.: The community-search problem and how to plan a successful cocktail party. In: Knowledge Discovery and Data Mining (2010)
11. Zhu, Q., Hu, H., Xu, C., Xu, J., Lee, W.C.: Geo-social group queries with minimum acquaintance constraints (2017)
12. Kai, W., Xin, C., Lin, X., Zhang, W., Lu, Q.: Efficient computing of radius-bounded k-cores. In: 2018 IEEE 34th International Conference on Data Engineering (ICDE) (2018)
13. Shi, C., Li, Y., Zhang, J., Sun, Y., Yu, P.S.: A survey of heterogeneous information network analysis. IEEE Trans. Knowl. Data Eng. **29**, 17–37 (2017)
14. Wang, Z., Yuan, Y., Zhou, X., Qin, H.: Effective and efficient community search in directed graphs across heterogeneous social networks. In: Borovica-Gajic, R., Qi, J., Wang, W. (eds.) ADC 2020. LNCS, vol. 12008, pp. 161–172. Springer, Cham (2020). https://doi.org/10.1007/978-3-030-39469-1_13
15. Fang, Y., Yang, Y., Zhang, W., Lin, X., Cao, X.: Effective and efficient community search over large heterogeneous information networks. Proc. VLDB Endow. **13**, 854–867 (2020)
16. Qiao, L., Zhang, Z., Yuan, Y., Chen, C., Wang, G.: Keyword-centric community search over large heterogeneous information networks. In: Jensen, C.S., et al. (eds.) DASFAA 2021. LNCS, vol. 12681, pp. 158–173. Springer, Cham (2021). https://doi.org/10.1007/978-3-030-73194-6_12
17. Jiang, Y., Fang, Y., Ma, C., Cao, X., Li, C.: Effective community search over large star-schema heterogeneous information networks. Proc. VLDB Endow. **15**, 2307–2320 (2022)
18. Sun, Y., Han, J., Yan, X., Yu, P.S., Wu, T.: PathSim: meta path-based top-k similarity search in heterogeneous information networks **4**, 992–1003 (2011)
19. Seidman, S.B.: Network structure and minimum degree (1983)
20. Liu, W., Jiang, X., Pellegrini, M., Wang, X.: Discovering communities in complex networks by edge label propagation. Sci. Reports (2006)
21. Amelio, A., Pizzuti, C.: Overlapping community discovery methods: a survey. In: Gündüz-Öğüdücü, Ş, Etaner-Uyar, A.Ş (eds.) Social Networks: Analysis and Case Studies. LNSN, pp. 105–125. Springer, Vienna (2014). https://doi.org/10.1007/978-3-7091-1797-2_6
22. Bao, X., Wang, L.: A clique-based approach for co-location pattern mining. Inf. Sci. **490**, 244–264 (2019)

Ship Classification Based on Trajectories Data and LightGBM Considering Offshore Distance Feature

Li Xu[1], Xiaohui Chen[1], Bowei Wen[1], Jingzhen Ma[1], Yujun Wang[2], and Qing Xu[1(✉)]

[1] University of Information Engineering, Zhengzhou 450000, China
xq1982_no.1@163.com
[2] 32022 Troops, Guangzhou 510080, China

Abstract. Ship classification based on AIS trajectory data is an important aspect of spatio-temporal trajectory data mining. Aiming at the fact that most of the features extracted by the existing ship classification methods are motion features, which ignore the spatial relation between the vessels and the coastline, a Method based on LightGBM (Light Gradient Boosting Machine) for ship classification considering the offshore distance features is proposed. First, the trajectory data is cleaned and segmented, then the basic motion features of the trajectory segment are extracted, and the features are further enhanced by combining the offshore distance of the vessels. After being normalized, the features are filtered by chi-square test method, and finally a LightGBM model is constructed. The selected features are used for classification training of five types of vessels: cargo, passenger, fishing, tug and yacht, and stable classification results are obtained by 5-fold cross-validation. The results show that the average accuracy of ship classification based on LightGBM model is 86.6% after the offshore distance feature is added, and the classification accuracy is improved by 3.1%, which is better than the traditional machine classification methods such as Random Forest, Decision Tree and KNN model.

Keywords: AIS Trajectory · Offshore Distance · LightGBM · Feature Extraction · Ship Classification

1 Introduction

Automatic Identification System (AIS) is a navigational aid system applied to maritime safety and communication between vessels, which plays an important role in reducing vessel collision accidents and other maritime services [1]. AIS trajectory data is generated when vessels loaded with AIS report their position, sailing speed, heading and other information at different frequencies [2]. With the help of shore-based or satellite communication networks, AIS trajectory data are pushed to AIS operation centers in quasi-real time, and global users can obtain these trajectory information in time, with low data acquisition cost and large coverage. The historical trajectory and quasi-real-time position of vessels can be obtained through AIS or other related network systems, and identifying the types of unknown vessels is helpful to quickly grasp the maritime situation information, which is of great significance for maritime traffic safety management. The AIS information sent by some ships that are engaged in illegal fishing or smuggling activities is artificially tampered, resulting in incorrect identification numbers and ship types contained in the AIS static information. In this case, the ship type can be identified according to the trajectory data to provide technical support for the identification of abnormal ship behaviors in the next step.

The types of vessels involved in the classification are generally divided into two categories. One is to classify small vessels in the same category, such as fishing vessels [3, 4]; the other is to classify vessels in different categories [5–7], such as fishing vessels, passenger vessels, sailing vessels, high-speed vessels, cargo vessels, oil tankers, tugs, etc.In terms of trajectory motion feature extraction, based on the four types of features of speed, acceleration, heading and heading change rate, the related secondary features, such as maximum acceleration) [4, 7–11], or the feature matrix based on trajectory points [5, 6, 12–17], are generally selected as the basic motion features of the trajectory for machine learning model training. In addition, on the premise of ensuring data quality, other auxiliary features, such as the length, width or area of the vessels or trajectory, can also be incorporated [10, 18, 19]. In terms of machine learning model construction, traditional machine learning models and deep learning models are usually used to classify vessels. The former includes least squares Support Vector Machine (SVM) [7], Decision Tree [4], Logistic Regression [8, 9], ensemble learning models [10, 11, 18, 19], etc. Among them, Random Forest has excellent performance in ship classification. More and more deep neural network models have been gradually applied to ship classification, including Convolutional Neural Network (CNN) [5, 12, 14–16, 20], Recurrent Neural Network (RNN) [6], Graph Neural Network (GNN) [13] and combined neural network model [17].

All these methods can effectively identify ship types for AIS trajectory. However, most of the existing studies only consider the geometry and motion information of the vessel trajectory in feature extraction, but ignore the marine geographic semantic information related to the vessel navigation. For example, some types of vessels operate near coastlines, while others require ocean-going operations. According to the above problem, the AIS trajectory data is used to identify cargo vessels, passenger vessels, fishing vessels, tugs and yachts. Considering geographical semantic information related to navigation of vessels, offshore distance features are included as the model input variables, and ship classification based on LightGBM model is built to explore the classification effect of different parameters combinations.

2 Research Method

2.1 Method of Model Establishment

LightGBM is an improved Gradient Boosting Decision Tree (GBDT) algorithm. GBDT algorithm is a Boosting ensemble learning framework based on decision tree classifier proposed by Professor Friedman of Stanford University in 2001 [21]. The main idea is to take the negative gradient value of the loss function of the model as the approximate value of the residual to fit the regression tree, and linearly combine the regression tree generated by each iteration through the additive model. Finally, The final classifier is obtained [22]. LightGBM is optimized on the basis of GBDT by histogram algorithm, leaf growth strategy with depth restriction, GOSS sampling method, independent feature bundling and histogram difference method. Compared with the traditional gradient lifting algorithm GDBT, LightGBM supports parallel learning and large data processing, with higher classification accuracy, less memory resources for training, and faster training efficiency [23, 24]. The main flow of LightGBM algorithm is as follows:

(1) Initialize the decision tree, set the number of decision trees as m and the weight of training samples as 1/m;
(2) Train each base classifier and set the base classifier as f(x);
(3) Initial weight of each base classifier;
(4) Update the weight of each base classifier e;
(5) Synthesize the results of each base classifier: $F(x) = \sum^e f(x)$.

In the model, the relation between trajectory features and vessel class is expressed as:

$$y = f_{LGBM}(x_1, x_2, \ldots, x_n, \alpha_1, \alpha_2, \ldots, \alpha_k) \tag{1}$$

f_{LGBM} is the mapping relation between the independent variable of trajectory features and the dependent variable of ship type. The mapping rule is LightGBM, x is the trajectory feature, α is the parameter in the mapping relation vessel, including the hyperparameter that needs to be set before training and the internal parameter determined during training. The process of model training is the process of determining parameter α.

2.2 Calculation of Loss Value

The loss value of the model is calculated through the loss function. Common loss functions include Mean Square Error (MSE), cross entropy, etc. No matter what type of network structure, if the loss function used is incorrect, it will be difficult to train the correct model.

Let LightGBM model be integrated by t decision trees, and the decision tree model corresponding to each tree is f_i. The prediction result generated by eigenvalue matrix X is $\hat{Y}^t$. The loss value O is expressed as:

$$O = LOSS\left(Y - \hat{Y}^t\right) = \sum_{i=1}^{m} loss(y_i, \hat{y}^t) + \sum_{i=1}^{t} \varphi(f_i) \tag{2}$$

$LOSS$ represents the loss function, and the Contrastive is selected as the loss function to calculate the loss value, and m represents the number of samples, φ Represents a regularized item. The forecast result $\hat{Y}^t$ reflects the decision tree growth process of gradient lifting algorithm:

$$\hat{Y}^t = \sum_{i=1}^{t} F_i(X) = \hat{Y}^{t-1} + F_t \tag{3}$$

The Taylor expansion of the loss function with respect to $\hat{Y}^{t-1}$ finally obtains:

$$O^t = \sum_{i=1}^{m} [loss\left(y_i, \hat{y}^{t-1}\right) + g_i f_t(x_i) + \frac{1}{2} h_i f_i^2(x_i)] + \varphi(F_t) + constant \tag{4}$$

g_i and h_i can be calculated as follows:

$$g_i = \frac{\partial loss\left(y_i, \hat{y}^{t-1}\right)}{\partial \left(\hat{y}^{t-1}\right)^2} \tag{5}$$

$$h_i = \frac{\partial^2 loss\left(y_i, \hat{y}^{t-1}\right)}{\partial \left(\hat{y}^{t-1}\right)^2} \tag{6}$$

3   AIS Data Preprocessing and Feature Extraction

3.1   AIS Data Preprocessing

3.1.1   Data Cleaning

Affected by objective or human factors such as sensor noise and object occlusion, AIS system will generate trajectory data loss, noise or error in the process of sending and receiving information. Cleaning the trajectory data to improve the quality of data can provide data guarantee for high-precision classification of vessels. Take the following steps to clean AIS data:

(1) Select the key attribute item. Select MMSI number, longitude, latitude, time, speed, vessel direction, sailing status, ship type code and other attribute items, and discard other irrelevant attributes.
(2) Handle missing values. To simplify the calculation, records containing missing values are deleted directly.
(3) Process property values that are outside the value range. Delete the record of the attribute that exceeds the value range.
(4) Select a record with a specific property value.

  ① Select the codes of five types of vessels corresponding to the attribute VesselType: cargo vessel, passenger vessel, fishing vessel, tug and yacht.
  ② Since only the moving trajectory points are selected as the information source, select trajectory point whose status is "Under way using engine" or "Engaged in fishing".

(5) Delete duplicates. Classify the trajectory points according to the MMSI number, and delete the time repeated records in each type of trajectory points.

3.1.2   Trajectory Segmentation and Data Resampling

In the phase of data cleaning, the stop points are deleted or the trajectory point record is missing due to AIS equipment signal or improper human operation, which makes the time interval between some adjacent trajectory points too large and the information is missing seriously. In order to reduce the impact of data loss on classification accuracy, the trajectories are segmented according to the time interval between trajectory points.

After the data is grouped by MMSI, each group of data represents a vessel trajectory. For each trajectory, the trajectory points are sorted from small to large according to the time attribute, and the time interval Δt between adjacent trajectory points is calculated. If $\Delta t > 15$ min, the trajectory is divided into two segments here, and the generated trajectory segment can be completed by repeatedly processing the last segment. After segmentation, some trajectories may contain fewer trajectory points. In order to ensure that the trajectories contain enough information for ship classification, the trajectories with the number of trajectory points more than 30 min are selected for experiment.

In general, the update frequency of AIS equipment changes according to the speed and status. The update interval of Class A equipment is specified as 2 s–3 min, and that of Class B equipment is 30 s–3 min. Because the actual time intervals between the trajectory points are not the same, in order to more accurately generate the statistical features of the trajectory, resample the trajectory at equal time intervals, and set the sampling time interval to 1 min in the experiment.

3.2 Feature Extraction

3.2.1 Basic Motion Features

A variety of parameters with physical significance are counted to represent the spatio-temporal features implied in the AIS trajectory segment, including speed, acceleration, heading and heading change rate.

(1) Speed. Each trajectory point contains a speed attribute. Sort the speed values included in the trajectory points, and calculate the maximum speed, minimum speed, average speed, 5th percentile speed, 10th percentile speed, 25th percentile speed, 50th percentile speed, 75th percentile speed, 90th percentile speed, 95th percentile speed, speed variance, speed skewness, and speed kurtosis as the preliminary features of ship classification. The average speed is calculated as follows:

$$\bar{v} = \frac{D}{T} \tag{7}$$

D is the total distance of the trajectory segment, and T is the total duration of the trajectory segment.

The calculation formula of speed variance is calculated as follows:

$$s^2 = \frac{\sum_{i=1}^{n}(v_i - \bar{v})^2}{n} \tag{8}$$

(2) Acceleration. Trajectory points do not contain acceleration attributes. The acceleration calculation formula of the i-th trajectory point is calculated as follows:

$$a_i = \frac{v_i - v_{i-1}}{\Delta t} \tag{9}$$

Δt is the time difference between trajectory points. Sort the acceleration values included in the trajectory points, and calculate the maximum acceleration, minimum acceleration, average acceleration, 10th percentile acceleration, 25th percentile acceleration, 50th percentile acceleration, 75th percentile acceleration, 90th percentile acceleration, deviation of acceleration variance, and acceleration kurtosis as the preliminary features of ship classification.

The average acceleration is calculated as follows:

$$\bar{a} = \frac{\sum_{i=2}^{n} |a_i|}{n-1} \tag{10}$$

The acceleration variance is calculated as follows:

$$\delta^2 = \frac{\sum_{i=2}^{n} (|a_i| - \bar{a})^2}{n-1} \tag{11}$$

(3) Heading. Trajectory points contain heading attributes. Calculate the maximum heading, minimum heading, average heading, 5th percentile heading, 10th percentile heading, 25th percentile heading, 50th percentile heading, 75th percentile heading, 90th percentile heading, 95th percentile heading, heading variance, heading deviation and heading kurtosis as the preliminary feature of ship classification.

(4) Heading change rate. The Trajectory point does not contain the heading change rate attribute. The acceleration of the i-th trajectory point is calculated as follows:

$$h_i = \left| \frac{c_i - c_{i-1}}{\Delta t} \right| \tag{12}$$

Calculate the maximum heading change rate, minimum heading change rate, average heading change rate, 5th percentile heading change rate, 10th percentile heading change rate, 25th percentile heading change rate, 50th percentile heading change rate, 75th percentile heading change rate, 90th percentile heading change rate, 95th percentile heading change rate, variance of heading change rate, deviation of heading change rate, and kurtosis of heading change rate as the preliminary feature of ship classification.

3.2.2 Offshore Distance Feature

Some vessels have obvious offshore distance feature. For example, yachts generally move near the coastline, while ocean vessels may travel far away from the coastline. The offshore distance features of the trajectory can be obtained by calculating the distance from the trajectory point to the coastline. However, the global coastline data consists of tens of millions of points, which makes the calculation of offshore distance very time-consuming, and ultimately affects the identification efficiency of the model. Based on the grid index of coastline, the following algorithm is adopted to improve the calculation speed of offshore distance of trajectory points:

```
Input: coastline grid data L, trajectory point p
Output: offshore distance d
1. Calculate the row number m and the column number n of
the grid where the trajectory points are located
2. Obtain the coastline data L' in grid (m, n)
3. If L' ≠ ∅
4.     d→The distance from p to L'
5.     output d
6. else
7.     Obtain the maximum row number R, C of the coastline
grid
8.     Set cardinality k of the outward expansion of the
grid where the trajectory point is located as 1
9.     while m+k ≤ R or m-k ≥ 0 or n+k ≤ C or n-k ≥ 0
10.         According to the range of row numbers (M-K,
m+k) and column numbers (N-k, n+k)
11.         Determine the range of valid grid numbers
12.         Obtain the corresponding coastline data L" ac-
cording to the valid grid number range.
13.         if   L" ≠ ∅
14.             d→The distance from p to L"
15.             output d
16.         else
17.             The grid where the track point is located
continues to expand outward by 1 cardinal number, 18.
i.e. k++
```

After calculating the offshore distance of each trajectory point, the offshore distance of each trajectory point is counted, and the maximum value is taken as the preliminary offshore feature of the trajectory.

3.2.3 Feature Selection

The above features are directly calculated artificial features, which need to be further screened according to the specific situation of the features, and redundant features that contribute less to the classification accuracy are deleted to form a feature subset that is most important for classification. Chi-square test is used to sort the features. The features are sorted according to chi-square statistics [27], and the features in the top 30 scores are selected as shown in Fig. 1. The top 30 features include 1 offshore distance characteristic, and 9 speed features and, 9 heading features, and 5 heading change rate features, and 6 acceleration features. Select the top k features for the experiment. The value of k is set to 5, 10, 15, 20, 25, 30, 35, 40 respectively for the experiment.

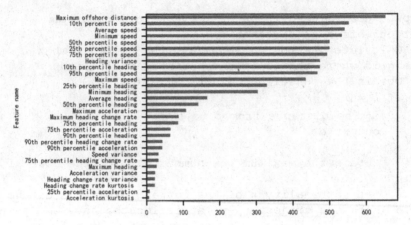

Fig. 1. The importance score of the top 30 features

4 Experiment and Analysis

4.1 Model Training

The AIS data of some North American regions in 2017 released by NOAA (National Oceanic and Atmospheric Administration) is selected as the experimental data. The types of vessels in this region are mainly cargo vessels, passenger vessels, fishing vessels, tugs and yachts. The AIS data is processed to obtain 29642 trajectories, of which the number of passenger vessel trajectories accounted for the smallest proportion, and the actual data volume is 4576, but it can meet the experimental requirements. In order to avoid the decline of recognition rate of some ship types due to data imbalance, 4576 trajectories of each type of ship are selected as samples, and the final sample data distribution is shown in Fig. 2.

In order to explore the relationship between different feature combinations and ship classification accuracy, different number of features is selected according to the importance ranking of features. At the same time, the grid search method is used to adjust the hyperparameters of LightGBM model to train the model, and the vessel identification accuracy under different feature combinations and different model hyperparameters are compared. In the experiment, the top 5, 10, 15, 20, 25, 30 and 35 features are selected as input vectors, and 5-fold cross-validation is used to segment the features to train the model. According to the features of the model, six hyperparameters are selected for adjustment.

Finally, the relationship between the number of features and the accuracy rate is shown in Fig. 4. It can be seen from Fig. 4 that since the correlation between the top features is small, increasing the number of features can significantly improve the accuracy of model classification. However, when the number of features increases to 25, the accuracy of model classification does not change significantly as the number of features continues to increase, indicating that redundant features do not contribute to the classification accuracy of the model. Therefore, it can be inferred that the top 25 features in importance ranking are the best combination of features. As the number of

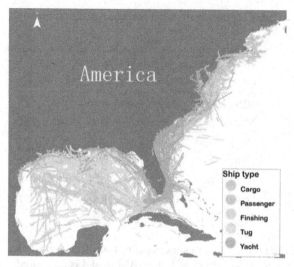

Fig. 2. The distribution of sample data

features involved in training increases. When learning_rate = 0.05, n_estimators = 380, max_depth = 7,num_leaves = 35, feature_fraction = 1, Bagging_fraction = 0.9, the identification accuracy of ship type is the highest.

Furthermore, confusion matrix is generated from the validation set results to analyze the identification effect of each ship type. The results are shown in Fig. 3.

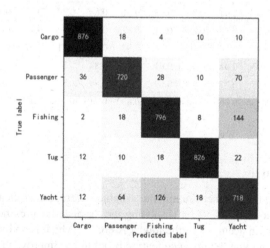

Fig. 3. The confusion matrix generated by the validation set results

The classification results of 5 types of ships correspond to 5 × 5 confusion matrix. The sample training results before and after adding the distance feature are compared, and the results are shown in Table 1. The results show that, on the whole, the classification effect of LightGBM model is significantly improved after adding distance features.

Table 1. The classification effect of LightGBM model

Types	No distance feature is added			Distance feature is added			Number of validations
	P	R	F1	P	R	F1	
Cargo	0.90	0.90	0.90	0.93	0.95	0.94	918
Passenger	0.85	0.81	0.83	0.87	0.84	0.85	864
Fishing	0.78	0.81	0.79	0.83	0.83	0.83	968
Tug	0.94	0.92	0.93	0.95	0.93	0.94	888
yacht	0.72	0.73	0.72	0.76	0.78	0.77	938
Weighted average value	0.835	0.833	0.834	0.866	0.866	0.866	4576

Furthermore, the top 25 features are used to train Random Forest, Decision Tree, and KNN. The classification effect of LightGBM model is compared. The final results are shown in Table 2. The results show that the LightGBM model is superior to the other three models in terms of classification Precision, Recall, and F1-score.

Table 2. The classification comparison of models

Types	LightGBM			Random Forest			Decision Tree			KNN		
	P	R	F1	P	R	F1	P	R	F1	P	R	F1
Cargo	0.93	0.95	0.94	0.89	0.93	0.91	0.84	0.80	0.82	0.83	0.91	0.87
Passenger	0.87	0.84	0.85	0.84	0.81	0.82	0.71	0.72	0.72	0.80	0.77	0.78
Fishing	0.83	0.83	0.83	0.79	0.81	0.80	0.63	0.71	0.67	0.72	0.73	0.72
Tug	0.95	0.93	0.94	0.93	0.91	0.92	0.84	0.8	0.82	0.81	0.90	0.85
yacht	0.76	0.78	0.77	0.71	0.69	0.70	0.59	0.56	0.57	0.67	0.55	0.60
Mean value	0.866	0.866	0.866	0.830	0.830	0.830	0.719	0.716	0.717	0.765	0.770	0.765

4.2 Results Analysis

(1) Before adding the distance feature, the weighted average classification accuracy of LightGBM model is 83.5%; after adding the distance feature, the weighted average classification accuracy of the model is 86.6%, which is an overall increase of 3.1%, indicating that the distance feature is helpful to improve the ship classification effect. Among them, the distance feature has the most obvious effect on the improvement of fishing vessels, with the classification accuracy increased by 5%, and the classification accuracy of other ships increased by 2%-4%.

(2) Compared with Random Forest, Decision Tree and KNN, LightGBM model has higher classification accuracy and better performance. Among them, the classification accuracy of Random Forest and LightGBM model is close to each other, which

also indicates that the classification performance of random forest is relatively excellent.

(3) After adding the distance feature, the classification accuracy of LightGBM model for various ships is more than 76%, among which cargo vessels and tugs have the best classification effect, with the classification accuracy reaching more than 90%. The classification effect of fishing vessels and yachts is a little poor, because these two types of vessels have strong mobility and the same movement features, which is easy to cause confusion in classification.

5 Conclusion and Future Work

An optimization method for ship type classification based on LightGBM is proposed. On the basis of existing research, the features of ships' offshore distance are added to further optimize the input features that affect the classification effect of LightGBM, and the recognition effects of different parameter combinations and related models are compared. The results show that the accuracy of ship type classification can be improved significantly by adding the feature of ships' off shore distance; Compared with Random Forest, Decision Tree, KNN, LightGBM model has higher accuracy in ship type classification.

The accuracy of ship classification based on AIS trajectory data needs to be improved, and it will be improved from two aspects in the future: first, in the aspect of trajectory feature processing, because the samples used in this experiment are part of the ships' trajectory segments, which cannot fully represent the overall motion features of the ships, it is necessary to further explore the overall features of the ships' trajectory to improve the contribution of the features to the classification. At the same time, other geographic information, such as routes, ports, berths and other auxiliary information, can be incorporated into the experiment of ship type classification to further improve the classification accuracy; Second, in the aspect of model construction, because the trajectory data has obvious features of time series and graph structure, it can combine the Recurrent Neural Network and Graph Neural Network in depth learning to classify vessels.

Acknowledgements. This project is supported by National Natural Science Foundation of China (41901397, 42101454, 42101455), and supported by Institute of Geospatial Information, University of Information Engineering.

References

1. Chen, R.L., Wang, Y.Q., Liu, B.J., et al.: Spatio-temporal features of vessel activities in the Bohai Sea based on GIS and AIS. Progr. Geogr. **39**(07), 1172–1181 (2020)
2. Zhen, R., Shao, Z.P., Pan, J.C.: Advance in character mining and prediction of vessel behavior based on AIS data. J. Geoinf. Sci. **23**(12), 2111–2127 (2021)
3. Zheng, Q.L., Fan, W., Zhang, S.M., et al.: Identification of fishing type from VMS data based on artificial neural network. South China Fish. Sci. **12**(02), 81–87 (2016)

4. Sánchez, P.D., Amigo, D., García, J., et al.: Architecture for trajectory-based fishing vessel classification with AIS data. Sensors **20**(13), 3782–3802 (2020)
5. Ljunggren, H.: Using deep learning for classifying vessel trajectories. In: 21st International Conference on Information Fusion, pp. 2158–2164. IEEE, Cambridge (2018)
6. Bakkegaard, S., Blixenkrone, M.J., Larsen, J.J., et al.: Target classification using kinematic data and a recurrent neural network. In: 19th International Radar Symposium (IRS), pp. 20–22. IEEE, Bonn (2018)
7. Yung, P.C., Irvine, J.M.: Passive identification of vessel type through track motion analysis. In: Geospatial Informatics X, pp. 20–40. SPIE, Washington (2020)
8. Feng, C., Fu, B., Luo, Y., et al.: The design and development of a vessel trajectory data management and analysis system based on AIS. Sensors **22**(1), 310–331 (2021)
9. Sheng, K., Liu, Z., Zhou, D., et al.: Research on vessel classification based on trajectory features. J. Navig. **71**(1), 100–116 (2018)
10. Kraus, P., Mohrdieck, C., Schwenker, F.: Ship classification based on trajectory data with machine-learning methods. In: 19th International Radar Symposium (IRS), pp. 1–10. IEEE, Bonn (2018)
11. Ginoulhac, R., Barbaresco, F., Schneider, J., et al.: Coastal radar target recognition based on kinematic data (AIS) with machine learning. In: 2019 International Radar Conference (RADAR), pp. 1–5. IEEE, Bonn (2019)
12. Yang, T., Wang, X., Liu, Z.: Ship type recognition based on vessel navigating trajectory and convolutional neural network. J. Mar. Sci. Eng. **10**(1), 84–104 (2022)
13. Li, T., Xu, H., Zeng, W.: Ship classification method for massive AIS trajectories based on GNN. J. Phys: Conf. Ser. **2025**(1), 12–24 (2021)
14. Wang, Y., Yang, L., Song, X.: Ship classification for space-based AIS data using 1D-CNN. In: 5th International Conference on Electronic Information Technology and Computer Engineering, pp. 840–844. ACM, Xiamen (2021)
15. Duan, H., Ma, F., Miao, L., et al.: A semi-supervised deep learning approach for vessel trajectory classification based on AIS data. Ocean Coast. Manag. **218**(3), 1–12 (2022)
16. Chang, J.L., Xie, L., Wei, Z.W., et al.: Research on vessel trajectory classification based on deep convolution neural network. J. Wuhan Univ. Technol. (Transp. Sci. Eng.) **1**(46), 160–165 (2022)
17. Cui, T.T., Wang, G.L., Gao, J.: Vessel trajectory classification method based on 1DCNN-LSTM. Comput. Sci. **47**(9), 175–184 (2020)
18. Damastuti, N., Aisjah, A.S., Masroeri, A.: Vessel classifying and trajectory based on automatic identification system data. IOP Conf. Ser.: Earth Environ. Sci. **830**(1), 12–49 (2021)
19. Zhong, H., Song, X., Yang, L.: Vessel classification from Space-based AIS data using random forest. In: 5th International Conference on Big Data and Information Analytics (BigDIA), pp. 9–12. IEEE, Kunming (2019)
20. Lin, J.Y., Zheng, B.L., Liu, J.: Ship classification model based on convolutional neural network. Inf. Technol. Inform. (2), 125–126 (2019)
21. Friedman, J.H.: Greedy function approximation: boosting machine. Annals 2001 **29**(5), 1189–1232 (2001)
22. Wang, H., Jiang, Y.N., Zhang, X., et al.: Lithology identification method based on gradient boosting algorithm. J. Jilin Univ. (Earth Sci. Ed.) **51**(3), 940–950 (2021)
23. Yu, Q., Huang, X.L.: Classification of heart sound signals based on LightGBM. J. Shaanxi Normal Univ. (Nat. Sci. Ed.) **48**(6), 47–55 (2020)
24. Singh, M., Nicholas, E., Singh, M., et al.: Using spectral acoustic features to identify abnormal heart sounds. In: 2016 Computing in Cardiology Conference (CinC), pp. 557–560. IEEE, Vancouver (2016)
25. Fang, M., Meng, X.F.: Data Mining Concepts and Technologies. China Machine Press, Beijing (2019)

26. Sang, L.Z., Wall, A., Mao, Z., et al.: A novel method for restoring the trajectory of the inland waterway vessel by using AIS data. Ocean Eng. **110**(1), 183–194 (2015)
27. Li, H.: Statistical Learning Methods, 2nd edn. Tsinghua University Press, Beijing (2019)

CDGCN: An Effective and Efficient Algorithm Based on Community Detection for Training Deep and Large Graph Convolutional Networks

Yulong Ma[1], Bing Kong[1(✉)], Lihua Zhou[1], Hongmei Chen[1], and Chongming Bao[2]

[1] School of Information Science and Engineering, Yunnan University, Kunming 650091, Yunnan, People's Republic of China
kongbing@ynu.edu.cn
[2] National Pilot School of Software, Yunnan University, Kunming 650091, Yunnan, People's Republic of China

Abstract. Graph convolution neural network (GCN) has become a critical tool to capture representations of graph nodes. At present, the graph convolution model for large scale graphs is trained by full-batch stochastic gradient descent, which causes two problems: over-smoothing and neighborhood expansion, which may lead to loss of model accuracy and high memory and computational overhead. To alleviate these two challenges, we propose CDGCN, a novel GCN algorithm. Through partitioning of the original graph with a community detection algorithm, the original graph is decoupled into many different communities. The decoupled communities restrict the message passing between certain communities, and the model can be trained by using mini-batch stochastic gradient descent. Meanwhile, to prevent the prediction accuracy of the model from decreasing due to over-decoupling, a shallow full-batch stochastic gradient descent GCN is added to the model. We have conducted extensive experiments on node classification tasks of multiple datasets. The experiments show that the model has excellent performance, especially in the dataset with a higher average clustering coefficient, and can achieve higher prediction accuracy.

Keywords: Graph Convolution Network · Community Detection · Deep Learning

1 Introduction

Graph convolutional neural networks (GCN) [1] is a critical tool for graph representation learning, so it is widely used in graph analysis and many prediction tasks about graphs, such as node classification, link prediction, and recommendation system [2]. GCN uses message passing technology to capture the neighbor information and structure information of nodes, reduce the representation dimension of nodes, and convert the high dimensional information of nodes into low dimensional dense vector embedding [3, 4]. GCN innovatively proposes a Full-batch stochastic gradient descent (SGD) training network in the field of graphs. However, when the depth of the network is slightly deeper, the messages received by the represented node and other nodes tend to be homogeneous, resulting in a decline in the representation ability, which is called over-smoothing [5, 6]. In the deeper GCN, more high-order neighbors and their calculated footprints are needed to support calculating the embeddings of the current node. Therefore, the number of supported nodes and intermediate embeddings will grow exponentially as the graph convolutional layer increases, a challenge known as neighborhood expansion [7], resulting in high computing and memory overhead.

ClusterGCN [8] proposes to cluster the dataset into subgraphs, and then perform Mini-batch SGD training according to the subgraphs. This method can reduce memory and computing overhead. However, this method directly deletes the edges between clusters when partitioning the original graph. This processing method may lead to the loss of a large number of edges, leading to over-decoupling, which affects the prediction accuracy of the model. Meanwhile, for different datasets, ClusterGCN needs to manually set the parameter of how many clusters the original data is partitioned into, and the model is very sensitive to this parameter, which brings challenges to the adjustment of model parameters [9].

Community detection is the finding of all community structures in a given graph, and it is often used in social networks, web graphs, and biological network analysis [10–12]. Community detection can decouple the graph into several subgraphs with cohesive relationships, and the algorithm can automatically determine how many communities the original data is divided into according to the dataset information.

In order to solve the over-smoothing and neighborhood expansion problems, this paper proposes CDGCN, which is a novel GCN based on community detection.

Our main contributions can be summarized as follows:

(1) We proposed a novel graph convolution neural network based on community detection (CDGCN). CDGCN which can limit the message passing to some specific communities to alleviate the over-smoothing and neighborhood expansion, thus reducing the memory and computing cost of model training.
(2) CDGCN has a mechanism to prevent over-decouple.
(3) CDGCN can automatically determine the number of subgraphs to be divided according to the modularity of the data. The subgraphs to be divided are more natural.
(4) We conducted an extensive sequence of experiments to evaluate the performance of CDGCN relative to baseline GCN. The experimental results show that our CDGCN is more accurate and efficient. On the data with a high average cluster coefficient (ACC) [13], CDGCN's performance is far higher than other models.

2 Related Works

2.1 Graph Convolutional Neural Networks

GCN is a neural network model that extends convolution operation to the graph domain, which is described as follows:

Let $G = (V, E, X)$ denote a graph constructed of n nodes, e edges, and d-dimensional features, where $V = [v_1, v_2, ..., v_n]$ is a set of n nodes, $E = \{e_{i,j}\}_{i,j=1}^{n}$ is the set of e edges, and $X \in \mathbb{R}^{n \times d}$ is the features matrix with d-dimensional for n nodes. The adjacency matrix of G is denote by an $n \times n$ sparse matrix $A \in \mathbb{R}^{n \times n}$, where $A_{i,j} = 1$ if $e_{i,j} \in E$, otherwise $A_{i,j} = 0$. The embedding of each node in the graph is calculated by the previous layer, which mixes the embeddings of the node's neighbors as follows:

$$X^{(l+1)} = \sigma(A'X^{(l)}W^{(l)}), \tag{1}$$

where $X^{(l)} \in \mathbb{R}^{n \times d_l}$ is d_l-dimensional embeddings at lth layer for all the nodes of the graph; A' is some normalization of A (the adjacency matrix of G); $W^{(l)} \in \mathbb{R}^{d_l \times d_{l+1}}$ is the weight matrix for transform $X^{(l)}$ to $X^{(l+1)}$ which will be learn in training of the l-layers GCN; σ is a nonlinear activation function and it is set to ReLU in most cases. GCN is greatly improved compared with the previous model. However, its Full-batch SGD training process requires a high computational and memory overhead.

The challenges of GCN, over-smoothing and neighborhood expansion, have attracted the attention of many researchers [5–7]. GraphSAGE proposes a strategy of aggregation after node-wise sampling, which alleviates the problem of neighborhood expansion to a certain extent. It also proposes Mini-batch SGD to train the model can update parameters many times in each epoch. FastGCN [14] uses layer-wise sampling. It no longer samples the graph, but samples the convolution layer, which further accelerates the speed of the model. Based on FastGCN, ASGCN [15] improved the layer-wise sampling method. An adaptive hierarchical sampling method is proposed. The sampling of each layer is not independent but realizes the information sharing between layers. GraphSAINT [15] proposes a method of subgraphs sampling of the original graph. This subgraphs sampling method is based on influence, influence is defined based on the connectivity of graph nodes, and GCN is constructed on the subgraphs obtained by sampling. The above methods control the number of nodes to, but there will still be over-smoothing and neighborhood expansion.

MarkovGCN [16] proposed a method based on the Markov diffusion dynamic graph to alleviate the over-smoothing problem. In this way, uses Markov diffusion process melts some edges in each layer of GCN for the purpose of obtaining the excellent structure of the community. Reducing some edges in each layer according to the Markov diffusion process can reduce the excessive passing of messages. This method requires a lot of memory overhead.

ClusterGCN uses METIS [17] to cluster the graph, which can decouple the graph into several subgraphs, and then train the model in the way of Mini-batch SGD. This model effectively alleviates the neighbor-expansion and over-smoothing problems, and accelerates the convergence speed of the model. However, the parameter of how many clusters of the original graph is divided in this model is very sensitive, which increases the difficulty of parameter adjustment. Meanwhile, this method of partitioning subgraphs will delete some edges of the original graph before the model starts training, which may lead to over-decoupling, so that much information is lost, reducing the accuracy of the model.

2.2 Community Detection

In real-world data, community structures naturally exist [10]. Community is a node-set with structural cohesion and attribute cohesion [18]. According to the connectivity of the graph, the original graph is divided into several subgraphs. The nodes within the same subgraph are densely connected, while the different subgraphs are sparsely connected or not connected.

In recent years, many algorithms of community detection have been developed. Among them, the time complexity of LOUVAIN [19] algorithm is $O(n \log n)$. Its calculation method mainly depends on optimizing modularity, and the concept of modularity is the measure of community division first proposed by Newman. Figure 1 shows the results of community detection. The original graph is divided into five subgraphs (communities), and the nodes in the subgraphs are densely connected and sparse in different subgraphs.

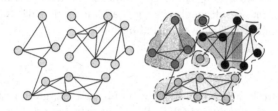

Fig. 1. Community Detection Demo.

3   Mothed

3.1   Motivation

In order to explain the motivation of the proposed algorithm, the limitations of the previously proposed training methods are first discussed.

ClusterGCN precomputes the original graph G into many different clusters $\overline{G} = [G_1, \cdots , G_c] = [\{V_1, \mathcal{E}_1\}, \cdots , \{V_c, \mathcal{E}_c\}]$, where the adjacency matrix is denotes as

$$\overline{A} = \begin{bmatrix} A_{11} & \cdots & 0 \\ \vdots & \ddots & \vdots \\ 0 & \cdots & A_{cc} \end{bmatrix}$$, where A_{tt} is the adjacency matrix of cluster V_t and the edges $\mathcal{E}_t$ is

the links between V_t. According to the recognized clusters $V = [V_1, V_2, \cdots , V_c]$, the feature matrix X and labels Y is partition into $[X_1, X_2, \cdots , X_c]$ and $[Y_1, Y_2, \cdots , Y_c]$. Then, the final embedding will be produced as:

$$Z^{(L)} = \overline{A}'\sigma\left(\overline{A}'\sigma\left(\cdots\sigma\left(\overline{A}'XW^{(0)}\right)W^{(1)}\right)\cdots\right)W^{(L-1)}$$

$$= \begin{bmatrix} \overline{A}'_{11}\sigma\left(\overline{A}'_{11}\sigma\left(\cdots\sigma\left(\overline{A}'_{11}X_1W^{(0)}\right)W^{(1)}\right)\cdots\right)W^{(L-1)} \\ \vdots \\ \overline{A}'_{cc}\sigma\left(\overline{A}'_{cc}\sigma\left(\cdots\sigma\left(\overline{A}'_{cc}X_cW^{(0)}\right)W^{(1)}\right)\cdots\right)W^{(L-1)} \end{bmatrix} \quad (2)$$

and the loss function is $\mathcal{L}_{\overline{A}'} = \sum_t \frac{|V_t|}{N}\mathcal{L}_{\overline{A}'_{tt}}$ and $\mathcal{L}_{\overline{A}'_{tt}} = \frac{1}{|V_t|}\sum_{i \in V_t} \text{loss}\left(y_i, z_i^{(L)}\right)$. Note: where $\overline{A}'$ is the normalized $\overline{A}$, c (the number of clusters) must be manually set, and ClusterGCN is sensitive to c. At each step, only a cluster V_t was used to emanate SGD for weight update based on the gradient of $\mathcal{L}_{\overline{A}_{tt}'}$.

ClusterGCN uses a clustering algorithm to decouple data and uses the clusters to construct graph convolution, alleviating the over-smoothing and neighborhood expansion to an extent. However, to divide the graph into many different clusters, it is necessary to delete some of the edges present in the original graph. Intuitively, the node itself is strongly correlated with its direct neighbors, so violently deleting some edges can result in the loss of important information.

In conclusion, our proposed model should have the following functions: 1) It can adaptively divide into several subgraphs to decouple the original data, thus alleviating the problems of over-smoothing and neighborhood expansion of the model; 2) It has a mechanism to prevent over-decouple; 3) Adopt a Mini-batch SGD strategy, which can reduce the computation and memory cost of the model.

3.2 CDGCN

The model framework of CDGCN is shown in Fig. 2. First, given graph data, use the community detection algorithm LOUVAIN to partition the graph into communities, and use the communities to construct the Mini-batch GCN, called Vanilla CDGCN. Its construction method is similar to ClusterGCN. Secondly, build a shallow Full-batch GCN, which captures the direct neighbor information of the nodes. Finally, use the mask function to select the current batch node embedding in the Full-batch GCN and combine them with the node embedding of Vanilla CDGCN.

Vanilla CDGCN. The proposed CDGCN aims to solve the problems of over-smoothing and neighborhood expansion.

In Fig. 2, given a graph data, its adjacency matrix is A, and its features matrix is $X^{(1)}$. LOUVAIN is used to precalculate A, the adjacency matrices corresponding to communities C_1 and C_2 are A_{C_1} and A_{C_2}, and the feature matrices are $X_{C_1}^{(1)}$ and $X_{C_2}^{(1)}$ respectively. Use the partitioned subgraphs C_1 and C_2 to construct a Mini-batch SGD GCN, called Vanilla CDGCN.

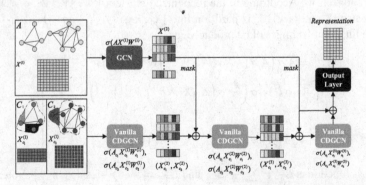

Fig. 2. The framework of the proposed CDGCN.

The model can limit message passing, so that the over-smoothing can be alleviated. Moreover, this method of building Mini-batch SGD GCN by using partitioned subgraphs just makes a specific number of the communities input model. Although the convolutional layer increases, the number of input nodes keeps small, and the number of the intermediate embedding of the nodes that need to be calculated and saved is small, thus alleviating the neighborhood expansion problem of the model. In addition, LOUVAIN automatically determines how many communities the data is divided into based on the modularity of the data. Figure 3 shows the message passing in the GCN and CDGCN depth models. When graph convolution layers reach the 4-layer, the GCN will message passing among 13 nodes, but the CDGCN is only among 7 nodes because it restricts message passing within the community.

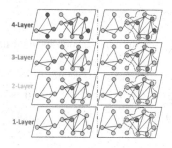

Fig. 3. GCN (left) and CDGCN (right) messaging processes.

Full-Batch SGD GCN. LOUVAIN and METIS directly delete some edges to partition the original graph into subgraphs. Considering there is important information between the nodes' direct neighbors and the nodes themself, the plain deletion of some edges may lead to a large amount of information loss, which leads to the occurrence of the over-decoupling problem. Therefore, we added a shallow Full-batch SGD GCN on the basis of Vanilla CDGCN. The shallow Full-batch SGD GCN can only consume a small amount of computing and memory overhead without losing the direct neighbor information. Then, use the mask function to select the current batch nodes embedding in Full-batch SGD GCN, and combine them with the nodes embedding of Mini-batch SGD GCN. Perform an embedded blend according to the following steps:

$$X_{full} = A'X^{(1)}W^l, \tag{3}$$

$$X^{(l+1)} = (1 - \alpha)A'_{C_t}X^{(l)}_{C_t}W^l + \alpha\phi(X_{full}), \tag{4}$$

where α is an adjustable hyperparameter, which can control the contribution of the Full-batch SGD GCN; X_{full} is an embedded matrix of Full-batch SGD GCN; ϕ A is a mask function used to select the embedding of current batch nodes in X_{full}.

4 Experiments

4.1 Datasets and Evaluation Measure

We conducted experiments on five small graphs to prove the effectiveness of CDGCN. In order to verify that CDGCN can effectively and efficiently conduct in-depth training on large graphs, this paper has carried out a node classification experiment on two large scale graphs. The ACC used to describe the clustering tendency of a graph and it is the average value of the clustering coefficients in all vertices of this graph [13]. The statistical information of the datasets used in the experiment is in Table 1.

The experiments calculate the micro F1-score of each model on different datasets to evaluate the accuracy of the model because the datasets used in this experiment have more than two label categories.

Table 1. Statistical information about the dataset.

Dataset	Nodes	Edges	Classes	Features	ACC	Training/Validation/Test
Chameleon	2,277	36,101	3	3,132	0.48	1,594/228/445
Squirrel	5,201	217,073	3	3,148	0.42	3,641/520/1,040
Cora	2,708	10,556	7	1,433	0.24	1,208/500/1,000
Citeseer	3,327	9,104	6	3,703	0.14	2,329/333/665
Actor	7,600	33,544	5	931	0.08	6,100/500/1,000
Pubmed	19,717	44,338	3	500	0.06	13,902/500/1,000
PPI	56,944	818,716	121	50	0.18	44,986/6,264/5,964

4.2 Baselines

In order to analyze the performance of the model in node classification tasks, this section compares Vanilla CDGCN (CDGCN (1)) and CDGCN with some baseline models. Specifically, 1) GCN, which extends the convolutional operation to graph data; 2) GraphSAGE, which uses node-wise sampling to train Mini-batch SGD based on GCN; 3) FastGCN adopts the layer-wise sampling method based on the convolution layer, which also improves the calculation efficiency of GCN; 4) ASGCN, which is improved on the basis of FastGCN, can adaptively determine the sampling rate of the convolution layer; 5) ClusterGCN, this model uses clustering precomputation to divide the datasets into several subgraphs and then train the Mini-batch SGD model, which saves a lot of memory and computing overhead; 6) MarkovGCN, this model takes into account the community structure, which to some extent alleviates the problem of over-smoothing; 7) GraphSAINT, this model uses graph sampling to reduce nodes input.

Table 2. Micro F1-scoreof Node classification of models on the small datasets.

Method	Chameleon	Squirrel	Cora	Citeseer	Actor
GCN	0.584	0.554	0.865	0.714	0.294
GraphSAGE	0.753	0.617	0.822	0.714	0.349
FastGCN	0.725	0.566	0.850	0.776	0.368
ASGCN	0.733	0.573	0.878	0.788	**0.374**
ClusterGCN	0.745	0.621	0.859	0.723	0.327
MarkovGCN	0.657	0.587	0.865	0.777	0.326
GraphSAINT	0.735	0.610	0.801	0.755	0.366
CDGCN(1)	0.766	0.666	0.861	0.729	0.241
CDGCN	**0.792**	**0.703**	**0.889**	**0.798**	0.293

4.3 Results

As shown in Table 2, CDGCN can achieve a higher micro F1-score on most datasets. In particular, compared with the best-performing data set in the baseline model, CDGCN increased the microF1 score of 0.039 and 0.082 in Chameleon and Squirrel, respectively. For data sets Cora and Citeseer, CDGCN also increased by 0.011 and 0.010 compared with the best-performing baseline model's micro F1-score. In the data set Actor, AS-GCN's micro F1-score is the highest, and CDGCN's performance in this dataset is not as good as ClusterGCN. Figure 4 shows the micro F1-score increment of CDGCN relative to the best baseline model on different ACC datasets. In general, on datasets with high ACC, the CDGCN will be higher than the baseline models' micro F1-score.

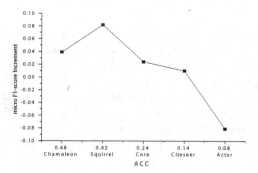

Fig. 4. Micro F1-score increment of CDGCN relative to the best baseline model on different ACC datasets

In order to explore the reason why CDGCN's micro F1-score on the Actor dataset is not performing well, Table 3 shows the number of edges deleted by ClusterGCN and CDGCN when partitioning subgraphs on different datasets and the micro F1-score of the final model. The results show that on the dataset of Chameleon, Squirrel, Cora, and Citeseer, CDGCN has fewer edges for subgraph division and deletion, and the CDGCN's micro F1-score is higher; On the dataset Actor, the CDGCN subgraph division removes more edges, and the CDGCN micro F1-score is lower. Obviously, when the parameters of the two models are adjusted to the best state on different datasets, the deletion of more edges in the subgraph division will lead to the reduction of the model's micro F1-score. On the Actor dataset, CDGCN removes more edges than ClusterGCN. This partition can lead to a large number of direct neighbor information loss and ultimately lead to poor performance of CDGCN on Actor.

Table 3. The precalculate the number of deleted edges and micro F1-score

Method		Chameleon	Squirrel	Cora	Citeseer	Actor	Pubmed
ClusterGCN	Removing edges	**20,757**	**132,492**	**658**	**363**	3,296	**9,400**
	micro F1-score	0.745	0.621	0.859	0.723	**0.327**	0.882
CDGCN	Removing edges	2,729	44,364	599	314	**7,722**	6,346
	micro F1-score	**0.792**	**0.703**	**0.889**	**0.798**	0.293	**0.908**

In Fig. 5, the data set Squirrel with high ACC and the data set Actor with low ACC are visualized according to the label, cluster, and community of the node to investigate the poor performance of CDGCN on the low ACC graph. The number of clusters can make ClusterGCN obtain the best accuracy. The number of labels, clusters, and communities in Squirrel is 3, 5, and 8, while that in Actor is 5, 7, and 24. Obviously, on Squirrel with high ACC, the graph divided by the community is highly similar to the graph divided by the label. However, on Actor with lower ACC, the community detection algorithm divides it into more communities and loses more direct neighbor information, resulting in over-decoupling. This over-decoupling of the graph will lose more edge information, which may be the reason why the CDGCN model performs poorly on data with low ACC.

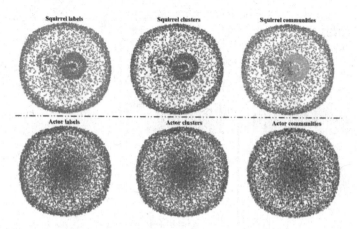

Fig. 5. Visual comparison of the label, cluster pre-computation, and community detection precomputation

4.4   Effect and Efficiency of CDGCN on Large Graphs

We conducted node classification experiments on large datasets Pubmed and PPI to analyze the memory cost, test accuracy, and time cost of each epoch during the training of ClusterGCN, GraphSAINT, CDGCN (1), and CDGCN. The reason why the comparison algorithm here only uses ClusterGCN and GraphSAINT is that the memory and time costs of the original GCN, GraphSAGE, MarkovGCN, FastGCN, and ASGCN during training are far greater than that of ClusterGCN and GraphSAINT, so they are not comparable.

Figure 6 shows the different performance of the time cost, memory cost, and test accuracy of ClusterGCN, GraphSAINT, CDGCN(1), and CDGCN on large graph datasets Pubmed and PPI with the increase of the graph convolution layer. The training time and memory cost of GraphSAINT are much higher than other models; ClusterGCN and Vanilla CDGCN have the least time and memory overhead; The time and memory cost of CDGCN is slightly higher than that of ClusterGCN. In addition, there is a phenomenon in GraphSAINT on Pubmed and PPI, that is, with the increase of the convolution layer, the micro F1-score first increases and then drops sharply, which is why GraphSAINT does not restrict message passing during model training. In ClusterGCN, Vanilla CDGCN, and CDGCN models, the micro F1-score is more stable with the increase of the convolutional layer, because these models limit the message passing during model training, which can better alleviate over-smoothing. Based on Vanilla CDGCN, the CDGCN combined with Full-batch GCN has the best prediction accuracy on the large datasets, because ClusterGCN and Vanilla CDGCN both lose some direct neighbor information during subgraphs partition, and Full-batch GCN can ensure that the model can capture the direct neighbor information.

The experimental results show that CDGCN alleviates neighborhood expansion and over-smoothing, thus reducing the time and memory overhead of the model in large graph training. In addition, CDGCN combined with shallow Full-batch GCN will increase the

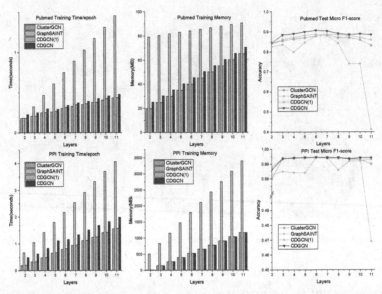

Fig. 6. The training time, memory overhead, and micro F1-score of the four models in the dataset Pubmed (upper) and PPI (lower)

time and memory costs, but it can avoid the loss of direct neighbor information so that the model can achieve better accuracy.

5 Conclusion

CDGCN has excellent representation learning performance on datasets with high ACC. The model constructed by using the decoupled subgraphs can limit the message passing during model training, thus alleviating the problem of over-smoothing and neighborhood expansion. In addition, in order to prevent the occurrence of over-decoupling, the CDGCN model combines the Full-batch GCN, which can ensure that the direct neighbors' information of the nodes is captured, thus preventing the possible over-decoupling of the community detection and bringing negative effects to the model. As the depth of the model increases, the CDGCN is always stable in the micro F1-score, and its stability is much higher than that of baselines. CDGCN maintains low time and memory overhead. In general, CDGCN is an effective and efficient graph convolution neural network, which can be trained in depth.

References

1. Kipf, T.N., Welling, M.: Semi-Supervised Classification with Graph Convolutional Networks (2017)
2. Zhang, Z., Cui, P., Zhu, W.: Deep Learning on Graphs: A Survey. CoRR abs/1812.04202 (2018)

3. Grover, A., Leskovec, J.: node2vec: Scalable Feature Learning for Networks, pp. 855–864 (2016)
4. Perozzi, B., Al-Rfou, R., Skiena, S.: Deepwalk: online learning of social representations. In: Proceedings of the 20th ACM SIGKDD International Conference on Knowledge Discovery and Data Mining, pp. 701–710 (2014)
5. Alon, U., Yahav, E.: On the Bottleneck of Graph Neural Networks and its Practical Implications (2021)
6. Oono, K., Suzuki, T.: Graph Neural Networks Exponentially Lose Expressive Power for Node Classification (2020)
7. Hamilton, W.L., Ying, Z., Leskovec, J.: Inductive Representation Learning on Large Graphs, pp. 1024–1034 (2017)
8. Chiang, W.-L., Liu, X., Si, S., Li, Y., Bengio, S., Hsieh, C.-J.: Cluster-GCN: An Efficient Algorithm for Training Deep and Large Graph Convolutional Networks, pp. 257–266 (2019)
9. Zeng, H., Zhou, H., Srivastava, A., Kannan, R., Prasanna, V.K.: GraphSAINT: Graph Sampling Based Inductive Learning Method (2020)
10. Girvan, M., Newman, M.E.: Community structure in social and biological networks. Proc. Natl. Acad. Sci. **99**, 7821–7826 (2002)
11. Guimera, R., Sales-Pardo, M., Amaral, L.A.N.: Modularity from fluctuations in random graphs and complex networks. Phys. Rev. E **70**, 025101 (2004)
12. Fortunato, S., Barthelemy, M.: Resolution limit in community detection. Proc. Natl. Acad. Sci. **104**, 36–41 (2007)
13. Kaiser, M.: Mean clustering coefficients: the role of isolated nodes and leafs on clustering measures for small-world networks. New J. Phys. **10**, 083042 (2008)
14. Chen, J., Ma, T., Xiao, C.: FastGCN: Fast Learning with Graph Convolutional Networks via Importance Sampling (2018)
15. Huang, W.-B., Zhang, T., Rong, Y., Huang, J.: Adaptive Sampling Towards Fast Graph Representation Learning, pp. 4563–4572 (2018)
16. Rahman, M.K., Agrawal, A., Azad, A.: MarkovGNN: Graph Neural Networks on Markov Diffusion, pp. 1019–1029 (2022)
17. Karypis, G., Kumar, V.: A fast and high quality multilevel scheme for partitioning irregular graphs. SIAM J. Sci. Comput. **20**, 359–392 (1998)
18. Radicchi, F., Castellano, C., Cecconi, F., Loreto, V., Parisi, D.: Defining and identifying communities in networks. Proc. Natl. Acad. Sci. **101**, 2658–2663 (2004)
19. Blondel, V.D., Guillaume, J.-L., Lambiotte, R., Lefebvre, E.: Fast unfolding of communities in large networks. J. Stat. Mech. Theory Exp. **2008**, P10008 (2008)

Investigate the Relationship Between Traumatic Occurrences and Socio-Economic Status Based on Geographic Information System (GIS): The Case of Qingpu in Shanghai, China

Huili Jin[1], Hongwei Xia[2], Joseph Mango[3], Jing Wang[1], Hong Yi[4], Xiaoming Yu[5], and Xiang Li[1,6(⊠)]

[1] Key Laboratory of Geographic Information Science (Ministry of Education) and School of Geographic Sciences, East China Normal University, Shanghai 200241, China
xli@geo.ecnu.edu.cn

[2] Department of Thoracic Surgery, Qingpu Branch of Zhongshan Hospital Affiliated to Fudan University, Shanghai 201700, China

[3] Department of Transportation and Geotechnical Engineering, University of Dar Es Salaam, Dar Es Salaam, Tanzania

[4] Faculty of Economics and Management, East China Normal University, Shanghai 200241, China

[5] Department of Radiology, Qingpu Branch of Zhongshan Hospital Affiliated to Fudan University, Shanghai 201700, China

[6] Chongqing Key Laboratory of Precision Optics, Chongqing Institute of East China Normal University, Chongqing 404100, China

Abstract. Numerous incidences in the world have been occurring and causing trauma to humans. Trauma that can be physical or psychological causes not only great harms and deaths to patients but also huge burdens of expenses to the families and public health sectors for due to treatments in China. Many studies have been researching on this subject. However, such studies lack to provide comprehensive information on the relationships between trauma incidences and their occurring environment. This study used GIS and trauma patients' data from Qingpu district in Shanghai to investigate the relationships between trauma incidences and their occurring environment. Such environments were studied in two levels of the socio-economic status (SES): Individual and sub-district. At the individual level, trauma incidences were studied with the housing prices, and at the sub-district level, were studied with the per capita disposable income in neighborhoods. We used descriptive and regression methods to count trauma incidences and analyze their relationships with SES. The results showed that trauma incidences are statistically negatively correlated with the the house prices and the per capita disposable income by the Pearson correlation coefficients of 0.71 and 0.72, respectively. The hot spot analyses showed that many trauma cases occurred in the Xiayang and Jinze streets as compared with other streets. When taken together, t These results provide a new baseline information that the researchers and health practitioners that could be used for learning and preparing effective measures for of mitigating and reducing trauma incidences and their resulting adverse impacts.

H. Jin and H. Xia—Contributed equally to this work.

© The Author(s), under exclusive license to Springer Nature Switzerland AG 2023
X. Meng et al. (Eds.): SpatialDI 2023, LNCS 13887, pp. 140–153, 2023.
https://doi.org/10.1007/978-3-031-32910-4_10

Keywords: Trauma incidences · Trauma patients · Socio-economic status · house prices · per capita disposable income · GIS

1 Introduction

The development of various sectors such as industries, housing, and transportation facilities and infrastructures in many countries has been coupled with serious incidences causing trauma for individuals and society. Such incidences cause not only great harm to patients but also huge burdens of expenses to the families and public health sectors for treatment. According to the World Health Organization (WHO) estimates, one out of 16,000 people dies every day due to trauma, and 90% of trauma incidences occur in the low- and middle-income countries [1–4] identified that in such countries, trauma that could be from physical and physiological injuries has also been causing more deaths to the young people of around 15 years old. Overall, this information shows that trauma patients among different social groups are unevenly distributed and a similar case is also noted economically for the rich and poorer [5–12]. Specifically, such socio-economic patterns have been studied mainly by considering the factors of age, gender, race, and socio-economic status (SES) of trauma patients [13–16]. In public health, SES is referred to as a general indicator used for measuring a person or an area's level of economy.

Several studies on SES and gender, for example have been studied and their main findings show that there are variations of types, death rates, care, post-traumatic disabilities, and return to work of trauma patients with low SES [5, 15–22]. These results imply that similar scenarios are also likely for trauma patients with high SES. The levels or quality of SES have been studied by different parameters. Maciel et al., for example, calculated the urban quality index of the community using four parameters: education, environment, housing, and economy in Victoria, Brazil [23]. Sehat et al. used the interview methods to measure patients' wealth index and house value index for the same purpose [9]. Vyas et al. derived the SES index of the permanent assets using the PCA method without the incomes data, which is often used for cases involving humans [5, 21, 24]. In general, these and other studies have focused more on studying SES with different subjects. Regarding trauma cases, all such studies lack comprehensive information that integrates, e.g., trauma patients, trauma incidences, and their relationships on space at different scales. The inadequacy of such information in China's studies is much more due to various restrictions, including the lack of relevant and sufficient data [25–28].

With the current development, online platforms and more advanced spatial methods based on GIS could be used for mining spatiotemporal data of various diseases [29–31]. Moreover, the descriptive analyses based on the GIS technology could also be done to discover essential information, such as areas with frequent trauma incidences and their causing factors [32]. Thus, this study addresses the identified problem using Qingpu district as the case study area. In particular, it investigates the relationships between trauma incidences (i.e. physical trauma) and the SES variables studied in two levels: Individual and sub-district. At the individual level, trauma incidences are studied with the housing prices of trauma patients. At the sub-district level, trauma incidences are studied with the per capita income in neighborhoods that are also used for population studies.

The realization of all these objectives is expected to provide new baseline information that could benefit various stakeholders such as researchers and governmental and non-governmental organizations when formulating injury prevention programs and policies. The main contributions of this study can be summarized as follows:

1. It extends knowledge on trauma incidences and their influencing factors in an area with scarce research.
2. It introduces a new GIS-based prototype with an additional of one variable of the community level and different socio-economic parameters for studying trauma cases and their related matters.

2 Materials and Methods

2.1 Study Region

Qingpu district is located in the west of Shanghai, China, and it borders with four other districts: Jiading, Minhang, Songjiang, and Jinshan (Fig. 1). This district has three streets and eight towns covering a total area of 676 square kilometers. Further, it has a population of over 1.219 million engaging in different activities such as agriculture, business, and manufacturing of industrial products. There are four vital industrial areas that together with other activities raise the Qingpu's economy: Qingpu Industrial Park (QIP), Zhangjiang Qingpu Park (ZQP), Export Processing Zone (EPZ), and Zhujiajiao Town. When looking at the neighborhood level, the economic developments in the Qingpu district vary from one place to another. The areas close to the downtown of Shanghai, such as the Xujing and Huaxin towns, have higher levels of economic development than others. This situation seems to be attributed by many factors, including the city's transportation network. Similarly, the house prices around the same areas are higher than in the outskirt areas. And the typical examples of this matter can be identified from the two house compounds of Green Wave Garden Villa, in Xujin and Xiayang New City, in Xiayang Street. The house prices in these two compounds are 102,062 CNY and 32,000 CNY per square meter, respectively.

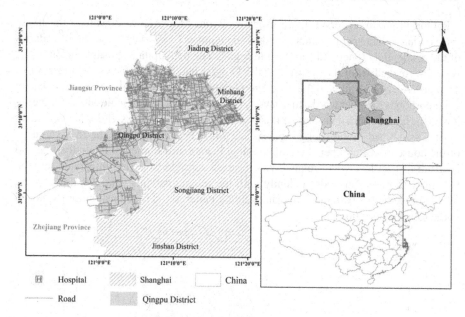

Fig. 1. Case study region

2.2 Data

2.2.1 Trauma Patients Data

Trauma patients data used in this study was obtained from the Zhongshan hospital which is affiliated with the Fudan University of Shanghai. According to the hierarchy of health facilities, the Zhongshan hospital is a tertiary hospital. And spatially, it is found in the central area of Qingpu district. As of 2019, this hospital received 2.11 million trauma patients, and among them, 41,300 were admitted and discharged. For our study, we acquired trauma patients data of adults from 2016 to 2020. The adults, in this case, refer to people with 18 years of age and above as classified by the population data. Next, we used the events' locational information recorded as the address for each patient to download geographical coordinates of trauma incidences. This exercise was done using the Baidu Map API, which besides the access, provides many other services such as geocoding and route planning for the spatially based features. All these data, i.e., the raw trauma patients data from the hospital and their positions by the Baidu Map API were synthesized in one file (i.e., a GIS shapefile) and used for studying different kinds of relationships with the SES variables.

2.2.2 SES Variables

The SES variables used in this research were the house prices and per capita disposable income in Qingpu. These variables are often used [1] and were both considered in our study to understand their total influence and relationships with trauma incidences. The house prices data was obtained from the Anjuke website at http://anjuke.com by running a Python program. Afterward, we used the Baidu Map API to download the house prices related data such as names, addresses, number of residents, and the boundaries of the residential compounds, as seen in Fig. 2. The per capita disposable income data was downloaded from the website of the Qingpu bureau of statistics at https://www.shqp.gov.cn/stat/tjzltjnj/ and this data was obtained together with the population data in neighborhoods. In other words, this data was acquired at the macro scale when comparing it with the house prices data, and for this reason, we regarded it as a sub-district parameter of SES as defined in the background of this work. For consistency, the SES variables of the house prices and per capita disposable income are studied at the individual and area/sub-district levels. All related data for each variable were first integrated into the GIS file and processed independently with the trauma patients data. Next, they were overlaid together to examine and visualize their patterns and relationships, as explained in the following sections.

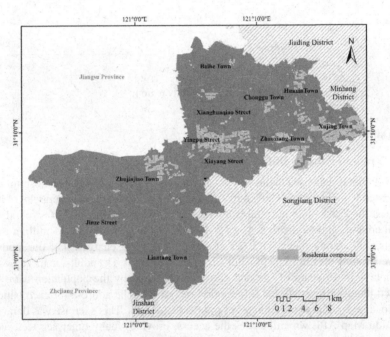

Fig. 2. Spatial distribution of the residential compounds in Qingpu District

2.3 Descriptive Statistics

Our study used three descriptive statistical methods to process the data of trauma incidences and evaluate their relationships with the SES variables. In the first method, the local Getis-Ord Gi* statistic (G*), which is available under the exploratory spatial data analysis (ESDA) tools in the ArcGIS software, was used to compute and visualize spatial distributions of the SES variables. In other words, this static was used to determine the cold and hot spot areas of the house prices and the per capita income in Qingpu, and according to this method, such areas are measured with two main parameters of the G* and p values. The low values of G* and p indicate that such variables are not significantly clustered, and they are referred to as the cold clusters. In contrast, they reveal the presence of significant clusters. The next statistical method was applied to determine spatial distributions and variations (i.e., magnitudes) of the trauma incidences. This objective was accomplished using the kernel density function available under the spatial analyst tools in the ArcGIS software. Lastly, we used a statistical analysis method of the Spearman Pearson, in the SPSS software to assess the relationships between trauma incidences and the SES variables. Such relationships are expressed using a variable ρ, which is computed by the following formula.

$$\rho = \frac{\sum_i (x_i - \bar{x})(y_i - \bar{y})}{\sqrt{\sum_i (x_i - \bar{x})^2 \sum_i (y_i - \bar{y})^2}} \tag{1}$$

Specifically, the ρ in this formula refers to the coefficient of correlation between two variables (i.e. x_i and y_i) and it ranges from -1 to 1. The ρ values range from 0 to 1 imply that the two variables are positively correlated. In contrast, they are negatively correlated, i.e., when the ρ values range between 0 to -1. If the value of ρ is equal to 0, then the two variables do not have a specific direction in their relationships.

3   Results and Analysis

In general, the results of data processed for four years (2016–2020) show that 1545 patients were attended by the Zhongshan hospital in Qingpu due to trauma. The annual incidence rate of all trauma cases was 40 per 10,000 person-years. In terms of gender, there was a high rate of trauma incidences for men (40 per 10,000 person-years) compared with women (20 per 10,000 person-years). This result corresponds with the raw data that also shows that, for the same period, men were 67.2%.

3.1   Results of Trauma Incidences at the Individual Level

The results explored by the Getis-Ord Gi* statistic (G*), shows that there are significant clusters of the house princes in Qingpu (Fig. 3). The areas with the highest house prices are found in the Xujing town as empirically spotted in Sect. 2.2.1. The results by the kernel density applied for the data of the house compounds trauma patients showed that more trauma incidences occurred in the Xiyang Street with cold clusters of the house prices (Fig. 4). When assessed with the population data which was also computed using kernel density, it showed that both areas of the Xujing town and Xiyang Street have large numbers of population compared with others. Thus, after factoring out population, we found that trauma incidences vary inversely proportional with the house prices. The Spearman Pearson coefficient which was calculated based on the two-sided test showed that trauma incidences and the house prices are statistically negatively correlated with the ρ value of - 0.71. This relationship is strong because it approaches to -1. Thus, when taken together, it can be inferred that, trauma incidences at the low level on the space relate more significantly with the socio economic status that is here referred to as the house prices.

Besides the relationships studied between them, we also analyzed trauma incidences to determine the frequency of their occurrence in different compounds (i.e. house compounds), and such compounds were divided into seven groups for the simplicity of our analysis: Q1, Q2, Q3, Q4, Q5, Q6, and Q7. The division of these groups followed the order of the house prices (in Chinese Yuan-CNY) from 15000–25000, 25000–35000, 30000–35000, 35000–40000, 40000–45000, 45000–50000, and 50000 + CNY, respectively. The results as presented in Fig. 5 and Table 1 showed that, trauma incidence rates vary differently between the studied groups. First, they show a rough decline trend from the cheapest compounds Q1 with 13 trauma incidence rate per 10,000 to the most expensive compounds, Q7 with 6 trauma incidence rate per 10,000.

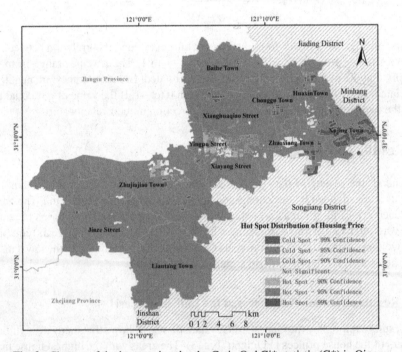

Fig. 3. Clusters of the house prices by the Getis-Ord Gi* statistic (G*) in Qingpu

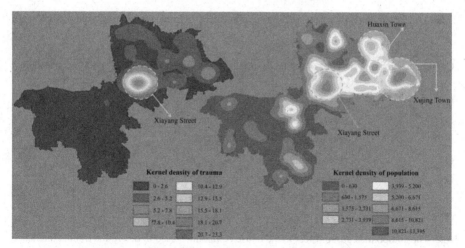

Fig. 4. Kernel density of trauma incidences and population in Qingpu from 2016 to 2020

This trend provides a general conclusion that the lower the house prices the higher the rates of trauma incidences at the micro level of the spatial results. When looking between the Q2 and Q6 compounds, the rates of trauma incidences show an 'arc' shape with low values at the center. In other words, it shows that the rates of trauma incidences for the immediate compounds with the low and high house prices are almost the same.

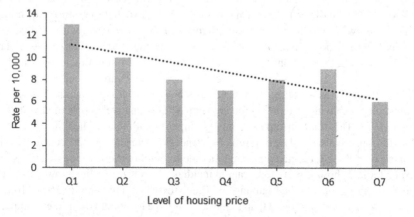

Fig. 5. Trauma incidence rates in Qingpu from 2016 to 2020

Table 1. Classification of trauma incidences and their occurrence rates in Qingpu from 2016 to 2020

Compounds group	Ranges of the house price (CNY)	Average Housing Price (CNY)	Rate per 10,000
Q1	5000–25000	19900	13
Q2	25000–30000	28400	10
Q3	30000–35000	32580	8
Q4	35000–40000	36470	7
Q5	40000–45000	41060	8
Q6	45000–50000	45770	9
Q7	>50000	60910	6

Note: The compounds group refers to the house compounds used to determine trauma incidence rates in Qingpu

3.2 Results of Trauma Incidences at the Sub-district Level

The first results of the Getis-Ord Gi* statistic (G*) at the sub-district level, showed that there are significant clusters of the per capita disposable income in Qingpu as presented in Fig. 6. The highest clusters are found in the Zhaoxiang town followed by the Chonggu town. Both towns are close to the Xujing town that has the highest clusters of the house prices. Thus, despite their closeness, these results imply that the SES variables studied in this research have different implications spatially. The spatial distribution of trauma incidences, showed that there were more trauma cases in Jinze street with cold clusters of the per capita disposable income followed by the Baihe town as seen in Fig. 7. This result shows a similar relationship as noted for the case of trauma incidences and the house prices explored at the individual level. The Spearman Pearson coefficient that was computed similarly as at the individual level, showed that trauma incidences and the per capita disposable income in Qingpu are statistically negatively correlated with the ρ value of - 0.72. This relationship is stronger compared with that of the house prices.

In addition, we also analyzed trauma incidences to determine their occurrence rates associated with the per capita disposable income in neighborhoods. The results as presented in Table 2 showed that more trauma incidences occurred in Jinze town, followed by the Xiayang Street, and the Liantang and Baihe towns with the rates of 16 per 10,000. When narrowed down, we found that all these areas have low population sizes compared with the Xujiang and Huang towns with the least trauma incidence rates. Put simply, this result also demonstrates that the areas with high socio-economic statuses in Qingpu experience little trauma incidences compared with others.

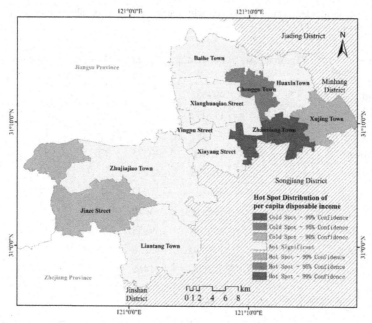

Fig. 6. Clusters of the per capita disposable income by the Getis-Ord Gi* statistic (G*) in Qingpu

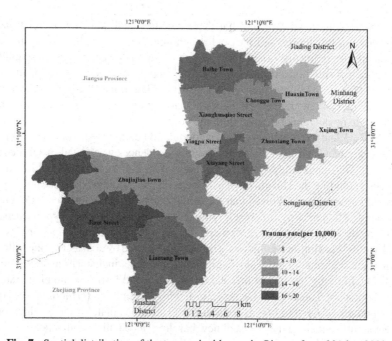

Fig. 7. Spatial distribution of the trauma incidences in Qingpu from 2016 to 2022

Table 2. Trauma incidence rates associated with the per capita disposable income in neighborhoods in Qingpu

Subdistrict	Trauma cases	Population	Per capita disposable income(CNY)	Rate per 10,000
Zhujiajiao Town	124	99568	32410	12
Yingpu Street	121	117442	42456	10
Baihe Town	155	97129	33609	16
Huaxin Town	184	193460	40275	9
Xujing Town	132	165398	48998	8
Chonggu Town	80	56922	37892	14
Xianghuaqiao Street	154	115313	36616	13
Zhaoxiang Town	138	102538	39855	13
Xiayang Street	240	149000	42456	16
Liantang Town	98	62259	31468	16
Jinze Town	115	55871	30611	21

4 Discussion and Limitations of the Study

This study's results have revealed that there are statistically negatively relationships between trauma incidences and the socio-economic statuses studied using the house prices and the per capita disposable income. Such relationships were studied spatially by the spatial-autocorrelation analysis tools used to compute and visualize trauma incidence cases in Qinpu. In addition, they were studied to determine their magnitudes using a statistical analysis method of the Pearson. The specific results showed that trauma incidences are negatively correlated with the house prices and the per capita disposable income by 71% and 72%, respectively. The population data was also studied along with these two variables, and its influence on trauma incidences was found insignificant. In other words, we found that there are some areas with high population and low trauma incidences, including the Huaxin town as seen in Fig. 4. The analysis of the house prices divided into seven groups showed that the trend (rates) of trauma incidences in Qingpu is not completely uniform. This result reminds that despite the clear hypothesizes that could be made on these studies, still there is a need for performing more analyses for optimal results. For simplicity, this could be well understood by considering the following scenario, that, the value of the relationship between trauma incidences and house prices was −0.71. Implying that the higher the house prices the lower the number (rates) of trauma incidences. This notion was however not in agreeable for the house prices of the two compounds of Q6 and Q7, as seen in Fig. 5. Besides that, all the findings of our study are significant since they present new baseline information in this field.

Despite its valuable results, there are some limitations that should be interpreted with the findings of this study. First, we have used only one parameter of the house prices to determine its influence on the occurrence of trauma incidences at the local level. There are several other socio-economic parameters at this level, including education, income and occupations of the family members in society. Such parameters were not included in this study which focused on identifying the influence of such variables and those at the regional scale. In addition, there could be many other socio-economic parameters at the regional level, besides the per capita disposable income used in this study. Thus, future studies should consider this observation to improve their findings. Moreover, they should also consider using other geo-statistical analysis tools to expand the knowledge of this research.

5 Conclusions

This study investigated the relationships between trauma incidences and the socio-economic statutes in two levels: Individual and sub-district. At the individual level, it explored the relationship between trauma incidences and the housing prices. At the sub-district level, it explored the relationships between trauma incidences were the per capita disposable income in neighborhoods. In both cases, it identified that trauma incidences are statistically negatively correlated with the house prices and the per capital disposable income by the Pearson coefficients of -0.71 and $-.0.72$, respectively. Through its analyses, it has revealed the hot spot areas with high incidence rates of trauma cases in Qingpu district that is used as the case study region. Further, it has shown that the rates of trauma incidences based on the house prices are not uniform. Overall, these results provide new baseline information that individuals, researchers and other stakeholders could use for further studies and appropriate measures for securing people's lives. Future studies should consider to extend this research by including many other socio-economic variables as discussed in the limitations of this studies in Sect. 4.

Acknowledgements. We thank the editors and reviewers for their valuable comments. This work is partially supported by the projects funded by the Chongqing Natural Science Foundation (Grant Number: CSTB2022NSCQMSX2069) and the Ministry of Education of China (Grant Number: 19JZD023).

References

1. World Health Organization. The Global burden of disease: 2004 Update. Geneva (2008)
2. Krug, E.G., Sharma, G.K., Lozano, R.: The global burden of injuries. Am. J. Public Health **90**(4), 523–526 (2000)
3. Hofman, K., Primack, A., Keusch, G., Hrynkow, S.: Addressing the growing burden of trauma and injury in low- and middle-income countries. Am. J. Public Health **95**(1), 13–17 (200). https://doi.org/10.2105/AJPH.2004.039354
4. Bonnie, R.J., Fulco, C., Liverman, C.: Reducing the Burden of Injury: Advancing Prevention and Treatment. Natl. Acad. Press, Washington (1999)
5. Ali, M.T., Hui, X., Hashmi, Z.G., et al.: Socioeconomic disparity in inpatient mortality after traumatic injury in adults. Surgery **154**(3), 461–467 (2013). https://doi.org/10.1016/j.surg.2013.05.036
6. Keppel, K., Pamuk, E., Lynch, J., et al.: Methodological issues in measuring health disparities. Vital Health Stat. **2**(141), 1–16 (2005)

7. Bhalla, K., Naghavi, M., Shahraz, S., Bartels, D., Murray, C.J.: Building national estimates of the burden of road traffic injuries in developing countries from all available data sources: Iran. Inj. Prev. **15**(3), 150–156 (2009). https://doi.org/10.1136/ip.2008.020826
8. Laflamme, L., Eilert-Petersson, E.: Injury risks and socioeconomic groups in different settings. Differences in morbidity between men and between women at working ages. Eur. J. Public Health **11**(3), 309–313 (2001). https://doi.org/10.1093/eurpub/11.3.309
9. Sehat, M., Naieni, K.H., Asadi-Lari, M., Foroushani, A.R., Malek-Afzali, H.: Socioeconomic status and incidence of traffic accidents in metropolitan Tehran: a population-based study. Int. J. Prev. Med. **3**(3), 181–190 (2012)
10. Sorenson, S.B.: Gender disparities in injury mortality: consistent, persistent, and larger than you'd think. Am. J. Public Health. **101**(Suppl 1), S353–S358 (2011). https://doi.org/10.2105/AJPH.2010.300029
11. Shahbazi, F., Hashemi-Nazari, S.S., Soori, H., Khodakarim, S.: Socioeconomic inequality in mortality from road traffic accident in Iran. J. Res. Health Sci. **19**(1), e00437 (2019)
12. Kacker, S., Bishai, D., Mballa, G.A., et al.: Socioeconomic correlates of trauma: an analysis of emergency ward patients in Yaoundé, Cameroon. Injury **47**(3), 658–664 (2016). https://doi.org/10.1016/j.injury.2015.12.011
13. Simpson, K., Janssen, I., Craig, W.M., Pickett, W.: Multilevel analysis of associations between socioeconomic status and injury among Canadian adolescents. J. Epidemiol. Community Health **59**(12), 1072–1077 (2005). https://doi.org/10.1136/jech.2005.036723
14. Klest, B., Freyd, J.J., Foynes, M.M.: Trauma exposure and posttraumatic symptoms in Hawaii: gender, ethnicity, and social context. Psychol. Trauma **5**(5), 409–416 (2013). https://doi.org/10.1037/a0029336
15. Adams, J., White, M., Heywood, P.: Time trends in socioeconomic inequalities in road traffic injuries to children, Northumberland and Tyne and Wear 1988–2003. Inj. Prev. **11**(2), 125–126 (2005). https://doi.org/10.1136/ip.2004.007823
16. Stirbu, I., Kunst, A.E., Bos, V., van Beeck., E.F.: Injury mortality among ethnic minority groups in the Netherlands. J. Epidemiol. Community Health **60**(3), 249–255 (2006). https://doi.org/10.1136/jech.2005.037325
17. MacKenzie, E.J., Morris Jr, J.A., Jurkovich, G.J., et al.: Return to work following injury: the role of economic, social, and job-related factors. Am. J. Public Health **88**(11), 1630–1637 (1998). https://doi.org/10.2105/ajph.88.11.1630
18. Hou, W.H., Tsauo, J.Y., Lin, C.H., Liang, H.W., Du, C.L.: Worker's compensation and return-to-work following orthopaedic injury to extremities. J. Rehabil. Med. **40**(6), 440–445 (2008). https://doi.org/10.2340/16501977-0194
19. Kendrick, D., Vinogradova, Y., Coupland, C., et al.: Getting back to work after injury: the UK Burden of Injury multicentre longitudinal study. BMC Public Health **12**, 584 (2012). https://doi.org/10.1186/1471-2458-12-584
20. MacKenzie, E.J., Morris, J.A., Jurkovich, G.J., et al.: Return to work following injury: the role of economic, social, and job-related factors. Am. J. Public Health **88**(11), 1630–1637 (1998)
21. MacKenzie, E.J., Shapiro, S., Smith, R.T., Siegel, J.H., Moody, M., Pitt, A.: Factors influencing return to work following hospitalization for traumatic injury. Am. J. Public Health **77**(3), 329–334 (1987). https://doi.org/10.2105/ajph.88.11.1630
22. Abedzadeh-Kalahroudi, M., Razi, E., Sehat, M.: The relationship between socioeconomic status and trauma outcomes. J. Public Health **40**(4), e431–e439 (2018)
23. Maciel, E.L., Pan, W., Dietze, R., et al.: Spatial patterns of pulmonary tuberculosis incidence and their relationship to socio-economic status in Vitoria, Brazil. Int. J. Tuberc. Lung Dis. **14**(11), 1395–1402 (2010)

24. Vyas, S., Kumaranayake, L.: Constructing socio-economic status indices: how to use principal components analysis. Health Policy Plan. **21**(6), 459–468 (2006). https://doi.org/10.1093/hea pol/czl029
25. Cheng, Y.F., Zhao, Y.H., Zheng, X.Y.: Association between socio-economic status and rehabilitation service utilization for adults with different disabilities. Chin. J. Rehabil. Theory Pract. **25**(03), 367–372 (2019)
26. Ma, W.J., Xu, Y.J., Li, J.S., et al.: A study on the relationship between injury and social economic status among primary and middle school students in Guangdong province. South China J. Prev. Med. **2**, 3–6 (2005)
27. Xue, X.D., Ge, K.X.: The effect of socioeconomic status on the health of the elderly in China: evidence from the Chinese longitudinal. Popul. Dev. **23**(02), 61–69 (2017)
28. Du, B.F., Wang, X.: Health inequality among the Chinese elderly: changes, regional disparities and determinants. Popul. Res. **37**(05), 81–90 (2013)
29. Sharma, N., Patil, M.M., Shamkuwar, M.: Why big data and what is it? Basic to advanced big data journey for the medical industry. Internet Things Biomed. Eng. 189–212 (2019)
30. Kearns, R.A.: Place and health: towards a reformed medical geography. Prof. Geogr. (1993). https://doi.org/10.1111/j.0033-0124.1993.00139.x
31. Khashoggi, B.F., Murad, A.: Issues of healthcare planning and GIS: a review. Int. J. Geo-Inf. **9**(6), 352 (2020). https://doi.org/10.3390/ijgi9060352
32. Keddem, S., Barg, F.K., Glanz, K., Jackson, T., Green, S., George, M.: Mapping the urban asthma experience: using qualitative GIS to understand contextual factors affecting asthma control. Soc. Sci. Med. **140**, 9–17 (2015). https://doi.org/10.1016/j.socscimed.2015.06.039

Contact Query Processing Based on Spatiotemporal Trajectory

Shuchang Zhang and Zhiming Ding$^{(\boxtimes)}$

Beijing University of Technology, Beijing 100022, China
zmding@bjut.edu.cn

Abstract. Due to the prevalence of location-based devices, user trajectories are widely available in daily life, and when an infectious disease out-
break occurs, contact tracking can be achieved by examining the trajectories of confirmed patients to identify other trajectories of direct or indirect contact. In this paper, we propose a generalized trajectory contact
search (TCS) query that models the contact tracking problem and other
similar trajectory-based problems. In addition, we propose a new method
for building spatio-temporal indexes and an algorithm for DBSCAN clustering based on spatio-temporal lattices to find all contact trajectories,
which iteratively performs a distance-based contact search to find all contact trajectories. The algorithm, which is able to downscale the location
and time of trajectories into a one-dimensional data and maintain the
spatio-temporal proximity of the data, reduces the dimensionality of the
search and improves the time and space efficiency. Extensive experiments
on large-scale real-world data demonstrate the effectiveness of our proposed solution compared to the baseline algorithm.

Keywords: Spatiotemporal index · Trajectory Contact Query ·
Trajectory data

1 Introduction

Our daily movements are collected in trajectory data by various devices such
as GPS, Bluetooth, cellular towers, etc. Among the different types of trajectory queries, there is a lack of research on the use of trajectory contact features, which occur when two objects are in close proximity to each other over
a period of time, allowing information (infectious diseases, chemical/radiation
spills, airborne materials, etc.) to be transmitted from one to the other. A direct
application is the tracking of contacts during the New Coronary Pneumonia pan-
demic. A large body of literature highlights the importance of contact tracking,
and applications for tracking contact events via Bluetooth connections between
devices have been established in some countries. However, this approach is hardly
practical because it requires strict user involvement and it cannot detect contact events with different radii due to hardware limitations. In contrast, contact

Supported by organization x.

tracking via traces is more applicable because the trace distance is measurable and the data is widely available.

Therefore, in this paper, we propose a new type of trajectory query, termed as Trajectory Contact Search (TCS), which finds all trajectories that directly and indirectly contact the query trajectory. Specifically, when two trajectories appear within a distance over a time period, we say they make a contact and one can influence the other. Then, given a query trajectory Tr_q, a distance ϵ, and the time step threshold k, we aim to find not only all trajectories R' it contacts, but also all the trajectories contacted by the influenced results R' subsequently. In fact, trajectory contact tracing is non-trivial. As pre-computing all contact events is not viable due to the flexibility of contact definition (ϵ and k), the query can only be answered by searching direct contacts to the influenced trajectory recursively. Besides, as a contact event requires both spatial and temporal continuity, new index and scanning algorithm are required to store and retrieve timestamp-level trajectories efficiently. Overall, our contributions are as follows:

- We propose a trajectory contact search query for the contact tracking problem.
- We propose a solution based on spatio-temporal grid partitioning to answer the contact search query without redundancy. In addition, we propose an algorithm based on DBSCAN clustering of spatio-temporal lattices to find all contact trajectories to further improve the temporal and spatial efficiency.
- Extensive experiments on large-scale real-world datasets show that our approach can answer TCS queries more efficiently than existing methods

2   Related Works

To the best of our knowledge, the travelling group discovery problem is closely related to TCS. Itfinds all groups of objects that move together over a period of time. Depending on how to define proximity (distance-based [1,2,4], or density-based [3,7,9]) and whether the time period is required to be consecutive [2,3,7] or not [5,9], various group patterns are identified. To discover the groups, the trajectories arefirst sliced into temporal snapshots, then a clustering algorithm or predefined criteria is applied to each snapshot tofind groups. Finally, the clusters from adjacent snapshots are intersected and concatenated until forming a long time sequence satisfying travel requirements. Besides, to enable distance comparison in every timestamp, linear interpolation is introduced to ensure an object to appear in every snapshot it crosses, which greatly inflates the input size and the processing cost. To reduce the cost, [3] uses trajectory segments instead of points, and it further simplifies trajectories using Douglas-Peucker algorithm. Meanwhile, [7] proposes a travelling buddy structure to capture the minimal groups of objects and perform intersection on buddies instead.

Geohash effectively defines an implicit, recursive quadtree over the world-wide longitude-latitude rectangle and divides this geographic rectangle into a hierarchical structure. The division continues along the longitude and latitude directions alternately until the desired resolution is achieved. During each division, if the target coordinate value is greater than the division point, a '1' bit is appended to the overall set of bits; otherwise, a '0' bit will be appended. So each node of the recursive quadtree can represent a fixed spatial bounding box. Finally, GeoHash uses a 1D string to represent a 2D rectangle from a given quadtree node. The GeoHash string is derived by interleaving bits obtained from latitude and longitude pairs and then converting the bits to a string using a Base 32 character map. For example, the point with coordinates of $45.557, 18.675$ falls within the GeoHash bounding box of "u2j70vx29gfu". GeoHash has been widely implemented in many geographic information systems (e.g. PostGIS), and also used as a spatial indexing method in some NoSQL databases (e.g. MongoDB).

3   Problem Statement

Definition 1 (Trajectory). A trajectory is a series of chronologically ordered points $Tr_o = \langle p_1 \rightarrow p_2 \rightarrow \cdots \rightarrow p_n \rangle$ representing the historical trace of an object o. Each point $p_i = \langle x, y, t \rangle$ indicates the location of o at time $p_i.t$.

As for a contact event, two objects are defined as contacted if their trajectories (1) are close to each other at a certain point in time, and (2) such proximity is kept for a continuous period of time, formally defined as follows:

Definition 2 (Contact Event). Given a distance threshold ϵ and a duration k, objects a and b are directly contacted during $[t_u, t_v]$ if $\forall t_i \in [t_u, t_v]$, $dist(a, b, t_i) \leq \epsilon$ and $t_v - t_u \geq k * \Delta t$, denoted as a contact event $C_{\epsilon,k}(a, b, [t_u, t_v])$.

Subsequently, we define the direct contact search problem below:

Definition 3 (Direct Contact Search (DCS)). Given a trajectory set R, a query trajectory Tr_q, a starting time t, a distance threshold ϵ and a duration k, a direct contact search $DCS(Tr_q, t, \epsilon, k)$ returns all trajectories T_o that satisfies: $\exists C_{\epsilon,k}(q, o, [t_u, t_v])$ where $t_u \geq t$ (direct contact).

Note that, if not specified, the query starting time t is assumed to set to the starting time of Tr_q. Now we are ready to define the trajectory contact search which further capture the indirect contacts:

Definition 4 (Trajectory Contact Search (TCS)). Given a trajectory set R, a query trajectory Tr_q, a distance threshold ϵ and a duration k, the trajectory contact search $TCS(Tr_q, \epsilon, k)$ returns all trajectories Tr_a which satisfy: there exists a sequence of trajectories $\langle Tr_0, Tr_1, \ldots, Tr_n \rangle$ where (1) $Tr_0 = Tr_q, Tr_n = Tr_a$, (2) $\forall i \in [1, n], Tr_i$ and Tr_{i-1} are contacted directly as $C_{\epsilon,k}(i-1, i, [c_i, c_i + k * \Delta t])$ and (3) $\forall i \in [2, n], ct_i \geq ct_{i-1} + k * \Delta t$.

4   Iteration-Based Trajectory Contact Search

A direct solution to address TCS follows the same routine of the disease transmission process. Starting from the query trajectory, it performs a DCS on a contacted trajectory in each iteration. Then trajectories retrieved by DCS are regarded as the newly contacted trajectories. The algorithm terminates when all contacted trajectories are examined. Intuitively, the iteration process may follow either Breath-First Search (BFS) or Depth-First Search (DFS) order. However, both can retrieve the result correctly but they may incur redundant computation, as one trajectory may contact multiple reported trajectories. We use a distance-based clustering algorithm to search for nearby trajectories to reduce the number of searches.

5   3DGeoHash-DB Contact Search Algorithm

5.1   3DGeoHash

GeoHash has been employed as an efficient indexing solution for massive 2D location data . But GeoHash only encodes the information of latitude and longitude. Our proposed 3DGeoHash method extends the idea of 3DGeoHash, and it includes the temporal dimension besides spatial dimensions. The core of the 3DGeoHash method is the encoding process that convert the items from the augmented 3D data structure into a sequence of characters, i.e. 1D string. Since the 3DGeoHash method defines a recursive octree on the temporally augmented world-wide geographic space, the maximum bounding box for this octree should be first established. The 3DGeoHash uses the following spatial and temporal extents:

Latitude and longitude: Since 3DGeoHash uses the WGS84 as the spatial references coordinate systems, the scope of longitude is $[-180°, 180°]$ while the scope of latitude is $[-90°, 90°]$

Time: Time is infinite and endless, while the 2D space has definite limits. Thus, a single year is divided in the 3DGeoHash encoding. There are two kinds of a single year, common year and leap year. The leap year contains 527040 min ($366 \times 24 \times 60$) while the common year has 525600 min ($365 \times 24 \times 60$). So the scope of a common year is $[0, 525600]$, and the scope of a leap year is $[0, 527040]$.

In Fig. 1, the longitude of one input point is $-40°$ and the division is carried out four times. As the total longitude scope is $[-180°, 180°]$, the longitude is split into two parts ($[-180°, 0°]$ and $[0°, 180°]$) in the first division. If the points belong to the left part $[-180°, 0°]$, then the points are marked as '0', or marked as '1'. Hence, $-40°$ belongs to $[-180°, 0°]$, so the first binary bit is '0'. In the second division, $[-180°, 0°]$ is split into $[-180°, -90°]$ and $[-90°, 0°]$. Because $-40°$ belongs to $[-90°, 0°]$, the second binary bit is '1'. The third and the forth divisions continue in the same way. Thus, the final binary code is "0110".

Since each child node has an extent equal to half of the interval of the parent node, a more direct calculation is formulated as the following. Given that the total scope in one dimension is $[X_{min}, X_{max}]$ and the total height of the final binary tree is h, the resolution of the leaf node will be r :

$$r = \frac{X_{max} - X_{min}}{2^h}$$

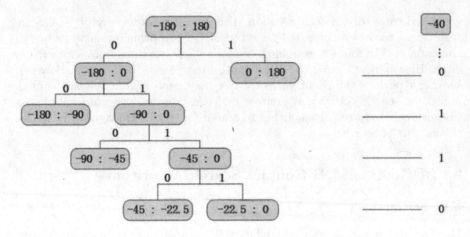

Fig. 1. The binary tree built by four divisions.

If the input value is X_i, the decimal code C_d can be derived as:

$$C_d = \left[\frac{X_i - X_{\min}}{r} \right]$$

In the above-mentioned example, if the longitude Xi is $-40°$, $X_{\max} = 180°$, $X_{\min} = -180°$, and $h = 4$. According to the Eq. 1, $r = 22.5°$ is obtained. Through the Eq. 2, the decimal code C_d is equal to 6. Finally, C_d can be transformed to the binary code $C_b = 0110$.

This encoding process is applied to all three dimensions, and yields three bit sequences, where the number of bits in each corresponds to the number of levels in the tree. For example, if the input data is $(-140°, 20°, 2015 - 6 - 1\ 00{:}00{:}00)$ and h is 10, then the input value of time '2015-6-1 00:00:00' will be transformed into a decimal value, 217440. The three derived bit sequences are:

$$longitude : 0001110001$$
$$latitude : \quad 1001110001$$
$$time : \qquad 0110100111$$

Finally, the three binary codes of the input trajectory point along the longitude, latitude, time dimensions are interleaved into one long binary code. The three bit sequences in this example are interleaved, and the complete binary code of the given trajectory point is listed as the following:

$$010001001110111110000001001111$$

B. The Base64 string of a trajectory point

The complete binary code of the given trajectory point is too long and cannot be directly stored in the target database. So the whole binary code is transformed to a Base64 string in a binary-to-text encoding schema to make it more convenient for database storage. During this encoding, six bits in the binary code are grouped into a corresponding character according to the Base64 map table. Thus the above-mentioned binary code in the Section 3.1 is transformed to a string "Re+BP", shown in Fig. 2. The detailed code-to-string transformation is illustrated as follows.

Binary code :	010001	001110	111110	000001	001111
Value :	17	30	62	1	15
String :	R	e	+	B	P

Fig. 2. The binary-code-to-string transformation process.

If the length of the transformed string is l and the height of binary tree is h, then the relationship between the l and h will be

$$h = 2l$$

The Eq. 3 indicates that each character in the 3DGeoHash string represents two levels in the octree. The resolution r of the octree leaf node in one dimension is

$$r == \frac{X_{\max} - X_{\min}}{2^{2l}}$$

If the spatiotemporal resolution r is known, the height h of the octree is obtained through the Eq. 5:

At last, C_d is transformed to a binary code C_b.

$$h = \left\lceil \frac{\ln\left((X_{\max} - X_{\min})/(r/2)\right)}{\ln(4)} \right\rceil$$

The string does not yet include the year information, so a prefix representing the year is appended to the string. Since the input data is $(-140°, 20°, 2015 - 6 - 100 : 00 : 00)$, the prefix is "2015-". Finally, the complete 3DGeoHash string is "2015Re+BP"

5.2 DBscanclustering Algorithm Based on Spatio-Temporal Grid

DBSCAN (Density-Based Spatial Clustering of Applications with Noise) is a more representative density-based clustering algorithm. Unlike division and hierarchical clustering methods, it defines clusters as the maximum set of density-connected points, is able to divide regions with sufficient density into clusters, and can discover clusters of arbitrary shapes in a spatial database of noise.

We use a set of neighborhoods to describe the closeness of the sample set, and the parameters $(\epsilon, MinPts)$ are used to describe the closeness of the sample distribution in the neighborhood. Where,ϵ describes the neighborhood distance threshold of a sample, and MinPts describes the threshold of the number of samples in the neighborhood of a sample with distance ϵ.

After generating the corresponding HASH codes for each trajectory point according to the 3DGEOHASH algorithm, for each HASH code corresponding to a different trajectory point, according to the distance given by ϵ, set the threshold of the number of samples in the neighborhood as 2, and perform DBSCAN clustering, and then generate different population classifications, the specific generated effect is shown in Fig.

Within a divided 3DGEOHASH spatio-temporal grid, all trajectory points satisfy the definition condition of contact, i.e., between trajectories, the distances are less than a given threshold, and the time interval is within the definition time of contact. Since the scale of the number of trajectory points in the same spatio-temporal grid is smaller, the trajectories are more uniformly distributed at each spatio-temporal scale, so the time required to perform the clustering algorithm is shorter.

After the DBSCAN method groups the people in the same spatio-temporal grid, all people in the same group are marked as contact as long as they are in contact or indirect contact when performing contact query, so that only one lookup is done for each group in query. Therefore, this method is easy to query, there will be no missing queries, and the number of queries is only once, so there is no need for multiple recursive queries, saving time and space.

6   Experiments

6.1   Experiment Settings

The experimental setup lacks public trajectory datasets with sufficient scale and density, especially for pedestrian trajectories, so we conducted 500 efficient trajectory contact query processing experiments on a real commercial dataset of cab trajectories in Beijing, China. We also experimented on an existing user location check-in dataset, Gowalla, a location-based social networking site where users can share their location by checking in. This dataset contains 6,442,890 check-ins from these users between February 2009 and October 2010. To ensure the correctness of the evaluation results, we randomly select 10, 20, 30, 40, 50 trajectories from the dataset as query trajectories, and evaluate the total runtime as well as evaluate the average query efficiency i.e., the number of contacts searched for a single trajectory query.

Our algorithms are implemented in Java and all experiments are performed on a single server. Our chosen solutions include 3DR-Tree [10] and R-Tree indexes + temporal indexes and HR-Tree [11], and our proposed algorithm for 3DGeoHash-DB.

6.2   Effectiveness Study

Figures 3 and 4 depict the total running time of TCS search using different algorithms and indexes on the two datasets, respectively. From the figure we are

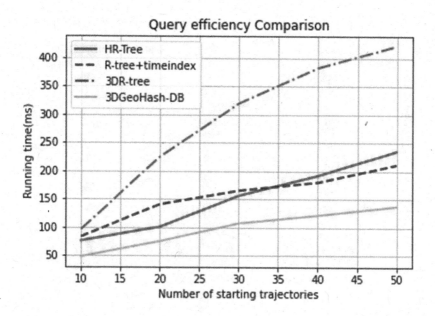

Fig. 3. Running time on T-Drive.

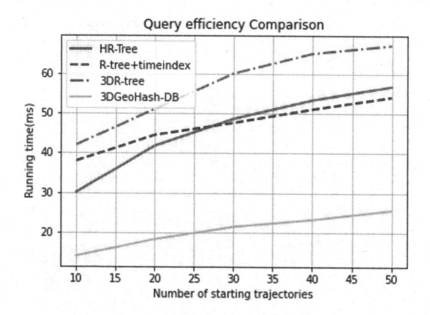

Fig. 4. Running time on Gowalla.

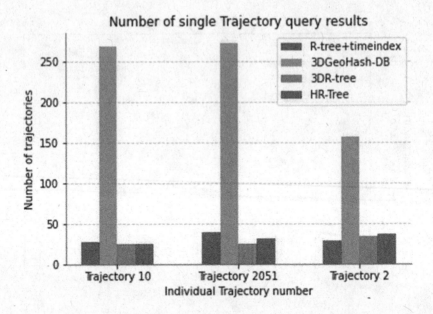

Fig. 5. Number of single track query results on T-Drive.

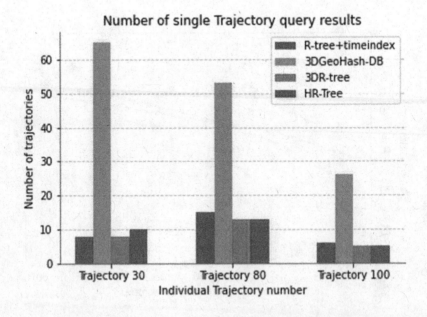

Fig. 6. Number of single track query results on Gowalla.

able to see that our proposed 3DGeoHash-DB algorithm consistently outperforms other traditional solutions, and the gap is larger as the number of query trajectories increases, which is in line with our expectation because more trajectories are queried to have more intersections in the contact result set, and our method only traverses the trajectory search results in the intersection once, preventing duplicate searches and saving time.

Figure 5 and 6 depicts the number of contacts that can be searched for a trajectory query using different algorithms and indexes. From the figure, we can see that our proposed 3DGeoHash-DB algorithm clearly outperforms the other two solutions, which is in line with our expectation, because the other methods search in a circle with a certain distance radius when querying, i.e., only direct contacts can be queried, and trajectories of indirect contacts cannot be queried. The single trajectory query will suffer from result omission. In contrast, our method uses distance-based clustering for trajectory grouping, and each query adds all trajectories within the same group to the results, which makes the average query efficiency improve.

7 Conclusion

In this paper, we introduce a new trajectory contact search query to model the trajectory contact problem. We propose a new spatio-temporal indexing method and a DBSCAN clustering algorithm based on a spatio-temporal grid to find all contact trajectories, which iteratively performs a distance-based contact search to find all contact trajectories. The algorithm, which can reduce the location and time of trajectories into a one-dimensional data and maintain the spatio-temporal proximity of the data, reduces the dimensionality of the search and is efficient in performing spatio-temporal proximity search. Experiments show that our scheme achieves faster query speed and less space consumption.

References

1. Buchin, K., Buchin, M., van Kreveld, M., Speckmann, B., Staals, F.: Trajectory grouping structure. In: Dehne, F., Solis-Oba, R., Sack, J.-R. (eds.) WADS 2013. LNCS, vol. 8037, pp. 219–230. Springer, Heidelberg (2013). https://doi.org/10.1007/978-3-642-40104-6_19
2. Gudmundsson, J., van Kreveld, M., Speckmann, B.: Efficient detection of motion patterns in spatio-temporal data sets. In: Proceedings of the 12th Annual ACM International Workshop on Geographic Information Systems, pp. 250–257 (2004)
3. Jeung, H., Shen, H.T., Zhou, X.: Convoy queries in spatio-temporal databases. In: ICDE, pp. 1457–1459. IEEE (2008)
4. van Kreveld, M., Löffler, M., Staals, F., Wiratma, L.: A refined definition for groups of moving entities and its computation. Int. J. Comput. Geom. Appl. 28(02), 181–196 (2018)
5. Li, Z., Ding, B., Han, J., Kays, R.: Swarm: mining relaxed temporal moving object clusters. PVLDB 3(1–2), 723–734 (2010)

6. Schmidt, J.M.: Interval stabbing problems in small integer ranges. In: Dong, Y., Du, D.-Z., Ibarra, O. (eds.) ISAAC 2009. LNCS, vol. 5878, pp. 163–172. Springer, Heidelberg (2009). https://doi.org/10.1007/978-3-642-10631-6_18

7. Tang, L.A., et al.: On discovery of traveling companions from streaming trajectories. In: ICDE, pp. 186–197. IEEE (2012)

8. Xu, J., Lu, H., Bao, Z.: IMO: a toolbox for simulating and querying "infected" moving objects. PVLDB 13(12), 2825–2828 (2020)

9. Zheng, K., Zheng, Y., Yuan, N.J., Shang, S., Zhou, X.: Online discovery of gathering patterns over trajectories. TKDE 26(8), 1974–1988 (2013)

10. Pfoser, D., Jensen, C., Theodoridis, Y.: Novel approaches to the indexing of moving object trajectories. In: Proceedings of VLDB, pp. 395–406 (2000)

11. van der Spek, S., van Schaick, J., de Bois, P., de Haan, R.: Sensing human activity: GPS tracking. Sensors 9(4), 3033–3055 (2009)

Influential Community Search Over Large Heterogeneous Information Networks

Xingyu Li[✉], Lihua Zhou, Bing Kong, and Lizhen Wang

School of Information Science and Engineering, Yunnan University, Kunming 650091, Yunnan, People's Republic of China
xingyuli1996@gmail.com

Abstract. Community search (CS) aims to find a cohesive community that satisfies query conditions in a given information network. Recent studies have introduced the CS problem into heterogeneous information networks (HINs) that are composed of multi-typed vertices and edges. However, existing works of community search in HINs ignore the influence of vertices and community. To solve this problem, we propose the concept of heterogeneous influence and a new model called heterogeneous k-influential community ($k\mathcal{P}$-HICs) which is designed by combining the concept of heterogeneous influence, meta-path, and k-core. Based on the model, we then develop three algorithms to find top-r $k\mathcal{P}$-HICs in the heterogeneous community containing the query vertex. The Basic-Peel and Advanced-Peel algorithms find top-r $k\mathcal{P}$-HICs by repeatedly peeling the low influential vertices. Considering the fact that top-r $k\mathcal{P}$-HICs are composed of vertices with high influence, the Reversed-Peel algorithm finds top-r $k\mathcal{P}$-HICs in a high influence vertices composed set and thus is more efficient. Extensive experiments have been performed on three real large HINs, and the results show that the proposed methods are effective for searching top-r $k\mathcal{P}$-HICs.

Keywords: Network Analysis · Heterogeneous Information Networks · Influential Community Search

1 Introduction

Many real-world networks have significant community structures, in which vertices are densely connected. Finding communities in a network is a fundamental problem in network analysis, which has attracted much attention in recent years. Exiting works can be classified into community detection (CD) [1, 2] and community search (CS) [3, 4]. Community detection aims to find all communities for a graph. Based on it, some scholars proposed the model and designed algorithms [9–11] to find the top-r influential communities in a network. However the proposed approaches need to traverse all the communities that exist in the network, it's time-consuming and not suitable for online query. Different from community detection, the community search problem focuses on the local structure and only searches the cohesive community containing the query vertex, thus is more suitable for query-based works. Although all the above studies can

X. Meng et al. (Eds.): SpatialDI 2023, LNCS 13887, pp. 165–176, 2023.
https://doi.org/10.1007/978-3-031-32910-4_12

effectively analyze the information network, they are not discussed in heterogeneous information networks (HINs) [5, 6] that are more similar to real-world networks.

Heterogeneous information networks are composed of multiple typed objects and multiple typed links denoting different relations. Figure 1(a) shows an HIN example of the DBLP network, which describes the relationships among entities of different types. There are four types of vertices in the HIN and those types are labeled by A, P, T, and V that represent author, paper, topic, and venue, respectively. The directed lines connecting the vertices denote their semantic relationships. For example, the authors a_1, a_2, and a_3 have written a paper p_4 involving the topic t_2, and it is accepted by the venue v_1. Some scholars have introduced the community search problem into HINs [6–8]. Based on the query vertex, it aims to find a dense community consisting of vertices of the same type. The CSH problem can find cohesive heterogeneous communities, however, it does not consider the influence of communities and vertices.

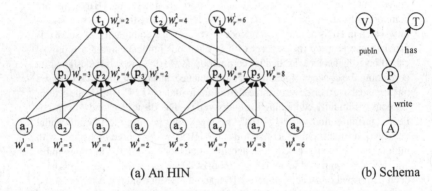

(a) An HIN   (b) Schema

Fig. 1. An HIN example with DBLP network Schema

In this paper, we study the problem of influential community search over HINs. To solve this problem, we propose a new model called heterogeneous k-influential communities ($k\mathcal{P}$-HIC). The $k\mathcal{P}$-HIC model ensures the cohesion and high influence of the community. We design three algorithms to find top-r heterogeneous k-influential communities (top-r $k\mathcal{P}$-HICs) in the heterogeneous community containing q. The Basic-Peel algorithm and the Advanced-Peel find top-r $k\mathcal{P}$-HICs by iteratively peeling vertices from the maximal $k\mathcal{P}$-HIC containing query vertex. The Reverse-Peel algorithm finds top-r $k\mathcal{P}$-HICs among the vertices with high influence and expands the searching range iteratively.

To sum up, in this paper, we make the following contributions:

(1) We propose heterogeneous influence, which is based on the heterogeneity of vertices in HINs. We further present $k\mathcal{P}$-HICs by combining the concepts of meta-path, heterogeneous influence, and k-core. Finally, we formulated the problem of influential community search in HINs;

(2) We design the Basic-Peel algorithm and the Advanced-Peel algorithm to find top-r $k\mathcal{P}$-HICs by iteratively peeling less influential vertices. To improve efficiency, We

further develop the Reverse-Peel algorithm which finds top-r $k\mathcal{P}$-HICs among the vertices with high influence;

(3) We conduct extensive experiments on three real datasets to evaluate the effectiveness and efficiency of our algorithms. The experimental results show all the proposed algorithms can find effective top-r $k\mathcal{P}$-HICs and the result communities are cohesive and composed of high-influence vertices.

2 Related Work

Community search aims to find a connected subgraph that contains all the given query vertices and satisfies the cohesive constraints. The cohesiveness of a community is measured by various metrics, and the k-core [9, 10] is the most frequent one used in the problem of community search. It requires that the degree of each vertex in the graph is at least k. Other metrics used in the field of community search include k-truss [11], k-clique [12], and K-ECC [13]. Based on the k-core metric, Sozio et al. [3] proposed a way to find a community containing the query vertex, in which all the vertices should be connected and have at least k neighbors. By considering the influence of vertices and community, Li et al. [14] presented the issue of influential community search and proposed algorithms to search the top-r influential communities. Furthermore, Bi et al. [15] proposed an optimized online search algorithm to find the top-r influential communities. Li et al. [16] proposed the maximal kr-Clique community and index-based algorithms. By considering multiple influence types in homogeneous networks, Seo et al. [17] proposed a method that finds the top-r most influential communities across multiple influence criteria. Although the community search has made some achievements, the communities studied are all in homogeneous information networks, which only contain one type of vertices and one type of edges.

However, the types of vertices and edges in real networks are complex and diverse, and only considering a single vertex type and edge type will cause information loss. To solve this problem, some scholars have proposed the concept of heterogeneous information network (HIN) [5] which contains various types of vertices and edges. Fang et al. first presented the problem of community search over HINs [6]. They defined the $(k, \mathcal{P})$-core model by combining k-core with meta-path [18] and then proposed online search algorithms and index-based algorithms to search $(k, \mathcal{P})$-core in HINs. Based on the meta-path [18], Yang et al. introduced k-truss into HINs and proposed two new models, namely $(k, \mathcal{P})$-Btruss and $(k, \mathcal{P})$-Ctruss [7], to find more densely heterogeneous communities. By considering the keyword in meta-path, Qiao et al. proposed a keyword-centric community search problem in HINs [19], it can find cohesive heterogeneous communities which also related to the keyword. Although all the above studies can find the corresponding heterogeneous communities, there is no research on influential community search in HINs.

3 Problem Definition

Definition 1: HIN [18, 20]. An HIN is a directed graph $G = (V, E)$ with a vertex type mapping function $\psi : V \rightarrow \mathcal{A}$ and an edge type mapping function $\phi{:}E \rightarrow \mathcal{R}$, where each vertex $v \in V$ belongs to a vertex type $\psi(v) \in \mathcal{A}$, and each edge $e \in E$ belongs to an edge type (also called relation) $\phi(e) \in \mathcal{R}$.

Definition 2: HIN Schema [18, 20]. Given an HIN $G = (V, E)$ with mapping $\psi :$ $V \rightarrow \mathcal{A}$ and $\phi{:}E \rightarrow \mathcal{R}$, its schema T_G is a directed graph defined over vertex types $\mathcal{A}$ and edge types (as relations) $\mathcal{R}$, i.e., $T_G = (\mathcal{A}, \mathcal{R})$.

Figure 1(b) is the schema of the HIN, in which the vertices labeled A, P, T, and V denote the author, paper, topic, and venue. The schema of an HIN describes all allowable edge types between vertex types.

Definition 3: Meta-path [18]. A meta-path $\mathcal{P}$ is a path defined on an HIN schema $T_G = (\mathcal{A}, \mathcal{R})$, and is denoted in the form $A_1 \xrightarrow{R_1} A_2 \xrightarrow{R_2} \cdots \xrightarrow{R_l} A_{l+1}$, where l is the length of $\mathcal{P}, A_i \in \mathcal{A}(1 \leq i \leq l+1)$, and $R_i \in \mathcal{R}(1 \leq i \leq l)$.

In the above definitions, we use upper-case letters (e.g., A) to denote vertex types in an HIN, and lower-case letters (e.g., a_1) to denote vertices, the same blow. We say a meta-path is symmetric if it is the same as its reverse path. For a certain meta-path $\mathcal{P}$, we call a path $p = a_1 \rightarrow a_2 \rightarrow \dots \rightarrow a_{l+1}$ between a_1 and a_{l+1} a path instance. We say vertex v is $\mathcal{P}$-neighbor of vertex u if existing a meta-path instance of $\mathcal{P}$ between them, and vice versa. We call vertices v and u are $\mathcal{P}$-connected if they can be connected by a chain of vertices between them, and each vertex should be $\mathcal{P}$-neighbor of its adjacent vertex in the chain.

Definition 4: Heterogeneous Influence. Given an HIN $G = (V, E)$ and a heterogeneous influence set W with mapping function $\varphi : W \rightarrow \mathcal{K}$, for any vertex $v_i \in V$, the heterogeneous influence of v_i is $w_A^i \in W$ and its influence type w_A associated with the vertex type of v_i, i.e. $\forall v_i \in V, f(v_i) = w_A^i$, and $\varphi(w_A^i) = w_A \in \mathcal{K}$.

In Definition 4, label A denotes the vertex type of v_i. For example, in Fig. 1(a), the four types A, P, V, and T are associated with four types of influence w_A, w_P, w_V, and w_T. Each vertex in HIN has a certain heterogeneous influence, such as the heterogeneous influence of vertices a_1 and p_2 is w_A^1 and w_P^2.

Definition 5: $\mathcal{P}$-$deg(v, S)$. Given an HIN, a set of vertices S and a meta-path $\mathcal{P}$, we define $\mathcal{P}$-$deg(v, S)$ as the number of path instances of $\mathcal{P}$ between v and all the other vertices in $S \backslash \{v\}$.

Definition 6: $k\mathcal{P}$-HIC. Given an HIN G, a heterogeneous influence set W, an integer k, and a set of $\mathcal{P}$-connected vertices S, we say S is a $k\mathcal{P}$-HIC, if $\forall v \in k\mathcal{P}$ - HIN, $\mathcal{P}-deg(v, S) \geq k$. The heterogeneous influence of S denoted by $f(S)$ is defined as the minimum heterogeneous influence of the vertices in S, i.e. $f(S) = \min_{v_i \in S} w_A^i$ in which $w_A^i \in W$ and $A = \psi(v_i)$.

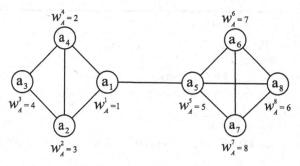

Fig. 2. An example of $k\mathcal{P}$-HIC

For example, in Fig. 1(a), let $q = a_6$, $\mathcal{P}\ominus = (APA)$, and $k = 2$, we can find a maximal $k\mathcal{P}$-HIC including query vertex a_6 shown in Fig. 2. According to Definition 6, each vertex in this $k\mathcal{P}$-HIC has at least two $\mathcal{P}$-neighbor, and all vertices are $\mathcal{P}$-connected. The influence of the $k\mathcal{P}$-HIC is determined by the vertex with minimal influence, which is a_1, thus the influence of the $k\mathcal{P}$-HIC is 1. Since $k\mathcal{P}$-HIC is not necessarily the maximal induced subgraph that satisfies the degree constraint, there also exist other $k\mathcal{P}$-HICs in the above example, such as $\{a_2, a_3, a_4\}$ and $\{a_5, a_6, a_7, a_8\}$.

Problem Statement. Given an HIN G, a heterogeneous influence set W, a query vertex q, a meta-path $\mathcal{P}$, and two integers k and r, the problem is to find top-r heterogeneous k-influential communities in the heterogeneous community containing q.

4 Search Algorithm

4.1 Basic-Peel Algorithm

The Basic-Peel algorithm searches the top-r $k\mathcal{P}$-HICs by peeling the vertex with the lowest influence and recalculating the degree of residual vertices in each iteration progress. In general, it consists of five steps: (1) find the maximal $k\mathcal{P}$-HIC which contains the query vertex and store it in G_t; (2) set the largest $k\mathcal{P}$-HIC with the lowest influence in G_t as a result and push it into R_S; (3) delete the vertex with the lowest influence in $k\mathcal{P}$-HIC found in step (2); (4) recalculate degree of all residual vertices in G_t, and if there still exist $k\mathcal{P}$-HICs, jump to step (2), else jump to step (5); (5) if the size of R_S is less than r, output all $k\mathcal{P}$-HIC in R_S, else output top-r $k\mathcal{P}$-HICs. Its pseudocode is shown in Algorithm 1. The time complexity of the Basic-Peel algorithm is $O(N_{HIC}M_c)$, in which N_{HIC} denotes the number of $k\mathcal{P}$-HICs existing in G_t and M_c denotes the number of edges in G_t.

Algorithm 1: Basic-Peel Algorithm

Input: G, W, q, $\mathcal{P}$, k, r;
Output: top-r $k\mathcal{P}$-HICs;

---
1   compute the maximal $k\mathcal{P}$-HIC containing q;
2   store the graph formed by vertices in the maximal $k\mathcal{P}$-HIC in G_t;
3    $R_s \leftarrow \varnothing$, $i = 0$;
4   **While** G_t contains $k\mathcal{P}$-HIC
5   set the largest $k\mathcal{P}$-HIC with the lowest influence in G_t as $k\mathcal{P}$-HIC$_i$;
6   R_s.push($k\mathcal{P}$-HIC$_i$);
7   let v be the vertex with the lowest influence in $k\mathcal{P}$-HIC$_i$;
8   delete v in G_t and recalculate the degree of vertices in G_t;
9       $i = i + 1$;
10   **If** $|R_s| \leq r$ **then** output all $k\mathcal{P}$-HICs in R_s **else** output last r $k\mathcal{P}$-HICs in R_s;

4.2 Advanced-Peel Algorithm

The Basic-Peel Algorithm, based on the simplest idea, has to recalculate the degrees of vertices, and this process is time-consuming. To optimize it, we propose the Advanced-Peel algorithm which is based on the DFS strategy to dynamically update the degrees of vertices and find the top-r $k\mathcal{P}$-HICs.

Algorithm 2: DeleteNode Algorithm

Input: v, G_t;
Output: the degree of vertices in G_t;

---
1    $S \leftarrow \varnothing$, S.push(v);
2   **While** S is not $\varnothing$;
3       $v_d = S$.pop( ), $U \leftarrow \{u \mid u$ *is* $\mathcal{P}$-neighbor of $v\}$;
4   delete v_d in G_t;
5   **for** each vertex $u \in U$ **do**
6   reduce the degree of u by one;
7   **If** $\mathcal{P}$-$deg(u) < k$
8   S.push(u);
9   Output the degree of vertices in G_t

The Advanced-Peel algorithm is similar to the Basic-Peel algorithm, while it does not recalculate the degrees of vertices in the iteration process, it uses the DeleteNode algorithm detailed in Algorithm 2 to update the degree of each vertex. After deleting the least influential vertex in each iteration, it updates the degrees of the neighbors of the deleted vertex, that is, the degree of each neighbor is reduced by one. Since the degrees of some vertices in $k\mathcal{P}$-HIC are not less than k, if the degrees of the neighbors do not satisfy this constraint after updating, those neighbor vertices will not appear in the following

$k\mathcal{P}$-HICs, therefore, we need to delete those vertices and repeat the above steps to update the degrees of their neighbors. The time complexity of the Advanced-Peel algorithm is $O(N_C + M_C)$, in which N_C and M_C respectively represent the number of vertices and edges in G_t.

4.3 Reversed-Peel Algorithm

Algorithm 3: Reversed-Peel Algorithm

Input: G, W, q, $\mathcal{P}$, k, r;
Output: top-r $k\mathcal{P}$-HICs;

---

1   compute the maximal $k\mathcal{P}$-HIC containing q;
2   store the graph formed by vertices in the maximal $k\mathcal{P}$-HIC in G_t;
3    $S \leftarrow \varnothing$, store influences of vertices in G_t in descending order in S;
4    $L = |G_t|$, $N_c = k+r$, $R_s \leftarrow \varnothing$, $S_t \leftarrow \varnothing$;
5   **While** $|R_s| < r$ AND $N_c \leq L$
6   store the graph formed by top N_c vertices in S in G_c;
7   calculate the degree of vertices in G_c;
8        $R_s \leftarrow \varnothing$, $i = 0$;
9   **While** G_c contains $k\mathcal{P}$-HIC
10   set the largest $k\mathcal{P}$-HIC with the lowest influence in G_c as $k\mathcal{P}$-HIC$_i$;
11   R_s.push($k\mathcal{P}$-HIC$_i$);
12   let v be the vertex with the lowest influence in $k\mathcal{P}$-HIC$_i$;
13   DeleteNode (v, G_c);
14           $i = i+1$;
15   If $N_c = L$ **then** exit the loop
16   If $N_c \times step \geq L$ **then** $N_c = L$ **else** $N_c = N_c \times step$
17   If $|R_s| \leq r$ **then** output all $k\mathcal{P}$-HICs in R_s **else** output last r $k\mathcal{P}$-HICs in R_s;

To find the most influential heterogeneous communities, in the algorithms above, we need to start from a huge vertex set and iteratively peel low influential vertices. The fact is that in real networks, the maximal $k\mathcal{P}$-HIC may have a large number of vertices, while the size of the result top-r $k\mathcal{P}$-HICs may be very small. Based on this idea, we propose the Reversed-Peel algorithm, which searches the top-r $k\mathcal{P}$-HICs by only considering vertices with high influence in the maximal $k\mathcal{P}$-HIC. The Reversed-Peel algorithm generally has five steps: (1) find the maximal $k\mathcal{P}$-HIC which contains the query vertex, and set $N_c = k + r$; (2) find the top N_c vertices with the highest influence in descending order and store the graph formed by these vertices as G_c; (3) set the G_c as input and apply the Advanced-Peel algorithm; (4) If the number of $k\mathcal{P}$-HICs in R_S is greater than r or the size of G_c equal to the maximal $k\mathcal{P}$-HIC, output the results, otherwise jump to step (5); (5) set $N_c = N_c \times step$, jump to step (2). The time complexity of the Reversed-Peel algorithm is $O(\sum_{j=1}^{C} N_j + M_j)$, in which C denotes the times that G_c need to be extended in order to find the top-r $k\mathcal{P}$-HICs, and N_j and M_j respectively represent the number of vertices and edges in G_c during the jth iteration. Note that in the algorithm we described above, we set the initial value of N_c equal to the sum of k and r. The reason is, to find top-r $k\mathcal{P}$-HICs, there should be at least $k + r$ nodes in G_c.

5 Experiments

We now present the experiments and results. We first discuss the setup in Sect. 5.1, and then we discuss the effectiveness testing and efficiency testing in Sect. 5.2 and Sect. 5.3.

Table 1. Datasets used in the following experiments

Dataset	Vertices	Edges	Vertex types	Edge types	Influence types
Foursquare	43198	810951	5	8	5
DBLP	682818	3902417	4	6	4
IMDB	2467802	15195181	4	6	4

5.1 Experimental Setup

We use three real datasets: Foursquare, DBLP, and IMDB. Their detailed information is shown in Table 1. Foursquare contains check-in records in the US, which has five types of vertices (user, venue, city, venue category, and date). In the following experiments, we use the meta-path $\mathcal{P} = (UVU)$ (user-venue-user), and the influence of the user is determined by the number of his check-in times in various venues, which reflects the user's activity. DBLP contains publication information in the computer science field, and it has four types of vertices (author, paper, venue, and topic). For this dataset, we use the meta-path $\mathcal{P} = (APA)$ (author-paper-author), and the influence of the author is evaluated by the number of papers that the author published. IMDB contains movie records since 2000, it has four types of vertices (movie, actor, director, and writer). We choose the meta-path $\mathcal{P} = (MAM)$ (movie-actor-movie) as the query parameter of the IMDB dataset. The influence of a movie is determined by the influence of actors, directors, and writers involved in the creation.

5.2 Effectiveness Testing

Core Analysis. To analyze the proposed $k\mathcal{P}$-HIC, we set $k = [16, 32, 64, 128, 256]$, and then examine the size distributions of top-1 $k\mathcal{P}$-HIC and Basic $(k, \mathcal{P})$-core [6]. The Basic $(k, \mathcal{P})$-core model searches heterogeneous community which is based on the concepts of meta-path and k-core. However, it does not consider the influence of communities and vertices. As shown in Fig. 3, since $k\mathcal{P}$-HIC comprehensively considers the cohesiveness and influence of communities, its community scale is smaller while ensuring community cohesion.

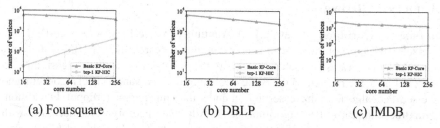

Fig. 3. Core Analysis for $k\mathcal{P}$-HIC

Case Study. To analyze the result top-r $k\mathcal{P}$-HICs, we used a small dataset which is more suitable for the case study. The dataset is extracted from DBLP dataset from 2017 to 2020, which includes 93,848 vertices and 412,404 edges. The influence of author comprehensively considers the influence of papers he contributed, and the influence of papers is determined by the influence of the venue it published.

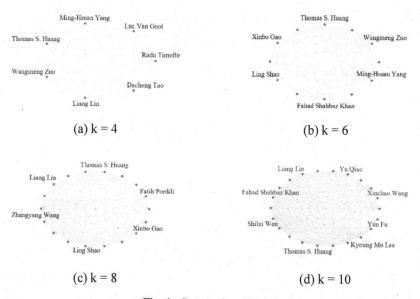

Fig. 4. Case study on DBLP

We set q = Prof. Dacheng Tao, $\mathcal{P}$ = (APA), $r = 1$, $k = [4, 6, 8, 10]$, and performed queries on the dataset we discussed above. As shown in Fig. 4, with the value of k increasing, the size of $k\mathcal{P}$-HIC shows an increasing trend. Prof. Dacheng Tao's main research fields include computer vision and machine learning, etc. After analyzing the results top-1 $k\mathcal{P}$-HIC, we found that the authors in the above four result communities mainly focus on the same field as the query vertex, and each author has a high number of citations.

5.3 Efficiency Testing

Runtime of Algorithms. We evaluate the runtime of Basic-Peel, Advanced-Peel, and Reversed-Peel algorithms for the influential community search query in HINs. Firstly, we set $r = 64$ and take k as a variable to compare the efficiency of the three algorithms. As shown in Fig. 5, the runtime of the Basic-Peel algorithm, Advanced-Peel algorithm, and Reversed-Peel algorithm decreases in turn under the same parameter input. In addition, the runtime of the Basic-Peel algorithm and the Advanced-Peel algorithm decreases with the increase of k. The reason for this phenomenon is that as the value of k increases, the maximal $k\mathcal{P}$-HIC contains query vertex will gradually become smaller, and these two algorithms peel vertices based on the maximal $k\mathcal{P}$-HIC, so the runtime shows a downward trend. Besides, since the size of the high-influence vertex set traversed by the Reversed-Peel algorithm is affected by k, its runtime shows an upward trend.

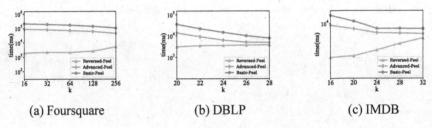

| (a) Foursquare | (b) DBLP | (c) IMDB |

Fig. 5. Runtime of different algorithms (Vary k)

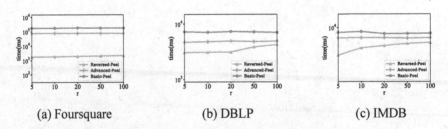

| (a) Foursquare | (b) DBLP | (c) IMDB |

Fig. 6. Runtime of different algorithms (Vary r)

We then set $k = 32$ and take r as a variable to compare the efficiency of the three algorithms. As shown in Fig. 6, the runtime of the three algorithms decreases in turn. In addition, with the value of k increase, the runtime of Reversed-Peel algorithms shows an upward trend, while the runtime of the other two algorithms does not fluctuate much. This is because the Basic-Peel algorithm and Advanced-Peel algorithm need to find all $k\mathcal{P}$-HICs, and then return the top-r $k\mathcal{P}$-HICs based on it. However, the Reversed-Peel algorithm only considers the vertices with high influence and does not find all $k\mathcal{P}$-HICs, so the runtime of the algorithm will increase with the increase of r.

Evaluate the Parameter *step*. In this section, we evaluate parameter *step* by setting it as a variable and keeping the value of k and r constant. As shown in Fig. 7, when the value of *step* increases within a reasonable range, the runtime of the algorithm can be slightly reduced, but as the value of *step* continues to increase, the candidate set to be searched is far larger than the set required by the target top-r $k\mathcal{P}$-HICs, so the algorithm time will increase significantly. When *step* reaches a certain threshold, the runtime of the algorithm tends to be stable. The reason is that the candidate set is too large, and its size approaches the size of the maximum $k\mathcal{P}$-HIC.

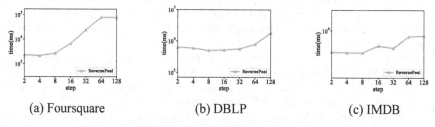

| (a) Foursquare | (b) DBLP | (c) IMDB |

Fig. 7. Runtime of the Reversed-Peel algorithm (Vary *step*)

6 Conclusion

In this paper, we study the problem of influential community search in HINs. Firstly, we propose the heterogeneous influence based on the heterogeneity of vertices in HINs. We then define $k\mathcal{P}$-HIC by combining the concept of heterogeneous influence, meta-path, and k-core. To find top-r $k\mathcal{P}$-HICs in HINs, we first design the Basic-Peel algorithm based on the simplest idea. By optimizing the recalculation process in the Basic-Peel algorithm, we develop the Advanced-Peel which updates the degree of vertices with the DFS strategy. Considering the fact that vertices in top-r $k\mathcal{P}$-HICs generally have high influence, we propose the Reverse-Peel algorithm. Extensive experiments on large real-world networks demonstrate the effectiveness and efficiency of our solutions. In future work, we are interested in designing an index algorithm to improve the efficiency of searching heterogeneous influence communities in HINs.

References

1. Fortunato, S.: Community detection in graphs. Phys. Rep. **486**(3–5), 75–174 (2010)
2. Javed, M.A., Younis, M.S., Latif, S., Qadir, J., Baig, A.: Community detection in networks: a multidisciplinary review. J. Netw. Comput. Appl. **108**, 87–111 (2018)
3. Sozio, M., Gionis, A.: The community-search problem and how to plan a successful cocktail party. In: Proceedings of the 16th ACM SIGKDD International Conference on Knowledge Discovery and Data Mining, pp. 939–948 (2010)

4. Cui, W., Xiao, Y., Wang, H., Wang, W.: Local search of communities in large graphs. In: Proceedings of the 2014 ACM SIGMOD International Conference on Management of Data, pp. 991–1002 (2014)

5. Shi, C., Li, Y., Zhang, J., Sun, Y., Philip, S.Y.: A survey of heterogeneous information network analysis. IEEE Trans. Knowl. Data Eng. **29**(1), 17–37 (2016)

6. Fang, Y., Yang, Y., Zhang, W., Lin, X., Cao, X.: Effective and efficient community search over large heterogeneous information networks. Proc. VLDB Endow. **13**(6), 854–867 (2020)

7. Yang, Y., Fang, Y., Lin, X., Zhang, W.: Effective and efficient truss computation over large heterogeneous information networks. In: 2020 IEEE 36th International Conference on Data Engineering (ICDE), pp. 901–912. IEEE (2020)

8. Jiang, Y., Fang, Y., Ma, C., Cao, X., Li, C.: Effective community search over large star-schema heterogeneous information networks. Proc. VLDB Endow. **15**(11), 2307–2320 (2022)

9. Seidman, S.B.: Network structure and minimum degree. Soc. Netw. **5**(3), 269–287 (1983)

10. Batagelj, V., Zaversnik, M.: An O (m) algorithm for cores decomposition of networks, arXiv preprint cs/0310049 (2003)

11. Akbas, E., Zhao, P.: Truss-based community search: a truss-equivalence based indexing approach. Proc. VLDB Endow. **10**(11), 1298–1309 (2017)

12. Yuan, L., Qin, L., Zhang, W., Chang, L., Yang, J.: Index-based densest clique percolation community search in networks. IEEE Trans. Knowl. Data Eng. **30**(5), 922–935 (2017)

13. Hu, J., Wu, X., Cheng, R., Luo, S., Fang, Y.: On minimal steiner maximum-connected subgraph queries. IEEE Trans. Knowl. Data Eng. **29**(11), 2455–2469 (2017)

14. Li, R.-H., Qin, L., Yu, J.X., Mao, R.: Finding influential communities in massive networks. VLDB J. **26**(6), 751–776 (2017). https://doi.org/10.1007/s00778-017-0467-4

15. Bi, F., Chang, L., Lin, X., Zhang, W.: An optimal and progressive approach to online search of top-k influential communities, arXiv preprint arXiv:1711.05857 (2017)

16. Li, J., Wang, X., Deng, K., Yang, X., Sellis, T., Yu, J.X.: Most influential community search over large social networks. In: 2017 IEEE 33rd International Conference on Data Engineering (ICDE), pp. 871–882. IEEE (2017)

17. Seo, J.H., Kim, M.H.: Finding influential communities in networks with multiple influence types. Inf. Sci. **548**, 254–274 (2021)

18. Sun, Y., Han, J., Yan, X., Yu, P.S., Wu, T.: Pathsim: Meta path-based top-k similarity search in heterogeneous information networks. Proc. VLDB Endow. **4**(11), 992–1003 (2011)

19. Qiao, L., Zhang, Z., Yuan, Y., Chen, C., Wang, G.: Keyword-centric community search over large heterogeneous information networks. In: Jensen, C.S., et al. (eds.) DASFAA 2021. LNCS, vol. 12681, pp. 158–173. Springer, Cham (2021). https://doi.org/10.1007/978-3-030-73194-6_12

20. Huang, Z., Zheng, Y., Cheng, R., Sun, Y., Mamoulis, N., Li, X.: Meta structure: computing relevance in large heterogeneous information networks. In: Proceedings of the 22nd ACM SIGKDD International Conference on Knowledge Discovery and Data Mining, pp. 1595–1604 (2016)

Spatiotemporal Data Mining

Fast Mining Prevalent Co-location Patterns Over Dense Spatial Datasets

Junyi Li[1], Lizhen Wang[1,2(✉)], Vanha Tran[3], Junyi Li[1], and Xiwen Jiang[1]

[1] School of Information Science and Engineering, Yunnan University, Kunming 650091, China
lzhwang@ynu.edu.cn
[2] Dianchi College of Yunnan University, Kunming 650228, China
[3] FPT University, Hanoi 155514, Vietnam

Abstract. Traditional prevalent co-location pattern mining (PCPM) methods generate complete table instances (TIs) of all candidates, which is both time and space consuming. Existing Apriori-like methods focus on improving the efficiency of TI generation, while existing Clique-based methods still contain many repeated traversing processes, and therefore neither of them can very well detect the overlap in TIs. To address these challenges, this paper first proposes the concept of extended maximal cliques (EMCs) to detect instance overlap situations, and designs a hash-based storage structure SSHT to reduce mining consumption. Second, a novel approach PCPM-EMC is introduced to detect all prevalent co-location patterns (PCPs), which uses the proposed P-BK$_{p,d}$ algorithm to generate EMCs, and adopts a bidirectional pruning strategy for PCP detection. Lastly, extensive experiments on both real-world and synthetic datasets show that the proposed approach is efficient, and reducing more over 80% space consumption and more than 50% time consumption than existing methods, especially in dense datasets.

Keywords: Spatial data mining · Prevalent co-location pattern · Extended maximal clique · Overlapping instance

1 Introduction

Prevalent co-location pattern mining (PCPM) aims to mine PCPs in given spatial datasets, where a co-location pattern is a subset of spatial features whose instances appear frequently adjacent in space, and a PCP is a co-location that satisfies the prevalent measurement. PCPM is an important technology of spatial data mining, which has many applications, such as plants protection [1], urban construction [2], and so on.

A spatial dataset usually contains a spatial feature set $F = \{f_1, f_2, ..., f_n\}$ and a spatial instance set $S = \{S_1, S_2, ..., S_n\}$ ($S_i = \{o_j \mid o_j.t = f_i\}$), where a *spatial feature f_i* represents a type of instances, and a *spatial instance o_j* with information < feature-type, instance-id, location > represents an appearance of its feature (i.e., $o_j.t$) in a particular location. Two instances satisfy the *neighbor relationship R*, if the distance between them does not exceed a given threshold d. An instance set $RI = \{o_1, o_2, ..., o_k\}$ is called a *row*

The first author is a student.

© The Author(s), under exclusive license to Springer Nature Switzerland AG 2023
X. Meng et al. (Eds.): SpatialDI 2023, LNCS 13887, pp. 179–191, 2023.
https://doi.org/10.1007/978-3-031-32910-4_13

instance of C, if (1) RI contains all the features in C and is of the same length as C, (2) all instances of RI form a clique under R. All instances in RI are *participating instance* (P-I) of C, and the participating instance set of f_i in C is denoted as $PIS(C, f_i)$. All RIs of C make up its *table instance* (TI). For evaluating the prevalence of co-locations, Shekhar et al. [3] defined *Participation Ratio* (PR) and *Participation Index* (PI), which are calculated as $PR(C, f_i) = \frac{|PIS(C,f_i)|}{|S_i|}$ and $PI(C) = min_{i=1}^n\{PR(C, f_i)\}$.

There are many works for PCPM, but still has the following weaknesses: Traditional PCPM method [4] generates complete TIs of all candidates, which has massive consumption; Apriori-like methods focus on reducing calculations of TI generation [5–7], Clique-based methods focus on speeding up MCs generation to calculate PI of candidates [8–13], but neither of them can detect well the overlap among RIs, so they contain many repeated traversal processes. In this paper, we attempt to address these problems.

1.1 Related Works

Apriori-Like Methods: Join-based algorithm [4] is a traditional PCPM method, which generates candidates and filters PCPs size-by-size, but it uses too much join operations to generate complete TIs of candidates, so many methods aim to reduce the calculations on generating TIs. Joinless algorithm [5] utilizes a star neighbor model to materialize the neighbor relationships between instances and a three-level strategy to avoid unnecessary computations. The algorithm based on iCPI-tree was presented in [6], which uses width-first strategy to generate all TIs. CPM-Col algorithm [7] designs several optimization and pruning strategies to best avoid visiting complete TIs. There are also many methods that focus on PCPM applying in other situations, such as methods for different data type [14], methods for condensed representation [15], and so on.

Clique-Based Methods: Wang et al. [8] proposed an order-clique-based method for mining maximal prevalent co-location patterns (MPCPs), which uses prefix tree structure to materialize neighbor relationships. Yao et al. [9] use a sparse undirected graph to store size-2 PCPs and further detect maximal cliques in the graph, they also designed a compress instance tree to reduce the space consumption. For mining all-size PCPs, Bao et al. [10] presented a clique-based framework for PCPM, using proposed complete cliques (I-clique and N-clique) and a C-hash structure. It is suitable for situation that the prevalence threshold changes repeatedly, but the process of generating complete cliques is time-consuming. Wu et al. [11] defined the concept of maximal ordered ego-cliques and designed a method based on geometric properties of instance spatial distributions. Methods based on maximal clique and hash table have been recently proposed, such as MCHT [12] and CPM-MCHM [13], which optimize the storage of MCs and use a two-level strategy to generate candidates and detect PCPs.

Maximal Clique Enumeration: Since the process of generating maximal cliques (MCs) is the important foundation of our proposed method, it is necessary to introduce its related work. The classical method for generating MCs in a given graph is Bron-Kerbosch algorithm (BK), which adopts the depth-first search strategy. There are many improved versions of BK, such as: BK with pivot selection [16], which can reduce a lot of unnecessary branching traversal; BK with recursive core decomposition [17], which adopts the strategy of eliminating a point with least neighbors in each iteration; BK with multi-level division [18], which can detect MCs in real-world graph datasets under limited memory. And there are many other works using other thoughts, such as methods based on breadth-first search, methods based on computational optimization. Since the BK series algorithms have better performance in most real datasets [19], we adopt their strategies for mining MCs in our approach.

1.2 Our Contributions

The principal contributions of this paper are as follows.

First, we define the extended maximal clique (EMC) concept to detect the instance overlap, and design the hash-based structure SSHT to reduce the consumption.

Second, we propose a novel approach PCPM-EMC, which generates EMCs by the proposed PCPM version of BK algorithm with pivot and division (P-BK$_{p,d}$), and adopts a bidirectional pruning strategy to detect all PCPs. The algorithm analysis is also given.

Finally, the extensive experiments on both real-world and synthetic datasets verify that the proposed approach is highly efficient, especially in dense datasets.

The remainder of the paper is organized as follows: Sect. 2 describes the research ideas by defining related concepts and proving several lemmas. The main algorithms and their analysis are presented in Sect. 3. Experimental results and analysis are presented in Sect. 4. Sect. 5 is for the conclusion and the future work.

2 Concepts and Principles

Traditional PCPM methods adopt Apriori-like strategy, which generate candidates size-by-size and generate all RIs of candidates by massive join operations, so they are both time and space consuming. In fact, many lower size RIs are actually included in higher size RIs, thus many instances repeatedly participating in multiple RIs, and we call this as instance overlap. Existing methods for improving the mining efficiency can fall into Apriori-like and Clique-based methods, but have such weaknesses: (1) CPM-Col is the most efficient Apriori-like algorithm in recent years, but it only work well with the special overlap that instances of some RIs are included in other RIs; (2) Clique-based methods first detect MCs replaced multiple size RIs, and then generate PCPs among the detected MCs, but they all ignore the instance overlap and thus cause a large number of mined MCs. Therefore, we analyze the causes behind the instance overlap situations and propose related concepts in Sect. 2.1, and introduce our approach in Sect. 2.2.

2.1 Discussion on Overlap Situations

In graph theory, MCs are generated from a given undirected graph, but the instances in spatial datasets are belong to distinct features·while all points in graph theory have no features. It will cause an overlap within MC. For an example in Fig. 1(a)-(2), denote the neighbor instance pairs with same feature as **SFIs-NR** (i.e., solid signs connected by dotted line, such as E.1 and E.2), and there are four MCs, i.e., {A.2, B.2, C.2, D.3,

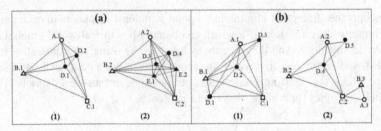

Fig. 1. Simple examples for SFIs-NR, OIs-MC, and combination of them. Each sign represents an instance. Neighbors are connected with solid line, and dotted line only for SFIs-NR.

E.1}, {A.2, B.2, C.2, D.3, E.2}, {A.2, B.2, C.2, D.4, E.1} and {A.2, B.2, C.2, D.4, E.2}, where the sub-clique {A.2, B.2, C.2} is repeated. The main reason of the overlap is: Existing co-location and MC concepts require that all features in same MC are different and ignore the large number of SFIs-NR in the dataset. If considering SFIs-NR, the number of generated MCs would be reduced, and there is only one special MC {A.2, B.2, C.2, D.3, D.4, E.1, E.2} in this example. We define such MCs in Definition 1.

Definition 1 (EC & EMC). *For an instance set $IS = \{o_1, ..., o_k\}$ and their feature set $C = \{f_1, ..., f_j\}$ $(j < k)$, if any instance in IS is neighboring with other instances with different features in IS, then IS is called an **extended clique** (EC). IS is an **extended maximal clique** (EMC), if it is an EC and not the subset of any other EC.*

SFIs-NR consideration can help reduce the calculation consumption due to the decrease in the number of generated MCs, but there are possible situations that partial overlapping instances participate in multiple MCs (as Fig. 1(b) shows), so we analysis the effects of overlapping instances in MCs and give its refined concept as follows, and the way for finding them is presented in Algorithm 2.

Definition 2 (OI-MC & NOI). *If an instance o_i is included in at least two MCs, then it is called an **overlapping instance among maximal cliques** (OI-MC). Otherwise, o_i is called a non-overlapping instance (NOI).*

For example, the instance C.2 in Fig. 1(b)-(2) is an OI-MC since it is included in two different MCs: {A.2, B.2, C.2, D.4} and {A.3, B.3, C.2}. OIs-MC have one common property that they all have more neighbors than other NOI in the same clique. Since this property is related to MCs, so we just show it in Fig. 1(b)-(2), not as dividing one feature or multiple features as Fig. 1(a). Therefore, when generating a size-k MC IS, all NOIs in IS can be found out by checking whether their neighbor number equal to k-1.

2.2 Proposed Approach

We note that the higher size cliques contain many lower size cliques and more information, thus we pay more attention to EMCs and employ top-down strategy to mine all PCPs. The strategy contains two phases: (1) Mine EMCs and store EMCs with same co-location together; (2) Generate candidate co-locations from the MC storage (CCMC) and check their prevalence. The basic process are similar to [10], here we only describe our improvements. Besides, this section describes the principles of our methods, and the detail of implementation will be explained with pseudo code in Sect. 3.

EMCs Storage: As Fig. 2 shows, we design a storage structure based on hash table (SSHT), and revise it to two parts: one part to store OIs-MC, called store set for overlapping instances (SSO); and other part to store NOIs, called count set for non-overlapping instances (CSN). Since a NOI will only participate in one EMC, it is only necessary to record the total number of them. Such structure greatly reduces the storage space from two aspects: (1) Massive cliques are stored as P-Is of features; (2) Many NOIs are integrated into a count. For an example in Fig. 1(b), due to generated EMC is {A.1, B.1, C.1, D.1, D.2, D.3}, its *key* in SSHT is {A, B, C, D}, and the *value* is { <A, {[1], []}>, <B, {[1], []}>, <C, {[1], []}>, <D, {[3], []}> }. When generating another EMC {A.2, B.2, C.2, D.4} with same *key*, the *value* will be updated to { <A, {[1], [A.2]}>, <B, {[2], []}>, <C, {[1], [C.2]}>, <D, {[3], [D.4]}> }.

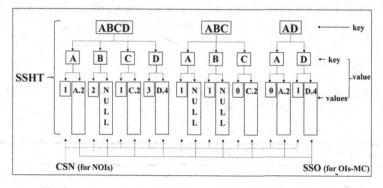

Fig. 2. An example for SSHT to store MCs (EMCs) in Fig. 1(b).

Lemma 1. *All participating instances (P-Is) of candidates can be found by SSHT.*

Proof: Since all EMCs are stored in SSHT, and each *key* represents a CCMC. If a co-location and its super-patterns are all not CCMCs, then there not exists any RI of it, and it cannot be a candidate. For a candidate C_k, denote the set of its super-patterns as $supC = \{C \mid C_k \subseteq C \wedge C \in SSHT\}$ and co-locations in $supC$ as $sups$, all its P-Is must be contained in total PIS of $sups$ based on the Priori Principle of co-locations [4].

PCPs Detection: The candidates are generated from the keyset of EMC storage, then the time consumption lies to finding P-Is for calculating PR value of each feature for each candidate. For a given candidate C_k, the existing methods finding its PIS by calculating the union of total PIS of $sups$ based in Lemma 1. By the proposed structure SSHT, NOIs number of $sups$ can directly be added in, and the union operation scope is narrowed among OIs-MC of them. The detail calculation is given as follows.

$$PR(C_k, f_i) = \frac{|PIS(C_k, f_i)|}{|S_i|} = \frac{\left|\sum\limits_{C \in \sup C} SSHT(C, f_i)\right|}{|S_i|} = \frac{\left|\bigcup\limits_{C \in \sup C} SSO(C, f_i)\right| + \sum\limits_{C \in \sup C} [CSN(C, f_i)]}{|S_i|}$$

(1)

When a candidate C is detected as a PCP, then all its sub-patterns are PCPs based on the Priori Principle of co-location [4], thus they can directly added to the result set and won't be accessed later (downward prune). If C is detected as an non-prevalent co-location pattern (NPCP), we try to remove all its super-patterns for reducing traversal since all of them must also be NPCPs (upward prune).

3   PCPM-EMC

In this section, we describe the proposed PCPM approach based on extended maximal clique (PCPM-EMC) in detail with pseudocode, whose main process has been introduced in the previous section. The complexity analysis is also given in this section.

3.1   General Framework

Algorithm 1 is the general framework of the PCPM-EMC, it can be summarized as two aspects: generate EMCs and detect PCPs.

Algorithm 1. General Framework for PCPM-EMC

Input: Instance set I, Feature set F, Neighbor relationship R, Prevalence threshold *min_prev*.
Output: all-size prevalent co-location patterns (PCPs).
Variables: *SSHT*: hash-based set of all-size EMCs; NP_2: set of size-2 NPCPs; *PCPS*: total result set of all-size detected PCPs; *CCMC*: set of all-size candidates from SSHT.
Steps:
1. $SSHT, NP_2$=P-BK$_{d,p}$($I, F, R, PCPS$);   //generate EMCs
2. $CCMC$=gen_sorted_Candidate_PCPs($SSHT$);
3. **While** $CCMC \neq \emptyset$ **do**
4.   push an unvisited candidate C;
5.   **If** contains_SubNPCP(C, NP_2) **then**   //upward prune
6.   **goto** Step 11;
7. $PI(C)$=cal_ParticipateIndex_Ck($C_k, SSHT, I$);
8.   **If** $PI(C) \geq min\_prev$ **then**   //downward prune
9.   prune_Unvisited_SubPatterns($C, CCMC, PCPS$);
10.   **Else**
11.   **For each** $C' \in$ add_Unvisited_Direct_SubPatterns($C, SSHT, PCPS, NP_2$) **do**
12. $C=C'$, **goto** Step 5;
13. **Return** *PCPS*;

Generate EMCs (Step 1): We adopt the generating strategy of an existing clique-based method [13], and make some improvements in Sect. 3.2.

Detect PCPs (Steps 2–12): Since the PCPs detection strategy has been given in Sect. 2.2, here we give some additional details: (1) In each iteration, take an unvisited candidate C with largest size from key set of SSHT, until there are no unvisited candidates (Steps 2–4); (2) If C has a size-2 NPCP, it must also be an NPCP, and it is unnecessary to calculate its PI value (Steps 5–6). Besides, NP_2 can be generated when building neighborhoods; (3) Calculating PI of C by count PR of each feature in C. If PR value of any feature lower than *min_prev*, then C must be an NPCP and the calculation can be terminated (Step 7); (4) If C is identified as a PCP, then all its sub-pattern must be PCPs. All of them can be added into the result set *PCP* (Steps 8–9); (5) If C is identified as an NPCP, all of its direct sub-patterns are added to the iteration, but not these sub-patterns the size below 3 or visited or contain the patterns in NP_2 (Steps 10–12).

3.2 Generate EMCs

Algorithm 2. P-BK$_{p,d}$: PCPM Version of BK Algorithm with Pivot, Division

---

Input: Instance set I, Feature set F, Spatial relationship R.
Output: all extended maximal cliques in the dataset.
Steps:
1. AGs=void_Assign_Grids(I, F, R), initialize $SSHT=\varnothing$, $PNS=\varnothing$, $NP_2=\varnothing$;
2. **For each** $gr \in AGs$ **do**
3.   randomly select a starting instance o_i;
4. SR, PR=gen_SeedandPartition_Region(o_i, gr, AGs, PNS, NP_2, $PCPS$);
5.   **Call** BKpivot_traversal($\varnothing$, PR, $\varnothing$, $SSHT$, PNS);
6.   void_Update_Visited_Sign(SR, $SSHT$, PNS);
7. **Return** $SSHT$, NP_2;

8. **Function** BKpivot_traversal(R, P, X, $SSHT$, PNS)   //BK$_p$ with traverse consideration
9.   **If** $P=\varnothing$ and $X=\varnothing$ **then**
10.   void_Update_Overlap_Sign(R, PNS);
11. $SSHT=SSHT \cup \{R\}$;
12.   **return**;
13.   **If** satify_EMC(P) **then**
14.   remove all instances from P to R, **goto** Step 10;
15. $PRNP$=gen_unvisitedP_Remove_NeighofPivot(P, X);
16.   **For each** $v \in PRNP$ **do**
17.   BKpivot_traverse($R \cup \{v\}$, $P \cap PNS(v)$, $X \cap PNS(v)$, $SSHT$, PNS);
18. $P=P-\{v\}$, $X=X \cup \{v\}$;
19.   **return**;

Since the BK algorithm with pivot and division have well performance [13, 19], thus we retain their generating strategy and further design an improved algorithm P-BK$_{p,d}$ based on above discussions, whose total generating strategy is partition first (Steps 1–4) and then generate EMCs in each partition (Step 5). The details are given as follows.

Generate Partitions: The total research area is divided into $\frac{\sqrt{2}}{2}d * \frac{\sqrt{2}}{2}d$ grids and all instances are assigned into these grids, and initialize the EMCs storage structure *SSHT* and partial neighbor set *PNS* (Step 1). Under such division, instances in same grid must form a clique, so they are directly added into *PNS*. For finding complete neighbors of an instance, it is only necessary to visit instances in neighbor 21 grids. Next, traverse all grids and generate EMCs (Steps 2–6). For each grid *gr*, first generate partition by three variables, i.e., starting instance o_i, seed region *SR*, and partition region *PR*, where o_i is an instance randomly selected in *gr* (Step 3), *SR* and *PR* are generated similar to [13, 18] (Step 4). And we further make several following changes: (1) The current grid will be skipped when o_i is visited, because all EMCs which contain instances in the grid must be generated before; (2) The visited instances will not be added into *SR*, since all EMCs which contain them must be generated before; (3) The *PNS* of instances in *SR* will be removed when the current iteration ends. Then, call function **BKpivot_traverse**() to generate EMCs in the partition *PR* (Step 5), and set all instances in *SR* as visited when the function execution is completed (Step 6).

Generate EMCs: In each partition, P-BK$_{d,p}$ executes strategy similar to [16], and the differences are given as follow: (1) If *R* is judged satisfying a EMC, all overlapping instances will be detected by checking whether they satisfy the property of OI-MC mentioned in Sect. 2.1, and store *R* into *SSHT* by strategy in Sect. 2.2 (Steps 9–12); (2) Step 10 also checks whether all instance of *R* are belong to the same feature, if it is, then *R* is not a EMC and will be skipped; (3) If all instances of *P* are belong to the same feature, it is necessary to check whether they are neighboring with each other, because *R* ∪ *P* must be an EMC (Steps 13–14); (4) The sub-recursion scope *PRNP* is determined based on conclusions in [16, 19], but the visited instances will not be added, because all EMCs contain them must be generated (Step 15). Remain executions are the same to existing methods (Steps 16–19).

3.3 Algorithm Analysis

Time Complexity Analysis: The time consumption of PCPM-EMC mainly comes from two aspects: (1) Generating all size EMCs by Algorithm 2. Since the complexity of BK with pivot is $O(3^{n/3})$ [16], denote the number of partitions as |P|, and the average number of instances of partitions as N_{aip}, thus the complexity is $O\left(|P| \cdot 3^{N_{aip}/3}\right)$; (2) Detecting all size PCPs (Steps 3–10). In most case, sub-patterns of all candidates are non-prevalent and disjoint with each other. Since traversal of sub-patterns is up to size-3, the complexity is $O\left(2^{S_{asc}-2} * S_{asc} * L_{alsc}\right)$, where S_{asc} is the average size of CCMCs and L_{alsc} is the average length of features in SSO of CCMCs.

Space Complexity Analysis: The space consumption of PCPM-EMC mainly comes from two aspects: (1) Storing P-Is of CCMCs by SSHT, which is $O(N_{ccmc} * S_{asc} * L_{alsc})$, where N_{ccmc} is number of CCMCs in SSHT, and S_{asc} and L_{alsc} are the same as above. Besides, consumption on CSN is $O(S_{asc})$ and can be negligible; (2) Storing visited candidates and their PI value, denoted as S_{vcpi}.

Lemma 2. *All extended maximal cliques can be found by Algorithm 2.*

Proof: The completeness of the generation strategy and visit consideration in Steps 4 and 15 were proved in [13, 18]. Steps 9 and 13 guarantee to generate all EMCs. Step 10 guarantees that all generated EMCs are correct.

Correctness: The correctness of PCPM-EMC is guaranteed by following aspects: (1) EMC generation and SSHT construction are correct by Lemmas 1 and 2; (2) Candidates generation and pruning strategies are correct as mentioned in Sect. 2.2; (3) Step 8 guarantees that all PI of output co-locations are not lower than *min_prev*.

Completeness: The completeness of PCPM-EMC is guaranteed by following aspects: (1) The generated EMCs are complete because of Lemma 2; (2) The generated candidates generated are complete due to Lemma 1.

4 Experimental Evaluation

4.1 Experimental Setup

Datasets: We conduct the experiments on both real-world and synthetic datasets. The real-world dataset is a plant distribution dataset of Three Parallel Rivers of Yunnan Protected Area, which contains 12 features and 3,855 instances. The synthetic datasets are generated by a generator similar to [5], the detail contains: (1) The research area is set to $D*D$ size and divided into grids with length gl, and set features number FN and instances number IN; (2) Then randomly generate co core co-locations with average size AS, and each core co-location has I RIs on average, and both AS and I follow Poisson distribution; (3) Each RI is randomly located in one grid, and instances of it are randomly distributed in the grid; (4) When a grid is selected to locate a RI, put other *clumpy* RIs into it. The remaining instances are randomly distributed and subject to aggregation θ. If there is no description, the parameters are set as: $D = 10$ km, $gl = 10$ m, $FN = 20$, $IN = 100$k, $co = 20$, $AS = 5$, $I = 1$k, *clumpy* $= 4$, $\theta = 0$ (1k $= 1,000$).

Comparison Algorithms: Since CPM-Col [7] is the most efficient Apriori-like algorithm according to our knowledge, Joinless [5] is one of the most widely used classical algorithms, and MCHT [13] has better performance than other Clique-based algorithm, thus we select them as the comparison algorithms. Besides, we also test the effectiveness of generating EMCs in PCPM-EMC by comparing it with BK, BK with pivot (BK_p) and BK with pivot and division based on bit operation ($BK_{p,d}$).

Platform: All algorithms are implemented in JAVA and run on a windows 10 operating system with Intel Core i7-8700K CPU @3.70 GHz and 16 GB memory.

4.2 EMCs Generation Comparison

In this part, we evaluate the EMCs generation efficiency of PCPM-EMC by comparing P-BK$_{p,d}$ with BK series enumeration methods mentioned above. The instances number and distance threshold directly affect EMC generation results, so we mainly test them.

First, we test the execution time and space of algorithms with the number of instances *IN* increases in dense datasets. As show in Fig. 3(a), the time consumption of all algorithms are increases, but only PCPM-EMC is fastest and stable. For the space consumption, PCPM-EMC is also the most advantageous. The main reason may contain: (1) P-BK$_{p,d}$ only holds partial neighbor set among partition iterations; (2) SSHT stores NOIs as count mentioned in Sect. 2.2; (3) Pruning strategies reduce the space consumption of unnecessary traversal and other temporary variables.

Next, we test the execution results of algorithms in real-world dataset. Since BK$_{p,d}$ has better space performance than other comparison algorithms, so we only display results of P-BK$_{p,d}$ and BK$_{p,d}$. As show in Fig. 3(c), PCPM-EMC still stable and has better performance in sparse dataset. When *d* reaches 1600 m, the execution time of BK$_{p,d}$ suddenly increases, the reason may be: More clique relationships will generate under the higher distance threshold, which makes the dataset show another kind of aggregation and is also related to the data distribution. EMC consideration in PCPM-EMC refers to the overlap situation between MCs due to aggregation, thus it still works well.

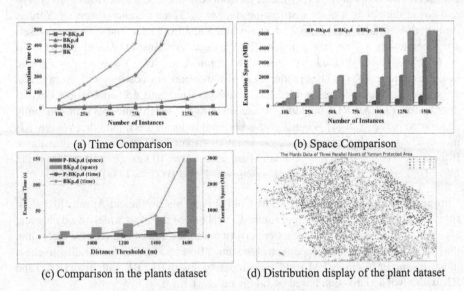

(a) Time Comparison	(b) Space Comparison
(c) Comparison in the plants dataset	(d) Distribution display of the plant dataset

Fig. 3. Comparison results of EMCs generation.

4.3 Performance

In this part, we evaluate the performance of proposed PCPM-EMC algorithm on synthetic datasets. In this experiment, we test the effects of different parameters, and randomly generate 10 datasets and summarize the results for each value of all parameters. If there is no description, the thresholds are set as: $d = 50$ m, $min\_prev = 0.3$.

Influence of the Number of Instances: Under a certain research area, if the number of instances *IN* increases, the data density increases and more neighbor relationships are generated. The execution time of all algorithms increase with *IN* increases. Joinless has the fastest growth because it takes much consumption on searching and generating all RIs for each candidate. PCPM-EMC works better than MCHT and CPM-Col, because that: The grid partition is used to reduce traversal when facing dense datasets, and SSHT is designed for reducing union operations when calculating PI of candidates.

Influence of the Number of Features: With instances number *IN* determined, if the number of features *FN* increases, then lower size co-location increases and higher size co-location decreases. As shown in Fig. 4(b), the execution time of Joinless decreases, because it cost less for scanning RIs of lower size candidate. MCHT works better than Joinless, because it only searches for MCs, and its execution time increases due to an increase in cliques' number when *FN* increases. PCPM-EMC and CPM-Col are stable, the main reason maybe: (1) They both use pruning steps to filter candidates; (2) In fact, PCPM-EMC finds P-Is by EMCs and SSHT, and CPM-Col finds P-Is by several search optimization strategies, and the total number of P-Is holds when *FN* changes.

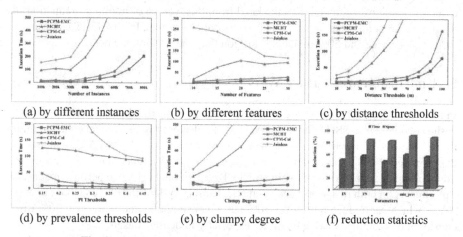

(a) by different instances   (b) by different features   (c) by distance thresholds

(d) by prevalence thresholds   (e) by clumpy degree   (f) reduction statistics

Fig. 4. Comparison by different parameters in synthetic datasets.

Influence of the Distance Threshold: When the distance threshold *d* increases, the more neighbor relationships will be generated, which means the number of RIs or EMCs increases. Figure 4(c) shows the execution time of algorithms under different distance thresholds, and all of them increase when *d* increases. Among them, Joinless costs most because it traverse all RIs of candidates; CPM-Col costs less than MCHT, because it uses the heuristic search strategy to reduce searching for part of RIs of candidates. PCPM-EMC performs better than CPM-Col, because the EMC number is much smaller than that of size-by-size RIs, and PCPM-EMC reduces traversing lots of MCs.

Influence of the Prevalence Threshold: If the PI threshold *min_prev* increases, more co-locations will be identified as non-prevalent, thus the mined PCPs number decreases. In Fig. 4(d), the execution time of CPM-Col and Joinless decrease with *min_prev* increases, but both PCPM-EMC and MCHT hold. The reason may be: (1) Apriori-like methods generate size-$(k + 1)$ candidates from size-k PCPs, the lower *min_prev* causes less mined size-k PCPs, thus less size-$(k + 1)$ candidates need to generate their RIs and the execution time decreases; (2) Clique-based methods materialize neighbor relationships by MCs, and only need to filter candidates from their MCs storage when *min_prev* changes, thus their performance hold.

Influence of the Clumpy Degree: The *clumpy* degree controls the RIs number in the same grid, if it increases, the data density and RIs number of candidates burst increase. Figure 4(e) shows the results, where PCPM-EMC and CPM-Col are stable, others increase fast when *clumpy* increases. The reason may be: Although higher *clumpy* causes more RIs or MCs in same neighborhood, the number of P-Is and EMCs are hold. Besides, the execution time of PCPM-EMC is a little larger than CPM-Col when *clumpy* equals to 1, because there are few instances participating in other RIs and few EMCs, thus PCPM-EMC also needs to traverse all MCs and has no advantage in this case.

The time and space reduction statistics of PCPM-EMC are shown in Fig. 4(f), each reduction value of parameters is calculated from the average of minimum reduction of the parameter at different values. Summarizing above results, PCPM-EMC can usually reduce 80% space and 50% time consumption than the existing methods.

5   Conclusion and Future Work

In this paper, we first propose the concept of extended maximal cliques (EMCs) and a hash-based structure SSHT for storing EMCs are also proposed, which can help reduce the mining consumption. Then, we present a novel approach PCPM-EMC, which uses the proposed P-BK$_{p,d}$ algorithm for accelerating the EMCs generation and a bidirectional pruning strategy for optimizing the PCPs detection. Lastly, we perform extensive experiments on both real-world and synthetic datasets to show the efficiency of our approach, which can reduce more over 80% space consumption and more than 50% time consumption than the existing methods, especially in dense datasets.

In future work, we plan to uncover the spatio-temporal properties of generating EMCs, and to explore incremental mining methods for dynamic EMC. Moreover, multi-level co-location pattern mining based on EMC also has promising.

Acknowledgments. This work was supported by the National Natural Science Foundation of China (62276227, 61966036, 62062066), the Project of Innovative Research Team of Yunnan Province (2018HC019), and the Yunnan Fundamental Research Projects (202201AS070015).

References

1. Wang, L., Fang, Y., Zhou, L.: Preference-Based Spatial Co-location Pattern Mining. Springer, Singapore (2022). https://doi.org/10.1007/978-981-16-7566-9

2. Chan, H.K., Long, C., Yan, D., Wong, R.C.: Fraction-score: a new support measure for co-location pattern mining. In: Proceedings of 35th IEEE International Conference on Data Engineering (ICDE), Macao, China, pp. 1514–1525. IEEE (2019)
3. Shekhar, S., Huang, Y.: Discovering spatial co-location patterns: a summary of results. In: Jensen, C.S., Schneider, M., Seeger, B., Tsotras, V.J. (eds.) SSTD 2001. LNCS, vol. 2121, pp. 236–256. Springer, Heidelberg (2001). https://doi.org/10.1007/3-540-47724-1_13
4. Huang, Y., Shekhar, S., Xiong, H.: Discovering colocation patterns from spatial data sets: a general approach. IEEE Trans. Knowl. Data Eng. 16(12), 1472–1485 (2004)
5. Yoo, J.S., Shekhar, S.: A joinless approach for mining spatial colocation patterns. IEEE Trans. Knowl. Data Eng. 18(10), 1323–1337 (2006)
6. Wang, L., Bao, Y., Lu, Z.: Efficient discovery of spatial co-location patterns using the iCPI-tree. Open Inf. Syst. J. 3(1), 69–80 (2009)
7. Yang, P., Wang, L., Wang, X., Zhou, L.: A spatial co-location pattern mining approach based on column calculation. Scientia Sinica Informationis 52(06), 1053–1068 (2022)
8. Wang, L., Zhou, L., Lu, J., Yip, J.: An order-clique-based approach for mining maximal co-locations. Inf. Sci. 179(19), 3370–3382 (2009)
9. Yao, X., Peng, L., Yang, L., Chi, T.: A fast space-saving algorithm for maximal co-location pattern mining. Expert Syst. Appl. 63, 310–323 (2016)
10. Bao, X., Wang, L.: A clique-based approach for co-location pattern mining. Inf. Sci. 490, 244–264 (2019)
11. Wu, P., Wang, L., Zou, M.: A maximal ordered ego-clique based approach for prevalent co-location pattern mining. Inf. Sci. 608, 630–654 (2022)
12. Tran, V., Wang, L., Chen, H., Xiao, Q.: MCHT: A maximal clique and hash table-based maximal prevalent co-location pattern mining algorithm. Expert Syst. Appl. 175, 114830 (2021)
13. Zhang, S., Wang, L., Tran, V.: CPM-MCHM: a spatial co-location pattern mining algorithm based on maximal clique and hash map. Chinese J. Comput. 45(3), 526–541 (2022)
14. Wang, X., Lei, L., Wang, L., Yang, P., Chen, H.: Spatial colocation pattern discovery incorporating fuzzy theory. IEEE Trans. Fuzzy Syst. 30(6), 2055–2072 (2021)
15. Wang, L., Bao, X., Zhou, L.: Redundancy reduction for prevalent co-location patterns. IEEE Trans. Knowl. Data Eng. 30(1), 142–155 (2018)
16. Tomita, E., Tanaka, A., Takahashi, H.: The worst-case time complexity for generating all maximal cliques and computational experiments. Theor. Comput. Sci. 363(1), 28–42 (2006)
17. Li, Y., Shao, Z., Yu, D., Liao, X., Jin, H.: Fast maximal clique enumeration for real-world graphs. In: Li, G., Yang, J., Gama, J., Natwichai, J., Tong, Y. (eds.) DASFAA 2019. LNCS, vol. 11446, pp. 641–658. Springer, Cham (2019). https://doi.org/10.1007/978-3-030-18576-3_38
18. Cheng, J., Zhu, L., Ke, Y., Chu, S.: Fast algorithms for maximal clique enumeration with limited memory. In: Proceedings of 18th ACM SIGKDD International Conference on Knowledge Discovery and Data Mining, Beijing, China, pp. 1240–1248. ACM (2012)
19. Xu, S., Liao, X., Shao, Z., Hua, Q., Jin, H.: Maximal clique enumeration problem on graphs: status and challenges. Scientia Sinica Informationis 52, 784–803 (2022)

Continuous Sub-prevalent Co-location Pattern Mining

Qilong Wang[1], Hongmei Chen[1,2(✉)], and Lizhen Wang[1,2]

[1] School of Information Science and Engineering, Yunnan University,
Kunming, China
hmchen@ynu.edu.cn
[2] Yunnan Key Laboratory of Intelligent Systems and Computing, Yunnan University,
Kunming, China

Abstract. Spatial co-location pattern represents a subset of spatial features whose instances are frequently located together in space. Sub-prevalent co-location pattern mining discovers patterns with richer spatial relationships based on star instance model instead of clique instance model. Further, discovering spatiotemporal sub-prevalent co-location pattern is important to reveal the spatiotemporal interaction between spatial features and promote the application of patterns. However, the methods for mining spatiotemporal sub-prevalent co-location pattern measure the interestingness of patterns by the frequency of patterns in time slice set, and ignore the duration of patterns which is an important spatiotemproal information in patterns. Thus, this paper presents mining spatiotemporal sub-prevalent co-location pattern by considering the duration and the frequency of patterns. Specifically, a novel pattern, is proposed by defining the continuous sub-prevalent index. Then, an efficient algorithm is designed to mine the proposed patterns by utilizing the anti-monotonicity of continuous sub-prevalent index to prune unpromising patterns. Extensive experiments on synthetic and real datasets verify the practicability of the proposed patterns and the effectiveness of the proposed algorithm.

Keywords: Spatiotemporal data mining · Spatial sub-prevalent
co-location pattern · Spatiotemporal sub-prevalent co-location pattern

1 Introduction

With the rapid development of spatial information technology such as the global positioning system, spatial data has shown an explosive growth. Spatial co-location pattern mining is an important branch of spatial data mining, which has draw the attention of researchers due to practicality of co-location patterns in environmental protection [1], public security [2] and public health [3]. A prevalent co-location pattern is a subset of spatial features whose instances are frequently collocated within a neighbourhood. For example, that Egyptian Plover occur frequently in near Nile Crocodile can be expressed as a prevalent co-location pattern {Egyptian Plover, Nile Crocodile}.

© The Author(s), under exclusive license to Springer Nature Switzerland AG 2023
X. Meng et al. (Eds.): SpatialDI 2023, LNCS 13887, pp. 192–203, 2023.
https://doi.org/10.1007/978-3-031-32910-4_14

Prevalent co-location pattern mining determines the neighbor relationship of spatial instances through the distance threshold, generates all row instances of patterns based on clique instance model(i.e., a row instance forms a clique), calculates the participation indices of patterns on the basis of row instances, and finally discovers all prevalent patterns through the participation index threshold [4]. In order to capture richer spatial relationships, sub-prevalent co-location pattern and star participation index based on star instance model are proposed, which loosen the clique constraint of spatial instances in a row instance.

Both prevalent co-location pattern and sub-prevalent co-location pattern ignore the time factor of patterns, i.e., patterns vary with time. For example, seagulls migrate to lakes in Yunnan to spend the cold winter, and leave from lakes when spring comes. This shows the pattern {Seagull, Lake} change with the season.

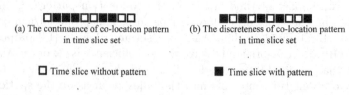

(a) The continuance of co-location pattern in time slice set   (b) The discreteness of co-location pattern in time slice set

☐ Time slice without pattern   ■ Time slice with pattern

Fig. 1. The distribution of co-location patterns in time slice set

To mine time-varying patterns, spatiotemporal co-location pattern mining was introduced. Celik et al. [5] mine co-location patterns on each time slice and finds patterns which appear on many time slices. Li et al. [6,7] mine sub-prevalent co-location patterns existing on many time slices. These spatiotemporal co-location patterns consider the frequency of patterns on time slices. However, besides the frequency of patterns, we argue that the duration of patterns is also important. Let us see Fig. 1. The frequencies of pattern in Fig. 1(a) and Fig. 1(b) are the same (i.e., 50%), but the duration of pattern in Fig. 1(a) is longer than that in Fig. 1(b). This implies the pattern lasts for a period of time besides repeatedly appearing. This kind of patterns is also meaningful. For instance, instead of passing by, seagulls spending the cold winter on lakes may be more meaningful for environmental protection.

Motivated by the above, we propose continuous sub-prevalent co-location pattern by taking into account the duration and the frequency of sub-prevalent co-location pattern. The main contributions of the paper are as follows:

- We define the continuous sub-prevalent index to measure pattern, and propose the novel continuous sub-prevalent co-location pattern.
- We prove the anti-monotonicity of the proposed measure, and design an efficient algorithm to mine the proposed patterns by utilizing the anti-monotonicity.
- We conduct extensive experiments on real and synthetic data sets. The experimental results show that the proposed pattern is practical and the proposed algorithm is efficient.

The rest of the paper is organized as follows. We review the related work in Sect. 2. Section 3 introduces preliminaries and defines the proposed continuous sub-prevalent co-location pattern. Section 4 describes the algorithm to mine the proposed patterns. Section 5 presents the experimental evaluation and Sect. 6 concludes the paper.

2   Related Work

2.1   Prevalent Co-location Pattern

Huang et al. [4] defined the prevalent co-location pattern based on clique instance model and proposed the Join-based mining algorithm, studies have proposed optimization algorithms [8–12] to solve the low efficiency issues of the Join-based algorithm.

Due to the impact of time factor on the co-location pattern, Celik et al. [5] analyzes the time-varying co-location pattern, and proposed a mixed spatiotemporal MDCOPs algorithm. Andrzejewski and Boinski [13] proposed the MAXMDCOP-Miner algorithm to solve the low efficiency issue of the MDCOPs algorithm. Qian et al. [14] proposed a sliding window model, which introduces the impact of event time intervals into the index to measure the spatiotemporal co-location pattern. Ma et al. [15] proposed a two-step framework to mine evolving pattern over time. Yang and Wang [16] proposed a spatiotemporal co-location congestion pattern mining method to discover the orderly set of roads with congestion propagation in urban traffic.

2.2   Sub-prevalent Co-location Pattern

To mine co-location pattern with richer spatial relationship, Wang et al. [17,18] proposed the sub-prevalent co-location pattern based on star instance model which loosens the clique constraint of spatial instances in a row instance, and designed the PTBA and PBA algorithms to mine sub-prevalent co-location patterns. Ma et al. [19] proposed the sub-prevalent co-location pattern with dominant feature. Xiong et al. [20] presented mining fuzzy sub-prevalent co-location pattern with dominant feature.

Taking into account the importance of time factor, Li et al. [6,7] proposed the spatiotemporal sub-prevalent co-location pattern by considering the frequency of pattern.

Distinct from the spatiotemporal sub-prevalent co-location pattern in [6,7], our proposed continuous sub-prevalent co-location pattern not only considers the frequency of pattern but also the duration of pattern.

3   Preliminaries and Problem Definition

3.1   Spatial Sub-prevalent Co-location Pattern

Let $F = \{f_1, f_2, ..., f_n\}$ be the set of spatial features in a spatial dataset, $S = S_1 \cup S_2 \cup ... \cup S_n$ be the set of spatial instances where S_i is the instance set of f_i, and d be a user-specified distance threshold. For two instances $i_i, i_j \in S$, if the Euclidean distance between them satisfies distance$(i_i, i_j) \leq d$, they satisfy the neighbor relationship $R(i_i, i_j)$. Figure 2(a) shows a spatial dataset, where $F = \{A, B, C, D\}$, $S = \{A.1, A.2, A.3, B.1, B.2, B.3, C.1, C.2, C.3, D.1, D.2\}$, and the neighbor relationships between instances are expressed by lines. A sub-prevalent co-location pattern c is a subset of the feature set, i.e., $c \subseteq F$, and the number of features in c is called the size k of c, i.e., $k = |c|$. The related definitions of sub-prevalent co-location pattern [17,18] is as follows.

Definition 1. *(Star Neighbodhoods Instance, SNsI). The set of star neighborhoods instances of an instance $i_j \in S$ is defined as $SNsI(i_j) = \{i_k | distance(i_j, i_k) \leq d, i_k \in S \}$.*

Definition 2. *(Star Participation Instance, SPIns). The star participation instance of a feature $f_i \in c$ is defined as $SPIns(f_i, c) = \{i_j | i_j \in f_i$ and the feature set of $SNsI(i_j)$ contains all features in $c\}$.*

In Fig. 2(a), $SNsI(A.1) = \{A.1, B.2, C.3\}$, $SPIns(A, \{A, B, C\}) = \{A.1, A.2\}$

Definition 3. *(Star Participation Ratio, SPR). The star participation ratio of a feature $f_i \in c$ is defined as the ratio of the number of star participation instances of f_i to the number of instances of f_i:*

$$SPR(f_i, c) = |SPIns(f_i, c)| / |S_i| \tag{1}$$

Definition 4. *(Star Participation Index, SPI). The star participation index of a pattern c is defined as the minimum of the star participation rates of all features in c:*

$$SPI(c) = \min_{f_i \in c}\{SPR(f_i, c)\} \tag{2}$$

Definition 5. *(Sub-prevalent Co-location Pattern, SCP). Given a user-specified star participation index threshold θ, if $SPI(c) \geq \theta$, the pattern c is called a sub-prevalent co-location pattern.*

In Fig. 2(a), for a pattern $\{A, B, C\}$, $SPR(A, \{A, B, C\}) = 0.67$, $SPR(B, \{A, B, C\}) = 0.67$, $SPR(C, \{A, B, C\}) = 0.67$ and $SPI(\{A, B, C\}) = \min\{0.67, 0.67, 0.67\} = 0.67$, if $\theta = 0.5$, the pattern $\{A, B, C\}$ is a SCP.

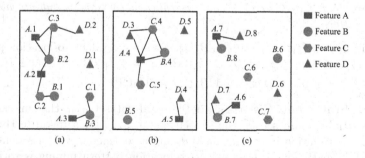

Fig. 2. A spatiotemporal dataset with three time slices

3.2 Continuous Sub-prevalent Co-location Pattern

Distinct from mining sub-prevalent co-location patterns from a spatial dataset, we propose mining continuous sub-prevalent co-location patterns from a spatiotemporal dataset by taking into account the duration and the frequency of patterns.

Let $T = \{t_1, t_2, ..., t_m\}$ be the set of time slices in a spatiotemporal dataset, $F = F^1 \bigcup F^2 \bigcup ... \bigcup F^m$ be the set of spatial features where $F^i = \{f_1^i, f_2^i, ..., f_n^i\}$ is the feature set on time slice t_i, $S = S^1 \bigcup S^2 \bigcup ... \bigcup S^m$ be the set of spatial instances where $S^i = S_1^i \bigcup S_2^i \bigcup ... \bigcup S_n^i$ be the instance set on t_i and S_j^i is the instance set of f_j, on t_i. Figure 2 shows a spatiotemporal dataset with 3 time slices each of which is Fig. 2(a), Fig. 2(b) and Fig. 2(c) respectively.

We define the related concepts of continuous sub-prevalent co-location pattern as follows.

Definition 6. *(Duration time slices, DTS). Given a sub-prevalent co-location pattern c, if it appears on time slice t_a, disappears on time slice t_d, and keeps on time slices $t_i(t_a \leq t_i < t_d)$, then a set of duration time slices $DTS(c)$ of c is defined as:*

$$DTS(c) = \{t_a, t_{a+1}, ..., t_{d-1}\} \tag{3}$$

Intuitively, a pattern may have multiple sets of duration time slices which can be noted by $DTSs(c) = \{DTS^1(c), DTS^2(c), ..., DTS^l(c)\}$.

Definition 7. *(Continuous sub-prevalent index, CSI). Given a sub-prevalent co-location pattern c, the continuous sub-prevalent index $CSI(c)$ of c is defined as:*

$$CSI(c) = \frac{\sum_{i=1}^{|DTSs(c)|} |DTS^i(c)| * \frac{|DTS^i(c)|}{|T|}}{Non(c) * \frac{1}{|T|} + \sum_{i=1}^{|DTSs(c)|} |DTS^i(c)| * \frac{|DTS^i(c)|}{|T|}} \tag{4}$$

Where $\frac{|DTS^i(c)|}{|T|}$ is the weight of duration time slice set $DTS^i(c)$ of c, $Non(c)$ is the number of time slices without c, i.e., $Non(c) = |T - \bigcup_{i=1}^{|DTSs(c)|} DTS^i(c)|$, and $\frac{1}{|T|}$ is the weight of time slices without c.

Definition 8. *(Continuous sub-prevalent co-location pattern, CSCP). Given a sub-prevalent co-location pattern c and a user-specified continuous sub-prevalent index threshold ρ, if $CSI(c) \geq \rho$, c is called a continuous sub-prevalent co-location pattern.*

In Fig. 2, $T = \{t_1, t_2, t_3\}$, if $\{A, B, C\}$ is a sub-prevalent co-location pattern on time slice t_1 and t_2, then $DTSs(\{A, B, C\}) = \{\{t_1, t_2\}\}$, $CSI(\{A, B, C\}) = \frac{2*\frac{2}{3}}{1*\frac{1}{3}+2*\frac{2}{3}} = 0.8$. if $\rho = 0.5$, then $\{A, B, C\}$ is a CSCP.

Problem Statement. Given a spatiotemporal dataset with the time slice set T, the spatial feature set F, the spatial instance set S, a distance threshold d, a star participation index threshold θ, and a continuous sub-prevalent index threshold ρ, continuous sub-prevalent co-location pattern mining is to find all CSCPs that satisfy all thresholds.

4 Mining Algorithm

Starting from size-2 patterns, all CSCPs can be mined level-by-level. To improve the efficiency of the algorithm, the anti-monotonicity of continuous sub-prevalent index will be proven, and be used for pruning unpromising patterns.

Lemma 1. *(Anti-monotonicity of continuous sub-prevalent index). Let c, c' be two co-location patterns such that $c \subset c'$, then $CSI(c) \geq CSI(c')$.*

Proof. (1) According the anti-monotonicity of star participation index [17,18], For $\forall t \in T$, $SPI^t(c) \geq SPI^t(c')$ holds. If c' is a SCP ($SPI^t(c') \geq \theta$), c is also a SCP ($SPI^t(c) \geq \theta$).

(2) Suppose $DTSs(c) = \{DTS^1(c), ..., DTS^l(c)\}$, $DTSs(c') = \{DTS^{1'}(c'), ..., DTS^{l'}(c')\}$. According to (1), for $\forall DTS^{i'}(c') \in DTSs(c')$, $\exists DTS^i(c) \in DTSs(c)$, $DTS^{i'}(c') \subseteq DTS^i(c)$ holds.

Suppose $DTS^{i1'}(c'), ..., DTS^{il'}(c') \subseteq DTS^i(c)$. For $\forall i1' \leq i', j' \leq il', i' \neq j'$, $DTS^{i'}(c') \cap DTS^{j'}(c') = \varnothing$ and $\bigcup_{i'=i1'}^{il'} DTS^{i'}(c') \subseteq DTS^i(c)$ hold.

Then, we have $\sum_{i'=i1'}^{il'} |DTS^{i'}(c')|^2 \leq |DTS^i(c)|^2$. Further, we have $\sum_{i=1}^{|DTSs(c')|} |DTS^i(c')|^2 \leq \sum_{i=1}^{|DTSs(c)|} |DTS^i(c)|^2$. On the other hand, we have $Non(c') \geq Non(c)$.

So, we have $\frac{Non(c)}{\sum_{i=1}^{|DTSs(c)|} |DTS^i(c)|^2} + 1 \leq \frac{Non(c')}{\sum_{i=1}^{|DTSs(c')|} |DTS^i(c')|^2} + 1$, i.e.,

$\frac{\sum_{i=1}^{|DTSs(c)|} |DTS^i(c)|^2}{Non(c) + \sum_{i=1}^{|DTSs(c)|} |DTS^i(c)|^2} \geq \frac{\sum_{i=1}^{|DTSs(c')|} |DTS^i(c')|^2}{Non(c') + \sum_{i=1}^{|DTSs(c')|} |DTS^i(c')|^2}$. Further, we have

$\frac{\sum_{i=1}^{|DTSs(c)|} |DTS^i(c)| * \frac{|DTS^i(c)|}{|T|}}{Non(c) * \frac{1}{|T|} + \sum_{i=1}^{|DTSs(c)|} |DTS^i(c)| * \frac{|DTS^i(c)|}{|T|}} \geq \frac{\sum_{i=1}^{|DTSs(c')|} |DTS^i(c')| * \frac{|DTS^i(c')|}{|T|}}{Non(c') * \frac{1}{|T|} + \sum_{i=1}^{|DTSs(c')|} |DTS^i(c')| * \frac{|DTS^i(c')|}{|T|}}$,

i.e., $CSI(c) \geq CSI(c')$. □

Pruning Strategy 1. If $c \subset c'$ and $CSI(c) < \rho$, then $CSI(c') < \rho$, i.e., c and its all supersets are not CSCPs, and can be pruned.

Based on lemma 1 and pruning strategy 1, we propose an efficient Continuous Sub-prevalent Co-location Pattern Mining Algorithm (CSCPMA) for mining all CSCPs. Generally, the CSCPMA adopts the level-by-level and generation-and-test method. Starting from size-2 patterns, it generates size-k candidate patterns based on size-$(k-1)$ patterns, and tests size-k candidate patterns to get size-k patterns.

Initialization (Step 1–4): The star neighbors instance set of each ·spatial instance in each time slice $t \in T$ is generated by Gen_SNsI(). All size-1 patterns, i.e., a subset of F, are the beginning the of the iterations(Step 5–13).

Generating Candidate Patterns and Sub-prevalent Patterns (Step 6–9): Size-k candidate patterns are generated by calling Gen_CCSCP(). In Gen_CCSCP(), size-k candidate patterns are generated based on the set

---

Algorithm 1. CSCPMA

Input :
   T: a set of time slices
   F: a set of spatial features
   S: a set of spatial instances
   d: a distance threshold
   θ: a star participation index threshold
   ρ: a continuous sub-prevalent index threshold
Output :
   $CSCP$: a set of CSCPs
Variables :
   k: a co-location size
   SCP_k: a set of size-k SCPs
   $CCSCP_k$: a set of size-k candidate patterns
   $CSCP_k$: a set of size-k CSCPs
Algorithm :
1: **for** each $t \in T$ **do**
2:    $SNsI^t = \text{Gen\_SNsI}(F, S, d)$
3: **end for**
4: $k = 2; SCP_1 = F; CSCP_1 = \text{Gen\_CSCP}(\rho, SCP_1)$
5: **while** $CSCP_{k-1} \neq \varnothing$ **do**
6:    $CCSCP_k = \text{Gen\_CCSCP}(CSCP_{k-1})$
7:    **for** each $t \in T$ **do**
8:       $SCP_k = SCP_k \cup \text{Gen\_SCP}(CCSCP_k, SNsI^t, \theta)$
9:    **end for**
10:   $CSCP_k = \text{Gen\_CSCP}(\rho, SCP_k)$
11:   $CSCP = CSCP \cup CSCP_k$
12:   $k = k + 1$
13: **end while**
14: **return** $CSCP$

$CSCP_{k-1}$ of size-$(k-1)$ CSCPs according to Lemma 1 and Pruning Strategy 1. Then, In Gen_SCP(), these candidate patterns are tested for generating size-k SCPs.

Generating Continuous Sub-prevalent Co-location Patterns (Step 10):
For each size-k SCP, Gen_CSCP() is called to calculate the continuous sub-prevalent index of the pattern according Definition 7. If the pattern satisfies the threshold ρ, it is a size-k CSCP.

The time cost of the CSCPMA mainly are Step 2, Step 8 and Step 10. The time complexity of Step 2 for generating star neighbor instance sets is $O(|T||S^i|^2)$, the time complexity of Step 8 for generating SCPs is $O(|T| \sum_{k=1} |C_k||S_j^i|^k)$, the time complexity of Step 10 for generating CSCP is $O(|T| \sum_{k=1} |SCP_k|)$, where C_k is the set of size-k candidate patterns and SCP_k is the set of size-k SCPs.

5   Experimental Results and Analysis

In this section, we conduct experiments to evaluate the efficiency of the proposed CSCPMA on synthetic datasets and compare the mining results with the STSCPMA [6,7] on real datasets.

Datasets. We analyze the patterns by two algorithms on two real datasets and evaluate the efficiency of two algorithms by 11 synthetic datasets. The synthetic datasets are randomly generated according to Poisson distribution with different number of features, the number of instances, the number of time slices or the range. The real datasets include the Tokyo-Checkin containing 14 POI types (features) and 115202 checkin (instances), and the ChicagoCrime dataset containing 19 crime types (features) and 373933 crime events (instances). The datasets are described in Table 1. The default parameters of both algorithms are shown in Table 2.

Environment Setting. Both the CSCPMA and the STSCPMA are coded in Python and run on a PC with Intel Core i7 CPU, 32 GB RAM and Windows 10.

Table 1. Experimental datasets

Data Sets	Number of Features	Number of Instances	Number of Time slices	Range
Tokyo-Checkin	14	115202	11	40000x40000
ChicagoCrime	19	373933	24	40000x40000
Synthetic 1/2/3/4	10/15/20/25	$8x10^4$	10	10000x10000
Synthetic 5/6/7	20	$(7/9/10)x10^4$	10	10000x10000
Synthetic 8/9/10	20	$10x10^4$	10/15/20/25	10000x10000
Synthetic 11	25	$8x10^4$	10	12000x12000

Table 2. The default parameters of CSCPMA and STSCPMA

Name	d	θ	ρ	TSF [6,7]
Tokyo-Checkin	1300	0.4	0.6	0.6
ChicagoCrime	800	0.4	0.6	0.6
Synthetic 1-11	350	0.4	0.6	0.6

5.1   Efficiency Analysis

Effect of Number of Features. We compare the running time of two algorithms on Synthetic 1–4 under different number of features. From Fig. 3 we can see that the running time of both algorithms increases as the number of features varies from 10 to 15, then the running time decreases when varying from 15 to 25. The reason may be that candidate patterns are generated and tested in plenty as the number of features varies from 10 to 15, then unpromising patterns are pruned effectively when varying from 15 to 25. The running time of CSCPMA is slightly higher than that of STSCPMA because CSCPMA spends more time discovering patterns that STSCPMA cannot find.

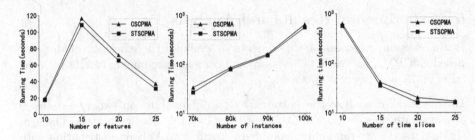

Fig. 3. Effect of number of features

Fig. 4. Effect of number of instances

Fig. 5. Effect of number of time slices

Effect of Number of Instances. We compare the running time of two algorithms on Synthetic 3 and 5–7 under different number of instances. In Fig. 4, as the number of instances gradually increases, the running time of both algorithms also increases. This is because more and denser instances lead to more star neighbors and patterns generated.

Effect of Number of Time Slices. We compare the running time of two algorithms on Synthetic 7–10 under different number of time slices. In Fig. 5, the running time of both algorithms decreases as the number of time slice increases, The reason is that sparser instances result in less patterns generated and tested.

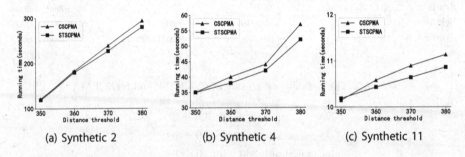

(a) Synthetic 2   (b) Synthetic 4   (c) Synthetic 11

Fig. 6. Effect of distance threshold

Effect of Distance Threshold. We compare the running time of two algorithms on Synthetic 2,4,11 under different distance thresholds. In Fig. 6, as distance thresholds gradually increases, the running time of both algorithms also increases. The reason is that more instances satisfy the neighbor relationship when increasing distance threshold, which leads to more star neighbors and more patterns.

Effect of Star Participation Index Threshold. We compare the running time of two algorithms on Synthetic 2,4,11 under different star participation index thresholds. In Fig. 7, both algorithms show a gradual decrease in running time as the star participation index threshold increases. This is because the larger star participation index threshold will lead to the fewer patterns satisfying the threshold.

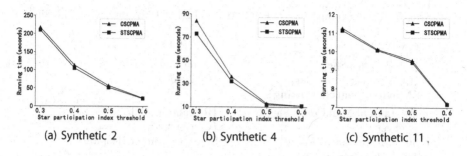

| (a) Synthetic 2 | (b) Synthetic 4 | (c) Synthetic 11 |

Fig. 7. Effect of star participation index threshold

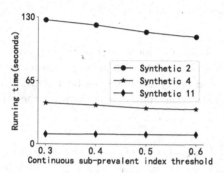

Fig. 8. Effect of continuous sub-prevalent index threshold

Effect of Continuous Sub-prevalent Index Threshold. We analyze the running time of the CSCPMA on datasets Synthetic 2,4,11 under different continuous sub-prevalent index thresholds as only the CSCPMA has this threshold. In Fig. 8, the running time of the CSCPMA on Synthetic 2 gradually decreases as the continuous sub-prevalent index threshold increases since the pruning strategy of CSCPs work effectively. The running time of the CSCPMA on Synthetic 4 and 11 is relatively flat, the reason is that generating candidate patterns costs a lot of time, but further generating CSCPs is relatively low-cost.

5.2 Case Analysis on Real Datasets

This section will analyze the cases on two real datasets to illustrate that the CSCPMA can mine more reasonable patterns by considering the duration and the frequency of patterns in time slice set.

On the Tokyo-Checkin Dataset. Table 3 list some size-2 and size-3 patterns mined by the CSCPMA and that mined by the STSCPMA on the Tokyo-Checkin dataset. We can see that the CSCPMA mines the size-2 pattern {Movie Theater,Parking} that cannot be mined by the STSCPMA, and the pattern is reasonable in real world. Usually, there are parkings near the movie theaters for convenience of audiences. The size-3 pattern {Bar,Parking,Hotel} indicates that

Table 3. Results comparison of CSCPMA and STSCPMA on Tokyo-Checkin

Size	CSCPMA	STSCPMA
2	{Hotel,Coffee Shop} {Convenience Store,Bar} **{Movie Theater,Parking}**	{Hotel,Coffee Shop} {Convenience Store,Bar}
3	{Restaurant,Mall,Coffee Shop} {Convenience Store,Restaurant,Hospital} **{Bar,Parking,Hotel}** **{Mall,Coffee Shop,Barbershop}**	{Restaurant,Mall,Coffee Shop} {Convenience Store,Restaurant,Hospital}

(Notes: the bold pattern is mined by the CSCPMA rather than STSCPMA)

consumers who have drunk alcohol should not drive, and should find hotels to rest. The size-3 pattern {Mall,Coffee Shop,Barbershop} shows that coffee shops and barbershops close to malls can have the benefit from malls. Therefore, the CSCPMA can mine more reasonable patterns than the STSCPMA on Tokyo-Checkin dataset.

On the ChicagoCrime Dataset. Let us take the pattern {Robbery, Sex Offense, Battery} as an example which is mined by the CSCPMA on ChicagoCrime dataset. The pattern indicates that robbery, sexual offense, and battery occur continuously and frequently in areas with poor public security.

6   Conclusion

This paper study the spatiotemporal sub-prevalent co-location pattern to better reveal the spatiotemporal relationship of patterns. First, we consider the duration and the frequency of patterns in time slice set, and propose the continuous sub-prevalent co-location pattern. Then, we propose an efficient mining algorithm to mine the proposed pattern. Extensive experiments on synthetic datasets and real datasets verify that the proposed algorithm can efficiently mine more reasonable patterns with richer spatiotemporal relationship.

Acknowledgements. This work is supported by the National Natural Science Foundation of China (62266050, 62276227), the Program for Young and Middle-aged Academic and Technical Reserve Leaders of Yunnan Province (202205AC160033), Yunnan Provincial Major Science and Technology Special Plan Projects (202202AD080003), the Open Project Program of Yunnan Key Laboratory of Intelligent Systems and Computing (ISC22Z02), Yunnan Fundamental Research Projects (202201AS070015).

References

1. Akbari, M., Samadzadegan, F., Weibel, R.: A generic regional spatio-temporal co-occurrence pattern mining model: a case study for air pollution. J. Geogr. Syst. **17**(3), 249–274 (2015)

2. Phillips, P., Lee, I.: Mining co-distribution patterns for large crime datasets. Expert Syst. Appl. **39**(14), 11556–11563 (2012)
3. Zeng, L., Wang, L., Zeng, Y., Li, X., Xiao, Q.: Discovering spatial co-location patterns with dominant influencing features in anomalous regions. In: Jensen, C.S., et al. (eds.) DASFAA 2021. LNCS, vol. 12680, pp. 267–282. Springer, Cham (2021). https://doi.org/10.1007/978-3-030-73216-5_19
4. Huang, Y., Shekhar, S., Xiong, H.: Discovering co-location patterns from spatial data sets: a general approach. IEEE Trans. Knowl. Data Eng. **16**(12), 1472–1485 (2004)
5. Celik, M., Shekhar, S., Rogers, J.P., Shine, J.A.: Mixed-drove spatiotemporal co-occurrence pattern mining. IEEE Trans. Knowl. Data Eng. **20**(10), 1322–1335 (2008)
6. Li, X., Chen, H., Xiao, Q., Wang, L.: Spatiotemporal sub-prevalent co-location pattern mining. J. Southwest Univ. Nat. Sci. Ed. **42**(11), 68–76 (2020)
7. Li, X.: Mining spatiotemporal sub-prevalent co-location patterns based on star model. Master's thesis, Yunnan University (2021)
8. Yoo, J.S., Shekhar, S.: A joinless approach for mining spatial colocation patterns. IEEE Trans. Knowl. Data Eng. **18**(10), 1323–1337 (2006)
9. Wang, L., Bao, Y., Lu, J., Yip, J.: A new join-less approach for co-location pattern mining. In: 2008 8th IEEE International Conference on Computer and Information Technology, pp. 197–202. IEEE (2008)
10. Wang, L., Bao, Y., Lu, Z.: Efficient discovery of spatial co-location patterns using the iCPI-tree. Open Inf. Syst. J. **3**(1) (2009)
11. Wang, L., Zhou, L., Lu, J., Yip, J.: An order-clique-based approach for mining maximal co-locations. Inf. Sci. **179**(19), 3370–3382 (2009)
12. Yang, P., Wang, L., Wang, X., Zhou, L.: A spatial co-location pattern mining approach based on column calculation. Sci. Sin. Inf. **52**(6), 1053–1068 (2022)
13. Andrzejewski, W., Boinski, P.: Maximal mixed-drove co-occurrence patterns. Inf. Syst. Front. 1–24 (2022)
14. Qian, F., Yin, L., He, Q., He, J.: Mining spatio-temporal co-location patterns with weighted sliding window. In: 2009 IEEE International Conference on Intelligent Computing and Intelligent Systems, vol. 3, pp. 181–185. IEEE (2009)
15. Ma, Y., Lu, J., Yang, D.: Mining evolving spatial co-location patterns from spatio-temporal databases. In: 2022 IEEE International Conference on Big Data and Smart Computing (BigComp), pp. 129–136. IEEE (2022)
16. Yang, L., Wang, L.: Mining traffic congestion propagation patterns based on spatio-temporal co-location patterns. Evol. Intel. **13**(2), 221–233 (2020)
17. Wang, L., Bao, X., Zhou, L., Chen, H.: Maximal sub-prevalent co-location patterns and efficient mining algorithms. In: Bouguettaya, A., et al. (eds.) WISE 2017. LNCS, vol. 10569, pp. 199–214. Springer, Cham (2017). https://doi.org/10.1007/978-3-319-68783-4_14
18. Wang, L., Bao, X., Zhou, L., Chen, H.: Mining maximal sub-prevalent co-location patterns. World Wide Web **22**(5), 1971–1997 (2019)
19. Ma, D., Chen, H., Wang, L., Xiao, Q.: Dominant feature mining of spatial sub-prevalent co-location patterns. J. Comput. Appl. **40**(2), 465–472 (2020)
20. Xiong, K., Chen, H., Wang, L., Xiao, Q.: Mining fuzzy sub-prevalent co-location pattern with dominant feature. In: Proceedings of the 30th International Conference on Advances in Geographic Information Systems, pp. 1–10 (2022)

The Abnormal Detection Method of Ship Trajectory with Adaptive Transformer Model Based on Migration Learning

Kexin Li[1]([✉]), Jian Guo[1], Ranchong Li[2], Yujun Wang[3], Zongming Li[4], Kun Miu[5], and Hui Chen[6]

[1] University of Information Engineering, Zhengzhou 450000, China
likexin_xxgcdx@163.com
[2] PLA 61221, Beijing 100000, China
[3] PLA 32022, Guangzhou 510000, China
[4] PLA 31682, Lanzhou 730000, China
[5] Army Special Operations College, Guilin 541000, China
[6] PLA 31438, Shenyang 110031, China

Abstract. The traditional modeling method of ship trajectory data is unable to deal with multiple features or ignore the temporal relationship. Moreover, due to the problems of data imbalance and lack of data labels, it is a great challenge to build ship behavior analysis and anomaly detection models based on trajectory data. Based on transfer learning and Transformer architecture, this paper proposes an anomaly detection method for adaptive Transformer model fitting trajectory timing distribution characteristics. Firstly, the trajectory data are preprocessed to simulate the characterization relationship of time-series data. Multiple different subsequences are divided by quantization of temporal distribution similarity and matching of temporal distribution. From the perspective of transfer learning, each subsequence is regarded as multiple source domains of independent distribution. The distribution correlation weight evaluation method is used to learn and fit the distribution characteristics of subsequences, to effectively describe the similarity and correlation effects between the distributions of each subsequence. At the same time, the attention mechanism is used to build the dynamic training Transformer network structure, mining the dependencies between data points in the sequence, and realizing a domain adaptive model that can effectively fit the multivariate characteristics of trajectory data. Finally, the anomaly detection task is completed by calculating the anomaly error. The example verification shows that, compared with the existing model, the model in this paper can more accurately realize the modeling of the normal trajectory motion characteristics, lay a foundation for the trajectory anomaly detection, and show a certain practical and engineering application value.

Keywords: Anomaly detection · Trajectory prediction · Transfer learning · Transformer · AIS

Kexin Li (1998-), master student.

X. Meng et al. (Eds.): SpatialDI 2023, LNCS 13887, pp. 204–220, 2023.
https://doi.org/10.1007/978-3-031-32910-4_15

1 Introduction

With the development of wireless communication, mobile sensor, and other technologies, knowledge mining based on massive trajectory big data has become a research hotspot in the construction of new service systems such as intelligent transportation [1] and intelligent ocean [2]. As an important part of world trade, Marine shipping is increasing in scale and density. At the same time, Marine safety and risk issues such as smuggling, piracy, and illegal fishing [3] are becoming more and more prominent. To strengthen the ability of maritime law enforcement and supervision, ensure maritime shipping safety and maritime territorial sovereignty, and improve the ability of Marine situation awareness [4], it is very important to conduct real-time monitoring of ships based on ship trajectory and identify abnormal behaviors to make active responses and establish an efficient and accurate ship anomaly detection system.

Automatic Identification System (AIS) [5] is a comprehensive digital navigation aid system and equipment, which can obtain and record the dynamic information of ships during navigation and transmit the data to shore-based or satellite. AIS data is the main data source for ship behavior analysis and maritime law enforcement supervision, including ship type, size, call sign, location, speed, heading, and other navigational information, providing important basic data for vessel abnormal behavior detection based on AIS data.

Chandola et al. [6] define an exception as a pattern that does not conform to normal behavior norms. Specifically, in the field of Marine shipping, ship anomaly refers to abnormal behaviors such as sudden change of speed, turning, driving in restricted areas, or deviating from the course based on behavior analysis of ship trajectory. Such behaviors are often related to smuggling, collision, illegal fishing, and piracy. Abnormal detection of ships is to analyze the ship's behavior based on the relevant data of the ship's movement, judge whether the ship's movement conforms to the normal rules of navigation activities, and then realize the judgment of the ship's abnormal behavior, and evaluate and warn the possible existence or occurrence of dangers. In recent years, research on trajectory anomaly detection mainly includes detection methods based on distance and density [7, 8], detection methods based on classification and clustering [9–11], and methods based on machine learning and pattern learning [12, 13]. The basic idea of the anomaly detection method based on the pattern is to carry out feature learning and modeling on the conventional trajectory and capture the dependence relationship of the sequential trajectory. The normal trajectory can usually maintain a good dependence relationship, while the abnormal trajectory usually violates these dependence relationships due to its mutability and low probability, making it unpredictable. Then, through the calculation error of the model-built track and the actual track, the difference is determined whether there is an anomaly in the track. With the development of deep learning technologies, Gated Recurrent Unit (GRU), Auto-Encoder (AE), Transformer, and other models are used to solve the problem. More attention is paid to adjusting and improving the parameter estimation and structural characteristics of the model through adaptive iterative learning of the model, so as to more accurately carry out the time sequence modeling and feature learning of the trajectory data and realize the trajectory anomaly detection task.

Meng et al. [14] took LSTM as the base predictor of the AdaBoost algorithm and built a combined model to realize accurate modeling of vehicle trajectory considering vehicle lane changing intention. Miguel et al. [15] take advantage of the generation characteristics VAE decoder to consider the influences of the surrounding subject behaviors in vehicle trajectory modeling. In order to overcome the limitations of a single model and build a more stable and practical sequential trajectory model, many combination models have been proposed. Wan et al. [16] built a combined model CNN-GRU based on a convolutional neural network and gated cycle unit and used AIS data to predict future ship trajectories. Cheng et al. [17] mapped the flight trajectory to the three-dimensional coordinate system in space, designed the CNN-LSTM model, organically combined the predicted trajectory with the conflict detection algorithm, and realized the conflict prediction, so as to improve the flight safety of aircraft. Wang et al. [18] studied the data-driven ship trajectory prediction and navigation intention recognition method based on the intersection waters of typical water traffic scenes. CNN + LSTM network was used as the encoder to extract its navigation environment and ship navigation temporal and spatial characteristics. The ship trajectory and navigation intention recognition model is formed. Lv et al. [19] proposed a GAN with transformers model, which uses a multi-head attention mechanism to better mine track features, and uses generators and discriminators to achieve reasonable simulation of pedestrian tracks.

As can be seen from the above research work, more and more algorithm models have been proposed in the aspect of trajectory data mining, but the detection effect of these methods largely depends on the data set and parameter Settings. In connection with the real world, it can be found that the proportion of positive and negative samples in training data is highly uneven due to the low frequency of abnormal events. Traditional model construction methods often assume that data sample distribution is ideal, but in actual situations, time series data often presents non-stationarity, nonlinear, and high complexity, and the model accuracy is limited.

To sum up, the anomaly detection methods for temporal trajectory still need further theoretical and methodological innovation. In this paper, the characteristics of ship trajectory data are fully considered. In view of the high cost of acquiring abnormal labels in the actual environment, the lack of abnormal labels, and the imbalance of data in the data set, the trajectory data is taken as the core drive for modeling. The wave characteristics, distribution trends, and characteristic rules of time series data are mastered through analysis. From the perspective of transfer learning, we focus on how to effectively model trajectory timing data from the perspective of adaptive data distribution, so as to build a method with wide applicability and high accuracy. The model firstly divides the original sequential data series effectively by quantification of temporal distribution similarity and temporal distribution matching and optimizes the distribution distance between each sub-sequence. The distribution correlation weight evaluation method is used to describe the domain similarity and correlation effect among the distributions effectively, so as to realize a distribution adaptive model. Meanwhile, combined with the Transformer model and the attention mechanism, the sequential dependence relationship between data points in the sequence can be mined to realize the accurate prediction of ship trajectory. Finally, the threshold value is determined by calculating the trajectory similarity and the abnormal trajectory is discovered. In this paper, the real AIS data set is selected for experiments, and the comparison with other benchmark models is fully analyzed. Experimental results show that the accuracy of the adaptive Transformer model proposed in this paper based on transfer learning has been improved, which has certain practical and engineering application value, and provides a novel research perspective for the analysis of offshore ship behavior.

2 Theory and Methodology

The process architecture of the ship trajectory anomaly detection method proposed in this paper based on migration learning adaptive Transformer model is shown in Fig. 1. The specific process of anomaly detection using AIS ship historical track data is as follows: Firstly, track data is preprocessed to remove noise data; In order to solve the distribution drift problem of time series data, the complete trajectory segment was divided into several least similar trajectory sequences based on the similarity quantization method of time series distribution, and the trajectory training data set was generated as the model input. Based on the idea of timing distribution matching, the model is trained to obtain a discrete model with adaptive feature distribution which can fully fit the trajectory distribution features. In order to avoid the loss of time sequence dependence due to transfer learning in the process of model training for different sequences, the multi-head attention mechanism of Transformer architecture is fully utilized to grasp the global relationship and implicit correlation information of time sequence trajectory data. Finally, the discriminant module is used to judge whether the trajectory data is abnormal. The combined model is used to model the ship trajectory, and the model is compared with other common models. Finally, based on the model, the ship track is constructed and the similarity is calculated, and the ship track anomaly detection is realized by calculating the outliers.

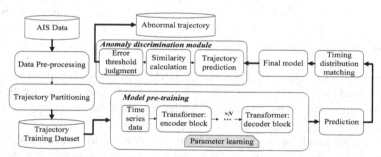

Fig. 1. Abnormal detection method of ship trajectory with adaptive Transformer model based on migration learning

2.1 Trajectory Anomaly Detection Based on AIS Data

2.1.1 AIS Data Preprocessing

AIS is a passive sensor, which may be affected by human operation, environment, signal loss, and other factors in the process of use, recording, and transmission, resulting in errors or missing data. However, the abnormal detection of ship trajectory requires modeling of normal data, so it is necessary to preprocess the original data and eliminate missing and abnormal data, so as to lay a foundation for better fitting the construction of a normal ship behavior model.

Firstly, the trace data with missing key values are removed. According to the literature [20] and the idea of the probability distribution, the arithmetic means to value and residual error are calculated for the key data of latitude and longitude, and the standard deviation is calculated to eliminate the data with excess residual error. In addition, in order to eliminate the influence of dimensions of different features in the multivariate data set on model training and improve the efficiency of model training while reducing the amount of training, the maximum and minimum value normalization is adopted to process the data and scale the data features to the same scale. The calculation formula is as follows.

$$x' = \frac{x - x_{\max}}{x_{\max} - x_{\min}} \tag{1}$$

where $x_{\max}$ and $x_{\min}$ are respectively the maximum and minimum values of this feature in the data set, x represents the original feature data, x' represents the feature data after normalization processing. In the process of result analysis, in order to make the predicted data have practical application value and guiding significance, we can carry on the reverse normalization of the predicted result data.

2.1.2 Anomaly Detection Task Based on Time Sequence Prediction

An Anomaly detection task based on sequential trajectory prediction aims to select attributes such as time, position, speed, and heading as input data through AIS trajectory data, and build a model to deeply dig into the correlation between characteristics and attributes to realize the modeling of general trajectory. Since abnormal trajectory usually does not accord with the behavior mode of general ships, Therefore, the model is often unable to accurately fit the abnormal trajectory. The abnormal trajectory can be judged and detected by comparing the difference between the predicted value and the real value of the model output.

Traditional time series prediction model ARIMA, progressive gradient regression tree GBRT and Facebook open source algorithm Prophet, etc., are suitable for the detection of a small amount of periodic data with relatively stable form, and cannot meet the challenges of increasing data volume and multi-vessel movement characteristics.

In this paper, a multivariate data set of ship trajectory is constructed based on AIS data as input, sequential similarity quantization, and time distribution matching methods are introduced to improve model generalization performance, and a ship trajectory prediction model is constructed based on the powerful feature extraction capability of Transformer combined with a multi-head attention mechanism. Then the error judgment is carried out by calculating the difference between the predicted value and the actual value to realize the abnormal detection task of ship trajectory, The anomaly detection roadmap is shown in Fig. 2.

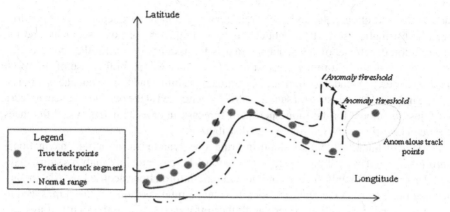

Fig. 2. Ship track point anomaly detection

2.2 Adaptive Transformer Model Based on Transfer Learning

The data feature distribution of time series data usually changes with time, showing non-stationarity and uncertainty, which is defined as concept drift [21]. In order to improve the accuracy of the model, it is very important to solve the problem of concept drift in the data set, make full use of the sequential trajectory data set, and make the model better fit the data distribution based on the historical trajectory data, so as to realize the accurate prediction of the future trajectory. In order to solve the drift problem of time series data, this paper constructs a time-independent discrete distribution strong generalization model that can capture the relationship of time series data to the greatest extent from the perspective of transfer learning. The model architecture is shown in Fig. 3.

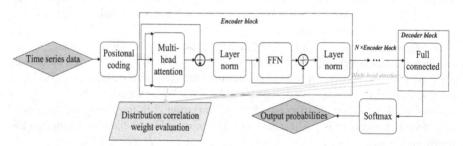

Fig. 3. Overall architecture of adaptive Transformer model based on transfer learning

2.2.1 Trajectory Segmentation Based on Temporal Distribution Similarity Quantization

The basic idea of the algorithm in this paper is to explore the common relationship characteristics of different sub-sequences, quantize the Distribution of track data based on Temporal Distribution Similarity Quantization, and divide the entire temporal track into i most dissimilar track segments. The number of assumed segments i is determined adaptively and effectively, and each trajectory segment is assumed to be subject to a certain distribution so that the model can fit the trajectory of this i segment, and the distribution difference of the sequence that is least similar to each other between the segments is minimized to the greatest extent. In other words, in the case of the worst probability drift, a model with strong generalization ability and time sequence invariance can be trained. Using historical samples already generated at the present moment to learn or adjust the model for the future period of forecast, in order to narrow the differences between historical data and future data distribution.

AIS data mainly includes static information, dynamic information, navigational information, and navigational safety information. This paper mainly analyzes ship behavior. Therefore, it mainly focuses on the dynamic information recorded by AIS in ship navigation, including the real-time longitude and latitude position of the ship, speed to the ground, heading to the ground, and other information. Since the rich features can more comprehensively feedback on the ship's motion characteristics, it is conducive to the representation learning of the model, and the multidimensional feature data set is constructed based on the basic information of AIS data. The data set is defined as follows:

$$Traj = \{Traj_1, Traj_2, ..., Traj_i\} \tag{2}$$

$$Traj_i = \{P_1, P_2, ..., P_n\} \tag{3}$$

$$P_m = [t_m, lat_m, lon_m, heading_m, sog_m, cog_m, distance_m, calc\_speed_m,$$
$$angle\_head_m, angle\_cog_m] \tag{4}$$

where $Traj$ represents the entire trajectory of a ship within a certain time range, which can be divided into the most dissimilar continuous and non-overlapping trajectory segments $Traj_i$. Each track segment $Traj_i$ is composed of n track points. t_m, lat_m, lon_m, $heading_m$, sog_m, cog_m represents AIS recording time, latitude, longitude, heading, speed, and course, respectively. $distance_m$, $calc\_speed_m$, $angle\_head_m$, $angle\_cog_m$ is the sailing distance between two points at adjacent moments calculated based on the AIS basic data, and calculates sailing speed, angular speed, and rudder speed.

Based on the idea of distributed robust optimization [22], the partitioning problem of trajectory sequences is transformed into an optimization problem, expressed in the following form:

$$\max_{0<i<I_0} \max_{L_1,...,L_i} \frac{1}{I} \sum_{1\leq\alpha\neq\beta\leq i} D(Traj_\alpha, Traj_\beta) \tag{5}$$

where I_0, δ_1 and δ_2 are the pre-defined parameters in order to avoid the nonsense of the solution value, and $D(,)$ is the distribution similarity measurement function, which is used to describe the distance of the different distributions mapped to the specific space. The paper uses the Maximum Mean Discrepancy (MMD) [23] as the distribution similarity measurement function.

2.3 Adaptive Transformer Model

Temporal Distribution Matching (TĐM) aims at matching the above temporal series distribution features, learning shared association information between different sequences, capturing and utilizing common features to the greatest extent, and constructing a transfer learning model to learn a model with distribution adaptability. The loss function of the timing distribution matching module is shown as follows:

$$loss_{pred}(\theta) = \frac{1}{i} \sum_{\beta=1}^{i} \frac{1}{|Traj_\beta|} \sum_{\alpha=1}^{|Traj_\beta|} loss(y_\alpha^\beta, pred(x_\alpha^\beta; \theta)) \tag{6}$$

where $loss(,)$ is the prediction loss function. Here, the mean square error is selected as the loss function, which is the parameter model to be learned. x_α^β and y_α^β respectively are the input and output data of the model. The distribution matching distance is introduced as a regularization factor to reduce the distribution difference between different subsequences. Combined with the multi-head attention mechanism, each attention module is used for distribution matching. $Att^{head} \in R, head \in [1, H]$ represents the output state of each encoder's multi-layer attention mechanism layer in a neural network structure containing one encoder, including the different distribution of characteristic information and time-dependent information learned by the attention mechanism layer. The weight vector $\varphi \in R^H$ is introduced to calculate the dependence relationship between the attention output states of each multi-head to dynamically reduce the cross-cycle distribution differences. Therefore, the matching degree of data distribution between the pairs of each subsequence can be expressed by the following formula:

$$loss_{tdm}(Traj_\alpha, Traj_\beta; \theta) = \sum_{head=1}^{H} \varphi_{\alpha,\beta}^{head} D(Att_\alpha^{head}, Att_\beta^{head}; \theta) \tag{7}$$

where $\varphi_{\alpha,\beta}^{head}$ represents the distribution correlation importance weight value between the distribution $Traj_\alpha$ and $Traj_\beta$ of the multi-head attention layers of the distribution.

The final optimization objective of timing distribution matching can be expressed as:

$$loss(\theta, \varphi) = \underset{\theta,\varphi}{\arg\min}\, loss_{pred}(\theta) + \lambda \frac{2}{i(i-1)} \sum_{\alpha,\beta}^{\alpha\neq\beta} loss_{tdm}(Traj_\alpha, Traj_\beta; \theta, \varphi) \tag{8}$$

where λ is the tradeoff coefficient.

First, according to the distributed similarity measure function, the model parameters are pre-trained with labeled data to better learn the hidden state representation of the network, so as to facilitate the subsequent learning and updating of the parameters φ. Here, define the parameter after pre-training as θ_0. The distribution correlation weight evaluation module is used to learn the importance correlation representation of the attention layer between different distributions and to help the model learn the common information between distributions. The weights will all be initialized $\varphi_{\alpha,\beta} = (\frac{1}{H})^H$. The segmented subsequences are regarded as different domains, and the calculation of cross-domain distribution distance and subsequence similarity were taken as optimization promotion indexes, and the weight parameters are updated based on Boosting strategy.

3 Experiments and Analysis

3.1 Experiment Data and Data Pre-processing

In the experimental part of this paper, data recorded and released by the US Coast Guard National AIS receiver on January 1, 2021, were selected, and the data records were filtered to 1 min. The initial data set contains 14,024 ships and 7,033,455 track points. After data cleaning and deletion of missing values, the data set contains 1,801 ships and 1,385,098 records in total, as shown in Fig. 4(a). Through data visualization, it can be found that the data after preliminary processing still contains obvious abnormal tracks such as position drift. In order to make the model better learn the behavior mode of general ships, the excessively short track segment is deleted and the residual error calculation is carried out to remove the outliers. The data set after preprocessing contains 564 ships, with a total of 836,200 track point data. The trajectory data after processing is shown in Fig. 4(b).

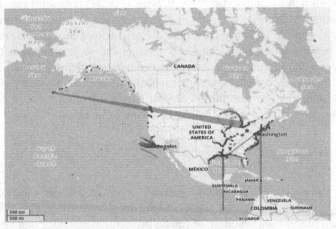

(a) Track data distribution before preprocessing

(b) Track data distribution after preprocessing

Fig. 4. The geographical location of experimental data. (Note: This figure is drawn based on the leaflet map component)

The raw data contains information on the ship's location, time of day, type of vessel, speed, course, length, beam, and draft. Considering the influence of various feature attributes on ship trajectory, based on the information of longitude, latitude, time, speed, and heading contained in the basic data set, multi-feature attributes are constructed as multivariate variables to constitute the input data, and the ship's longitude and latitude at a future time are taken as output labels. After data preprocessing, the basic statistics and distribution information of the multivariate input data set are shown in Table 1 and Fig. 5.

Table 1. Multiple input data set basic information

Characteristic attributes	Unit	Maximum	Minimum	Mean	Standard deviation
Latitude	Degree (°)	60.9984	21.3074	39.9244	8.2901
Longitude	Degree (°)	−69.1030	−176.6380	−99.8279	26.7073
Heading	Degree (°)	359.0	0.0	172.66	113.7799
Reporting Speed	Meters per second (m/s)	52.0412	0.0	2.4497	6.2175
Course	Degree (°)	204.7	−179.9	−18.9988	103.5629
Steering angular speed	Radians per second (°/s)	5.9833	0.0	2.8776	1.8964
Sailing angular speed	Radians per second (rad/s)	3.4117	0.0	1.5188	0.8791
Distance	Kilometer (km)	1.63975	0.0	0.0417	0.1069
Calculating speed	Kilometers per hour (km/h)	13475.5218	0.0	0.3027	26.6717

Note: Heading is the direction indicated by the ship's bow and the ship's bow, and COG is the ship's heading refers to the actual sailing direction of the ship's trajectory. The original AIS data recorded speed in units of knots (knot), which was converted to kilometers per hour (km/h) in this paper (1 knot = 1.852 km/h)

Taking the ship track with MMSI No. 212348000 within the experimental area as an example, the track data features are shown in the figure after the original track data is preprocessed through track cleaning and dimensional processing. As can be seen from Fig. 6, after the preprocessing, the trajectory data becomes smoother and conforms to the normal mode. Besides, the normalization process eliminates the dimensional influence, making the fluctuation range of the sequence data smaller, making it easier for the model to obtain the geometric distribution of the sequence data, and improving the convergence rate of model optimization.

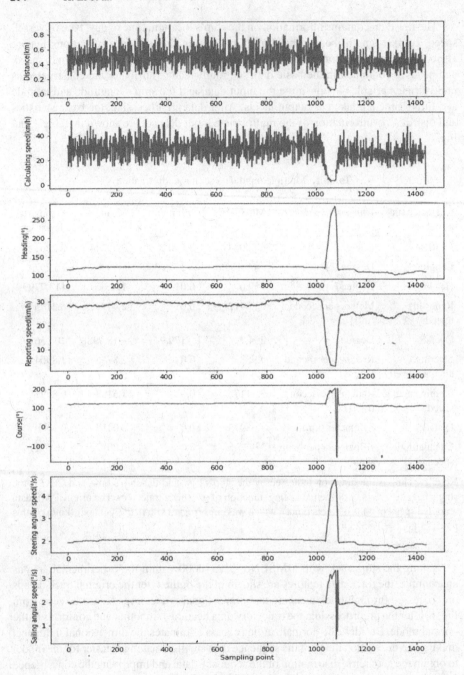

Fig. 5. Multivariate dataset

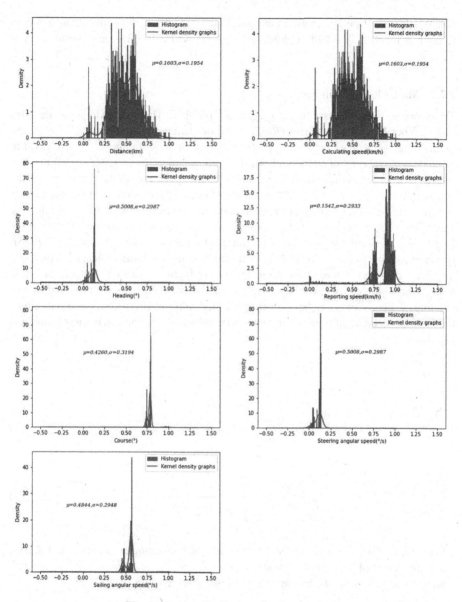

Fig. 6. Feature distribution of trajectory data

3.2 Experimental Results and Analysis

3.2.1 Experimental Environment

In this paper, the deep learning framework PyTorch is adopted to realize the adaptive Transformer model, and model training is completed on the NVIDIA GeForce RTX3090 Ti graphics card. Python programming language, Jupyterlab development environment, and Windows 10 operating system are adopted. The experimental environment is configured as follows: The CPU is Intel (R) i9-12900K@ 3.19 GHz, and the memory is 32 GB.

3.2.2 Model Evaluation Index

Trajectory prediction is essentially a regression problem. Therefore, Mean Square Error *(MSE)*, Root Mean Square Error *(RMSE)*, and determination coefficient (R^2) are commonly used to evaluate regression problems in machine learning. R^2 is performed to evaluate the accuracy of the model. *MSE* is the square of the true value and the predicted value and then the sum average. *RMSE* is the square root of the ratio between the square of the deviation between the predicted value and the true value and the number of observations m, which measures the deviation between the predicted value and the true value. The higher the number of times, the more the calculation result is related to the larger value, while the smaller value is ignored. Therefore, compared with *MSE, RMSE* is more sensitive to the outliers in the data. The smaller the value of the two indicators, the more accurate the prediction result. The determination coefficient reflects the linear relationship between two variables. The accuracy of the model can be measured by calculating the degree of fitting between the predicted value and the actual value. The closer the R^2 is to 1, the higher the accuracy of the model will be. The calculation formula is as follows.

$$MSE = \frac{1}{m} \sum_{i=1}^{m} (\text{traj}_i - p_i)^2 \tag{9}$$

$$RMSE = \sqrt{\frac{1}{m} \sum_{i=1}^{m} (traj_i - p_i)^2} = \sqrt{MSE} \tag{10}$$

$$R^2 = 1 - \frac{\sum_{i=1}^{m} (traj_i - p_i)^2}{\sum_{i=1}^{m} (traj_i - \overline{traj})^2} \tag{11}$$

where i represents the serial number of input data, m is the number of data samples, $traj_i$ is the true value of the i ith observed data, p_i is the predicted value of the ith observed data and $\overline{traj}$ represents the average value of the observed data.

3.2.3 Experimental Analysis

In order to take into account the complexity and accuracy of the model, the number of encoders in the integrated attention mechanism neural network is set as 2, in which the multi-head attention mechanism layer is set as the double-headed attention, and the decoder part is the multi-layer fully connected neural network. The backpropagation algorithm is used to update the network parameters. Adaptive optimizer Adam was used to optimize the network model parameters, and the learning rate of the Adam optimizer was set at 0.002. In the experiment, the data set was divided into the training set, verification set, and test set according to the proportion of 85%, 10%, and 5%. In order to avoid model overfitting and generalization decline caused by overtraining, we introduce the Dropout mechanism and early stop mechanism in the experiment. When using the training set to train the model, we verify each training round on the verification set and compare the verification effect. When the verification result is no longer improved for five consecutive rounds, we stop the training. First-timetime model parameters with the best verification effect were saved and used for ship trajectory sequence prediction. In the experiment, the regularization Dropout ratio of the model is set at 0.2.

In order to verify the effectiveness of the prediction model, the transfer learning adaptive Transformer model proposed in this chapter was compared with LSTM, CNN, GRU, CNN-GRU, CNN-LS,TM, and other classical models for ship trajectory prediction, and ablation experiments were set. In order to explore the image of the input step size on the model accuracy, the track sequence of consecutive step size was taken as the model input, and the same training method was used to predict. Calculate the distance difference between the output latitude and the actual latitude and longitude, and then evaluate the accuracy. The experimental results are shown in Table 2.

Table 2. Comparison of model prediction effect

Predicted step	Evaluation index	LSTM	CNN	GRU	CNN-GRU	CNN-LSTM	Adaptive Transformer
2	MSE	1.7982	3.7252	1.5997	**0.7326**	1.0259	0.7925
	RMSE	1.3410	1.9301	1.2648	**0.8559**	1.0129	0.8902
	R^2	0.8743	0.8052	0.8873	**0.9301**	0.8998	0.9217
4	MSE	3.2388	5.3259	3.1468	2.0211	3.0257	**1.1453**
	RMSE	1.7997	2.3078	1.7739	1.4217	1.7395	**1.0702**
	R^2	0.8118	0.7725	0.8223	0.8542	0.8470	**0.9065**
8	MSE	3.7584	6.3544	3.6562	3.0125	3.5799	**1.8846**
	RMSE	1.9387	2.5208	1.9121	1.7357	1.8921	**1.3728**
	R^2	0.7352	0.6649	0.7715	0.7899	0.7844	**0.8365**
12	MSE	4.0122	7.3083	3.9472	3.5963	3.8751	**2.1123**
	RMSE	2.0030	2.7034	1.9868	1.8964	1.9685	**1.4534**
	R^2	0.6419	0.5817	0.6651	0.6807	0.6759	**0.7893**
16	MSE	4.4782	8.8952	4.3026	3.9822	4.2598	**3.0571**
	RMSE	2.1162	2.9825	2.0743	1.9955	2.0639	**1.7485**
	R^2	0.5517	0.4928	0.5773	0.5991	0.5889	**0.7280**

As can be seen from the table, with the increase of prediction step length, the prediction accuracy of each model decreases to varying degrees, indicating that with the increase of time span, the uncertainty of time training increases, and the variability of time series is difficult to be accurately described by the model. Through comparison experiments with LSTM, CNN, GRU, CNNGRU, CNN-LSTM, and other benchmark models, it can be seen that when the step size is 2, Adaptive Transformer is second only to the CNN-GRU model. However, with the increase in step size, Adaptive Transformer will become more adaptive than the CNN-GRU model. The Adaptive Transformer model proposed in this paper has better predictive performance than all other models, indicating that the domain generalization model based on the idea of transfer learning has a better adaptive learning ability of sequence distribution, smaller actual deviation from the real value in the long time span prediction, and smaller performance degradation. It has stronger temporal stability in temporal trajectory prediction.

3.2.4 Anomaly Detection Visualization

In order to further explore whether the model proposed in this paper can realize the detection of ship trajectory anomalies, the original unprocessed trajectory data is brought into the model for training based on the well-trained transfer learning adaptive Transformer model, and several groups of trajectory points with predicted and actual values exceeding the abnormal threshold are randomly selected for visualization, as shown in Fig. 7. It can be seen from the figure that the model proposed in this paper can better fit the trajectory of normal ships and realize the detection of abnormal trajectory points.

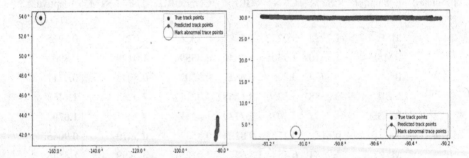

Fig. 7. Anomaly track point visualization

4 Conclusions

With the globalization of trade and the rapid development of mobile sensor equipment, the scale and density of maritime shipping are increasing day by day. Efficient and accurate ship behavior prediction and identification play an extremely important guiding role in improving maritime situation awareness, strengthening maritime control and law enforcement supervision, as well as the formulation and deployment of management and decision-making schemes. Based on the basic concepts and theories of transfer learning and domain generalization, this paper proposes a transformation-learning adaptive ship trajectory anomaly detection model in Transformer. Multiple attention modules are introduced in Transformer to mine the local and complex correlation information of trajectory sequence in a parallel computing way and effectively represent the complex trajectory data model. The accuracy of prediction is improved.

In this paper, the AIS data recorded and released by the national AIS receiver of the United States Coast Guard was used for parameter training. Through the comparative analysis of prediction experiments, it can be concluded that, based on the idea of neighborhood learning, molecular trajectory segments can be delimited adaptively and considered as multiple source domains according to the characteristics of dynamic changes in the distribution of ship trajectory time series data over time. By ensuring that the distribution difference of source domain data is minimized in a specific feature space, the generalization ability of the model can be significantly enhanced. Compared with the existing widely used LSTM, GRU, CNN, CNN-LSTM, CNN-GRU, and other models, the prediction accuracy of the Transformer has been significantly improved. This method is based on the multi-source input feature vector of AIS data, avoiding complex feature engineering, treating sub-track segments as different neighborhoods, and introducing multiple attention mechanisms, which can fully realize the learning and mining of multivariate data features, so as to realize the prediction of trajectory, and the detection, detection, and discovery of abnormal trajectory can be realized according to the difference between the predicted value and the actual value.

In the transfer learning adaptive Transformer model proposed in this paper, the time complexity of parameter calculation is still relatively high, and it will take a long time to train and learn the model. In future research, it can be further considered to reduce the time complexity by combining models, knowledge distillation, and other methods to improve the efficiency of model training. In order to avoid the problem that model training is only applicable to small samples and lacks generalization, the transfer learning method based on the model "pre-training and fine-tuning" can be adopted in future research to conduct the pre-training of the deep learning model at the observation points with sufficient sample data. At the same time, the characteristics of different spatial points can be grasped to realize the rapid deployment and effective prediction of the model in the new environment.

References

1. Zhang: Construction of intelligent transportation platform based on 5G vehicle network. Commun. Inf. Technol. (S2), 28–31 (2022)
2. Feng, W.: Exploration of 5G ultra-remote coverage technology and application scenarios. Commun. World **16**, 47–49 (2022)
3. Theodoropoulos, P., Spandonidis, C.C., Giannopoulos, F., Fassois, S.: A deep learning-based fault detection model for optimization of shipping operations and enhancement of maritime safety. Sensors **21**(16), 5658 (2021)
4. Tu, E., Zhang, G., Rachmawati, L., Rajabally, E., Huang, G.B.: Exploiting AIS data for intelligent maritime navigation: a comprehensive survey from data to methodology. IEEE Trans. Intell. Transp. Syst. **19**(5), 1559–1582 (2017)
5. Lee, W., Cho, S.W.: AIS trajectories simplification algorithm considering topographic information. Sensors **22**(18), 7036 (2022)
6. Chandola, V., Banerjee, A., Kumar, V.: Anomaly detection: a survey. ACM Comput. Surv. (CSUR) **41**(3), 1–58 (2009)

7. Gupta, M., Gao, J., Aggarwal, C.C., Han, J.: Outlier detection for temporal data: a survey. IEEE Trans. Knowl. Data Eng. **26**(9), 2250–2267 (2013)
8. Liu, H., Li, X., Li, J., Zhang, S.: Efficient outlier detection for high-dimensional data. IEEE Trans. Syst. Man Cybern. Syst. **48**(12), 2451–2461 (2017)
9. Zhang, Z., Zhu, M., Qiu, J., Liu, C., Zhang, D., Qi, J.: Outlier detection based on cluster outlier factor and mutual density. In: Peng, Hu., Deng, C., Wu, Z., Liu, Y. (eds.) ISICA 2018. CCIS, vol. 986, pp. 319–329. Springer, Singapore (2019). https://doi.org/10.1007/978-981-13-6473-0_28
10. Liu, H., Qiao, Y., Zhao, G., Cheng, J., Meng, Z.: Agricultural machinery abnormal trajectory recognition. Int. J. Mach. Learn. Comput. **11**(4), 291–297 (2021)
11. Qiao, Z., Zhao, L., Gu, L., Jiang, X., Li, R., Ge, L.: Research on abnormal pedestrian trajectory detection of dynamic crowds in public scenarios. IEEE Sens. J. **21**(20), 23046–23054 (2021)
12. Du, X., Yu, J., Chu, Z., Jin, L., Chen, J.: Graph autoencoder-based unsupervised outlier detection. Inf. Sci. **608**, 532–550 (2022)
13. Wu, H., Tang, X., Wang, Z., Wang, N.: Uncovering abnormal behavior patterns from mobility trajectories. Sensors **21**(10), 3520 (2021)
14. Meng, Tang, Wang: LSTM-AdaBoost vehicle trajectory prediction model considering lane change intention. Comput. Eng. Appl. **58**(13), 280–287 (2022)
15. Wan, Pan, Zhen, Ship: Ship trajectory prediction based on CNN-GRU. J. Guangzhou Inst. Navig. **30**(02), 12–18 (2022)
16. Cheng: Research on Collision Avoidance and Trajectory Prediction Technology of Aircraft Based on Machine Learning. Nanjing University of Posts and Telecommunications (2022)
17. Wang, Yuan, Li, Xiao: Ship trajectory prediction and navigation intention recognition in intersection waters. Traffic Inf. Saf. **40**(04), 101–109 (2022)
18. Miguel, Á.D.M., José, M.A., Fernando, G.: Vehicles trajectory prediction using recurrent VAE network. IEEE Access **10**, 32742–32749 (2022)
19. Lv, Z., Huang, X., Cao, W.: An improved GAN with transformers for pedestrian trajectory prediction models. Int. J. Intell. Syst. **37**(8), 4417–4436 (2022)
20. Chen, Zhu, Yan: Ship track prediction based on LSTM. Mar. Eng. (06), 121–125 (2019)
21. Lu, J., Liu, A., Dong, F., Gu, F., Gama, J., Zhang, G.: Learning under concept drift: a review. IEEE Trans. Knowl. Data Eng. **31**(12), 2346–2363 (2018)
22. Bertsimas, D., Sim, M., Zhang: Adaptive distributionally robust optimization. Manag. Sci. **65**(2), 604–618 (2019)
23. Borgwardt, K.M., Gretton, A., Rasch, M.J.: Integrating structured biological data by kernel maximum mean discrepancy. Bioinformatics **22**(14), 49–57 (2006)

Spatiotemporal Data Storage

A Comparative Study of Row and Column Storage for Time Series Data

Lu Li, Feifan Pu, Yi Li, and Jianqiu Xu[✉]

Nanjing University of Aeronautics and Astronautics, Nanjing 210016, China
jianqiu@nuaa.edu.cn

Abstract. Over the past few decades, researchers have done massive research on data storage structures of relational databases. The existing research mainly focuses on the analysis and optimization of row and column storage structures in relational databases. It is discovered that row and column storage techniques are acceptable for relational database operations in a variety of goal and usage scenarios. However, with the generation of massive time series data, researchers ignore experimental analysis for specific storage structures for time series data in databases. In order to provide comprehensive verification, we compare and analyze the space and time consumed in the process of bulk loading and insertion, range query, and aggregate calculation of time series data under openGauss-based row and column storage. The purpose is to provide a storage design basis for extending time series data management capabilities in relational databases or developing time series databases. The results show that the choice of storage for time series should be based on the specific application scenarios.

Keywords: Time Series · Row-oriented · Column-oriented · Database Storage

1 Introduction

Time series data refers to data monitored and recorded in chronological order. With the development of sensor technology and the large-scale investment in various fields such as transportation, finance, environmental quality, medical care, and industry, countless terabytes of time series data are generated constantly. With such complex, diverse, and large time series data, it is essential to achieve efficient and accurate data analysis capabilities in databases.

Due to the huge data volume and other characteristics of time series data, its requirements for storage capacity and computing performance pose greater challenges to relational databases. The users' operation for time series data usually emphasizes on statistical analysis functions. Therefore, the traditional relational databases based on row storage have some limitations in managing time series data with the characteristics of massive data storage, variable data structure, and high requirements for historical data query. Researchers rarely pay attention to time series data storage methods based on a relational database and comprehensive comparative analysis for data storage modes is scarce.

Common data storage structures are divided into row-based storage and column-based storage. Row-oriented storage stores values of each attribute of tuples continuously (see Fig. 1) while column-oriented storage divides each column into several compression units and each compression unit (CU) will be compressed and stored (see Fig. 2). Due to the different storage structures, the data access process is also different for the two. For example, we input a query statement to find tuples whose time is greater than t1 and less than t3 and whose O3 is greater than 75. Row storage databases will scan all tuples and attributes continuously while column storage databases can only scan time and O3 CUs to get target tupleids. According to their characteristics, these two storage structures are applicable to OLTP and OLAP business scenarios respectively. Row storage reads and writes all data in each row at one time, while column storage only scans data of related columns. Records in row-oriented stores are easy to read and write while write operations are slower in column-oriented stores. Column stores perform better while making aggregation operations on time series datasets. However, in some certain application scenarios, it is more in line with business requirements to have both row and column storage methods available simultaneously. For example, in a financial institution, various financial indicators of different clients at different time points need to be analyzed, including clients' financial status, borrowing records, income and expenditure situation, etc. In this case, the data of all financial indicators of each client at each point in time can be stored by row for time-series analysis. Meanwhile, the data of all clients for each financial indicator at each point in time can be stored by column for comparative analysis which allows for personalized analysis of each client as well as comparison of differences among different clients. In the aspect of space occupation, the compression rate of column-oriented storage mode is much higher than that of the row-oriented especially.

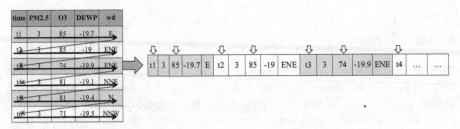

Fig. 1. Row-oriented storage structure and data access procedure.

The openGauss is a domestic enterprise-level open-source relational database built on Linux operating system, including several common database modules such as storage engine, SQL engine, communication management, and security management. It benefits from high levels of performance, security, dependability, and intelligence. OpenGauss is developed based on the mature relational database PostgreSQL and both row-oriented and column-oriented storage are included in the underlying data storage structure. As a result, for examining the effects of various data storage architectures on time series data, this program and platform work well.

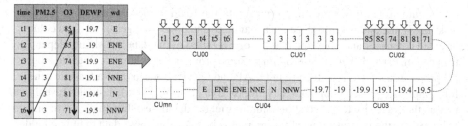

Fig. 2. Column-oriented storage structure and data access procedure.

Inspired by these observations above, we will conduct an all-round comparison of time and space consumption in aspects of bulk loading, one-by-one inserting process of time series data, and various query and aggregate operations in open-Gauss. This study will provide a basis for integrating time series data management capabilities into relational databases or creating time series databases.

The rest of this paper is organized as follows. Section 2 reviews the related work about time series and row and column storage structures. Section 3 introduces characteristics of time series scenarios and details about accessing and querying analysis of row and column storage. Section 4 presents the main contribution of this work–the results of experimental evaluations of different storage structures, respectively. The discussion and conclusion are presented in Sect. 5 and Sect. 6.

2 Related Work

In this section, we analyze the existing research work on database storage structures and time series.

Traditional databases are based on row-oriented storage and store each tuple [1] in continuous space. In [2], the author provides a brief overview of row-oriented storage databases' development history. Due to the storage layout, such databases are generally suitable for OLTP scenarios [3] which contain a large number of short online transactions such as insert, update, and delete operations. In [1] and [4], in addition to highlighting the benefits of row-oriented storage, those articles also noted certain disadvantages: with the generation of increasingly large data, for example, when users want to query the value of a specific attribute, the databases will still get every attribute value of tuples, which increases the extra costs. Is row-oriented storage still relevant today? In [5], they demonstrate that row stores can be optimized for read-heavy query workloads and that they can even outperform column stores in terms of efficiency. A hybrid row/column approach is proposed by [6] named the fracture mirrors approach which achieves efficiency by allowing each storage mode to handle the transactions they are good at.

Another storage structure mainly used for relational databases is column-oriented storage. In 2005, Mike Stonebraker et al. [7] present a read-optimized relational DBMS and introduce column-oriented storage which is faster than popular commercial products. In [4], Daniel J. et al. present that the row storage primarily processes updates and the column store primarily processes reads. Harizopoulos et al. [8] compare the performance of a row and column store built from scratch and demonstrate that column stores outperform row stores in proportion to the fraction of columns they read from disk. In [3], the authors introduce the advantages and disadvantages of row and column-oriented databases and point out that the organization of the database should depend on the need. In [9] and [10], authors optimize some problems of column-oriented databases. [9] proposes a shared architecture in OLAP and OLTP scenarios and a feasible scheme for compression of column storage is proposed in [10]. In [11], their studies reveal two factors that gave rise to a revival of column-oriented databases: the rapid growth of data volumes and the increasing need for interactively analyzing these data to utilize hidden information. They introduce a storage advisor tool on SAP HANA database to decide which storage method (row or column) to use in different scenarios.

Time series data is prevalent and has a wide range of uses in the Internet of Things (IoT), finance, healthcare, and other industries. However, time series data is quite enormous and gathers several indicators together (for example, CPU, memory, network statistics, and battery life). We need to explore the most effective way to store this enormous amount of data in order to determine if traditional row or column storage will accommodate our increasing requirements. In [12], the authors discuss the evolution of time series data management in the era of big data and examine the benefits and shortcomings of SQL and NoSQL for managing time series data. In [13], the authors introduce the new time series database named IoTDB. In order to organize data more effectively, reduce data size, and improve query speed with time series data, it uses column storage as the primary storage mode and offers a column file format called TsFile. In [14], The authors provide a summary of a few of the most common time series database storage types, highlighting the various feature sets for each. [15] proposes an approach of model transformation from an object-relational database to a NoSQL column-based database. In [16] and [17], the authors offer two different types of time series databases, namely LittleTable and HeteroTSDB, and discuss their shared properties and storage methods.

There are various time-series databases both domestically and internationally. Some of the popular international time-series databases include InfluxDB, TimescaleDB, OpenTSDB, and Graphite. As for the storage methods, different databases may offer different options. For example, InfluxDB supports both row and column storage through its "tag-value" and "field" concepts, while TimescaleDB utilizes a hybrid storage model that combines row-based storage for metadata and columnar storage for time-series data. OpenTSDB, on the other hand, is columnar-oriented and stores data in a compressed form to minimize disk usage. Graphite, meanwhile, uses a fixed-size, ring-buffer-style data structure with row-based storage. In China, there are several time-series databases developed including TDengine, Open-Falcon, HBase, and so on. TDengine supports both row-based and columnar storage, and uses a hybrid compression algorithm to reduce data storage size. Open-Falcon supports row-based storage and has a fixed storage structure for time-series data. HBase is a popular database that uses columnar storage to manage time-series data. These databases generally offer a mix of row-based and columnar storage options to optimize performance and minimize storage requirements.

3 Data Features and Storage Structure Analysis

Multiple storage structures can be used to store time series data. Different organizational structures of storage are suitable for different businesses and have different data scanning methods. In this section, the application scenarios and common features of time series data in the database will be analyzed firstly based on its business characteristics. Then, two data storage structures are demonstrated including row-oriented storage and column-oriented storage. Generally, the row storage is used for OLTP (online transaction processing) scenarios while the column storage is used for the execution of complex queries in OLAP (online analytical processing) scenarios with a large amount of data. Each of them will be described in this section respectively.

3.1 Time Series Data Features

Time series data is represented by a sequence of time-stamped values, denoted by $TS = \langle (t_1, x[1]), (t_2, x[2]), \ldots (t_n, x[n]) \rangle$. Every timestamp t_i is associated with m attribute values. The length of TS is n and all data in the same data column must be of the same data type and comparable.

The application scenarios of time series data are mainly divided into the following two types: OLAP (Online Analytical Processing) and OLTP (Online Transaction Processing). OLAP refers to a type of database system that is designed to support complex data analysis and queries. For example, a healthcare company uses an OLAP system to analyze patient data from different perspectives, such as demographics, medical history, and treatment outcomes. The system enables researchers to quickly identify trends and patterns in the data, and to generate insights that can inform clinical decision-making and improve patient care. OLTP systems are typically used for transactional tasks, such as recording sales, tracking inventory, or processing customer orders. These systems are optimized for fast data input and retrieval, with the goal of maintaining data accuracy and consistency. For instance, A retail company uses an OLTP system to process customer orders and manage inventory in real-time. The system captures transactional data such as product details, customer information, and payment details, and updates the inventory and financial records accordingly. According to the application scenarios, time series databases tend to focus on the following technical cores:

(i) **High throughput capability of writing.** It is generally accepted that row storage is better suited than column storage for quick writing and updating of time series data. This can be testified with insert DML.

(ii) **High compression ratio.** Giving users a high compression ratio includes two reasons. The first is the ability to reduce costs, and the second is the efficiency with which memory storage of the compressed data may be assured. Bulk loading processes may testify to the fact that column-oriented storage has a substantially greater compression rate than row storage.

(iii) **Multi-dimensional query capability.** Scenarios regarding time series data usually need analyze data with multiple dimensions. It is crucial to find a solution for the issue of how to more effectively query and compute numerous dimensions. It always involves searches for points and intervals that involve one or more tuple attributes.

(iv) **Efficient aggregation capabilities.** Aggregating statistical report queries is a common requirement for time series services, and it takes time to accomplish. This can be testified with common aggregate calculations such as count, max, sum, and so on.

According to the business characteristics of time series data, the related operations on time series data tables mainly include bulk load, tuple insert, range query, and aggregations. In the experimental part, detailed experiments will be implemented in this sequence.

3.2 Row-Oriented Storage Structure

The default storage mode of a relational database is row-oriented storage. Row storage means that all columns of a row or all attributes of a tuple are stored continuously. The entire row can be read or written at one I/O which is a good implementation of the ACID principle. Multiple consecutive row records form a single data block for organizational storage. There are two main ways to access data, one is sequential access that scans every data block in sequence, while the other is to index a column or multiple columns of data for quick access. The index will return regarding key and ctid of a given query with block number and offset. The data access procedure of the row-oriented storage database can be shown in Fig. 3 and the access algorithm can be seen in Algorithm 1. The input contains a piece of time series data (TS), Q_t and Q_a which refer to time and other attribute parameters, and P which presents predicates of conditions. The algorithm can obtain result tuples by index scan method (lines 1–4) and sequential scan method (lines 5–14).

The technique associated with data compression in row storage procedures is called TOAST which stands for The Oversized attribute Storage Technique. The block is the basic storage unit of data in file storage and some row storage databases like PostgreSQL do not allow one row of data to be stored across blocks. For much long row data, those databases will start TOAST which aims at compressing or slicing large attribute values into multiple physical rows and storing them in another system table which is called the TOAST table. This special storage method is named out-of-row storage. However, since the data types of attributes of time series data are commonly the basic ones such as int and float and are rarely variable-length data types like text, there is generally no opportunity to use TOAST which indicates that it will save little storage space for time series data.

The indexes supported by row-oriented storage mainly include B-tree, GIN, and GIST. Different indexes use different algorithms suited to different queries. By default, row storage databases will create B-tree indexes on columns specified by users. Generally, B-tree is suitable for equivalent and range queries on data that could be sorted in order. GIN is usually applied to text searches. In the GIN table, every keyword will record the location it appears in order to search rapidly. Though, the building procedure of GIN is time-consuming. GIST is a balanced search tree like B-tree. Unlike the B-tree, it is allowed to define any type of data and operator in GIST for users to access data. For spatial data, it is impossible for B-tree to search a point or space of a given condition. However, it can be achieved by using GIST to implement an R-tree on spatial data for point or space searching.

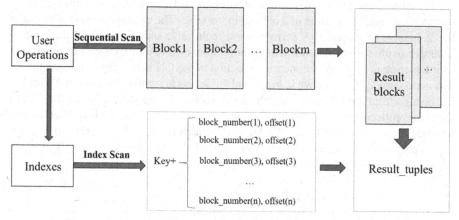

Fig. 3. Data access procedure of row-oriented storage.

Algorithm 1: *Row-access* procedure

Input: Time series data TS, time parameter Q_t, other attribute parameters Q_a, predicates P
Output: R
1 blocklist←TS; //*blocklist is the collection of all data blocks*
2 **if** index exists **then** //*suppose the index is B-tree built on Q_t*
3   collection C(key,ctid(block_number, offset))←index scan(Q_t,P);
4   R←search(sort(C),blocklist,filter(Q_a, P));
5 **else**   //*sequential scan on all data blocks without any index*
6 | **for** block in blocklist **do**
7 | | **for** tuple in block **do**
8 | | | **if** tuple satisfies conditions(Q_t, Q_a, P) **then**
9 | | | R+=tuple;
10 | | | **end if;**
11 | | **end for;**
12 | **end for;**
13 **end if;**
14 **return** R;

3.3 Column-Oriented Storage Structure

A column storage database organizes data in columns. Due to the low data compression rate of traditional row storage, in the case of analytical works, row storage often reads and loads data columns that are not related to the business target resulting in a large amount of waste of I/O and poor performance. Therefore, some databases offer both row-oriented storage and column-oriented storage engines for users to choose from such as openGauss.

The basic storage unit of the column store engine is CU, which is a compressed block of data composed of a portion of a column in the table. The division method is shown in Fig. 2. In order to manage CUs corresponding to the table and interface with the actuator layer to provide various functions, the column store engine uses CUDesc (Compression Unit Descriptor) to record the meta information of the CU in a column store table. The data access procedure is shown in Fig. 4 and the access algorithm is shown in Algorithm 2. The algorithm starts by obtaining the result tuples with an index built on time (lines 1–5). The collection of key and ctid is found based on the B-tree index. After sorting for ctids, we search target CUs in CUDesc and search result tuples by other filters. The access procedure can also be achieved by sequential scan (lines 6–10) on CUDesc by getting target tupleids and tuples with all filters.

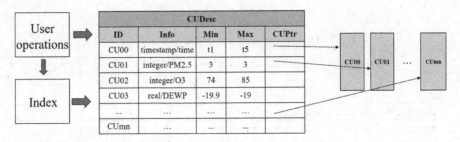

Fig. 4. Data access procedure of column-oriented storage.

Algorithm 2: *Column-access* procedure

Input: Time series data TS, time parameter Q_t, other attribute parameters Q_a, predicates P

Output: R

1 CUDesc←TS;

2 **if** index exists **then**   *//suppose the index is B-tree built on time*

3   collection C(key,ctid(CUid, offset))←index scan(Q_t, P);

4   CUs(Q_a)←search(sort(C), CUDesc);

    //CUs(Q_a) is the collection of CU storing Q_a data

5   R←collection(tupleid)←search(CUs(Q_a),key,filter(Q_a,P));

6 **else**   *//sequential scan on all data blocks without any index*

7   CUs(Q_t, Q_a)←search(CUDesc);

8   R←collection(tupleid)←search(CUs(Q_t, Q_a),filters(Q_t, Q_a, P));

9 **end if;**

10 **return R;**

In terms of data compression, column storage has much better spatial compression rate on time series data than that of row storage. The column store engine supports low, medium, and high compression levels separately and users can specify the compression level while creating a table. Each column will select compression methods adaptively according to the data type, including delta value encoding, run length encoding, dictionary encoding, LZ4, zlib, and etc.

The indexes supported by column store mainly are B-tree, sparse index, and clustered index. For column store engines, which are generally used to cope with large data analytical calculations, B-tree indexes can help column stores greatly improve their point query efficiency. In leaf nodes of a B-tree index, the mapping of key values to CUid and offset is stored in order to query the CUDesc table to obtain result data. Sparse indexes are filtered by the maximum and minimum values of each CU, and only CUs with query conditions in the range will be read, which greatly reduces the consumption of I/O reads. The clustered index is mainly to solve the problem that the range between min and max of every CU is too clustered so that a large number of CUs are misread. The clustered index sorts the data in some intervals accordingly which can ensure that the intersection of CUs is as small as possible and can greatly improve the efficiency of sparse indexes in data discrete scenarios.

4   Experiment

In this section, we present our experimental evaluation of space occupancy and efficiency of different storage structures in openGauss. Firstly, the experimental environment and datasets are described. Then, the experiments are illustrated and the relative results are discussed respectively.

4.1   OpenGauss

OpenGauss is an open-source relational database management system that has multi-core high-performance, complete link security, intelligent operation and maintenance for enterprise features. The openGauss, originated from PostgreSQL, integrates Huawei's technology accumulated over the years in databases. It enhances the storage engine, transaction, optimizer, and ARM architecture of PostgreSQL. In the meantime, as a global database open-source community, openGauss has the characteristics of high performance, high availability, high security, and easy operation and maintenance compared with other open-source databases. It strives to expand and improve the ecosystem of database software and hardware applications. OpenGauss, which simultaneously has row-based and column-based storage, will be used to implement our experiment.

4.2 Datasets and Experimental Settings

In our experiments, we will use three open-source time series datasets. The properties of these three datasets are listed in Table 1, and the details of each dataset are described as follows:

(i)   Air quality dataset (AQD): this dataset contains hourly air quality indices from March 2013 to March 2017. The volume is around 35,000 tuples with 15 dimensions. The attributes consist of No, time, station, relative meteorological data and a series of air quality indices. Data types include integer, timestamp, float and variable character.

(ii) Room occupancy detection dataset (RODD): this dataset describes the occupancy of the room. 2665 one-minute observations were made from February 2–4, 2015. It has 2665 tuples and 7 attributes. This includes date, temperature, humidity, light, CO2, humidity ratio, and ground truth occupancy which was obtained from time-stamped photographs taken every minute.

(iii) Environmental monitoring dataset (EMD): This dataset comes from the IOT monitoring equipment of Jiangsu Academy of Sciences, which is used to monitor 19 kinds of data such as air quality and water quality. The dataset is real-time monitoring data every 2 min from October to December 2021 in the northern area of the wetland park. The quantity is more than 3 hundred thousand and there are 3 attributes.

The missing values of all datasets are completed by linear interpolation. All time-relative attributes are consolidated into a timestamp format and some useless attributes are deleted.

We will implement four kinds of operations including bulk loading, insertion, range query and aggregate calculation to compare time and space consumed by row-oriented storage and column-oriented storage with statements supported by openGauss. The bulk loading operation will verify the space occupation condition of two kinds of storage structures whereas the rest will compare time consumed of the row-oriented storage and the column-oriented storage while working with time series data. The metrics and subdivision information of each operation is shown in Table 2.

Table 1. Datasets description

Dataset Name	#tuples	#attributes	temporal frequency
Air quality	35065	15	1 h
Room occupancy detection	2665	7	1 min
Environmental monitoring	353744	3	2 min

Table 2. Workload of experiments

Metrics	Operation	Subdivision	Transaction
storage size	bulk load		OLTP
time	insert		
	range query	point	OLAP
		interval	
	aggregate operators	count	
		max	
		sum	
		average	

4.3 Experimental Evaluation

(1) Bulk loading and insertion

The space occupied by time series data in row-oriented storage tables and column-oriented storage tables is different. Different compression rates of column storage tables also affect the space occupation. The compression rate cannot be set for row-oriented storage(R) tables while users can customize the compression rate of column storage tables to three degrees of compression containing no(C_N), low(C_L), and high(C_H). After comparing the space occupation of three datasets, we find that the space occupied by column storage is much smaller than that of the row, and with the increase of column-oriented storage compression rate, time series data occupies less space, even up to one-fifth of the row storage. The storage size results of row and column storage are shown in Fig. 5.

Inserting a row of time series data is a common operation in time series data services. Distinct storage structures of time series data can lead to large differences in the time taken for insert operations. Since tuples under the row store structure are all stored in a single block, it is convenient to insert all attribute values at once. For column storage, since attribute values are stored in different CUs, an inserting operation requires access to multiple CUs which takes much more time. Because the insertion position is always at the end of the time series according to the characteristics of the time series business, it can be searched sequentially to find the insertion location without indexes. The following Fig. 6 the time consumption comparison results of the insertion process in row storage and uncompressed column storage.

It is obvious that the time consumption of insertion to the row-oriented storage databases is much less than that of the column-oriented storage databases because the insert process can be done in one block in a row store, while it needs to be done in multiple CUs in a column store.

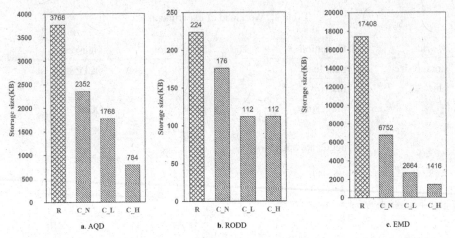

Fig. 5. Occupation of row and column storage databases on three datasets.

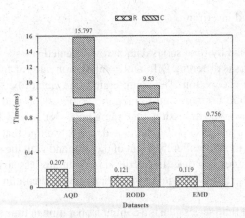

Fig. 6. Comparison of time consumption of insert operation.

(2) Range Query

In scenarios of time series, the range query for time dimension is much more common such as searching for a tuple at a certain point or tuples of a certain time period. In this section, we will comprehensively compare the time consumption of point query and range query under the two storage structures.

Figure 7 and Fig. 8 show the time consumption situation of point queries and interval queries respectively where * presents all attributes in a tuple. While performing point queries on time series, the search time and the number of search blocks of the time series data table in the column structure are less than those in the row structure. For interval queries, the searching procedure of row storage tables performs more stable and the search time consumption of column storage tables varies with the number of resulting tuples. Generally, the more result tuples, the more time consumed.

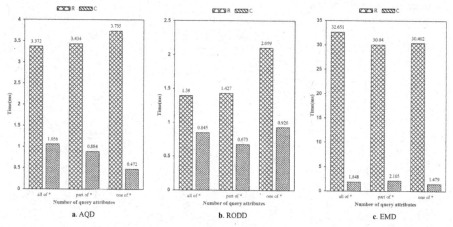

Fig. 7. Comparison of time consumption of point query.

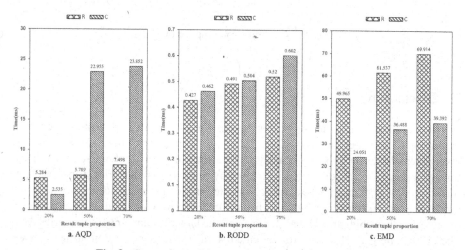

Fig. 8. Comparison of time consumption of interval query.

(3) Aggregate calculation

The aggregation functions compute data with the same dimension and are frequently applied in time series scenarios to statistically examine the data. The following aggregate functions are frequently used: count, sum, max, etc. In this section, we will compare the time consumption of several aggregate function processes under different row storage and column storage.

Figure 9 demonstrates that in time series scenarios, basic aggregate functions without filters can outperform row-oriented ones in column-oriented storage. If users need to filter time and other dimensions before completing aggregation calculations, the time required is similar to interval queries.

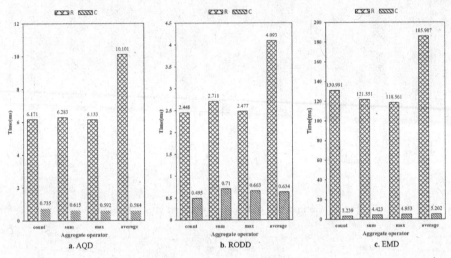

Fig. 9. Comparison of time consumption of aggregations.

5   Discussion

Various storage formats are suited for various time series data application scenarios, according to the experiment's findings. Taking three open source time series datasets as experimental data, the experiment analyzes the effects of row and column storage formats in four application procedures that are frequently employed in time series scenarios. First, in terms of OLTP transactions, we make statistics on the time and space requirements for tuple insertion and bulk loading respectively. Obviously, row-oriented storage consumes more space than column-oriented storage, and the larger the amount of time series data, the greater the gap. However, row-oriented storage takes far less time to insert rows than column-oriented storage does. Row storage is therefore better suited for real-time time series databases with large storage capacities. Furthermore, in terms of OLAP transactions, we statistics the time consumption of range query and aggregate operators. We found that point query is more efficient in the case of row storage regardless of the number of target attributes queried. In the interval query scenario, the effectiveness of different datasets in different storage structures is not always the same. The percentage of query results in relation to the total quantity will have a significant impact on the query efficiency of row and column storage for high-dimensional time series data. For low-dimensional time series data, the results show that the lower the dimension, the better the column storage effect. The result will not be changed with the increased proportion of query results. The statistical results of aggregate operators show that column-oriented storage has an absolute advantage in computing efficiency. Therefore, when dealing with time-series data services, it is necessary to comprehensively consider application requirements to select a more suitable storage structure.

6 Conclusion

In this study, we compare the space consumption of three time series datasets in the case of row storage and column storage, and the time consumption of business scenarios such as row-by-row insertion, range query, and aggregation calculation. Experimental results show that different time series data business scenarios are suitable for different storage structures. Firstly, for real-time time series databases that focus on data recording instantly and correctly, it is more suitable to use row storage as the underlying data storage structure to ensure the accuracy and efficiency of data recording. Then, for analytical time series databases mainly used for statistical analysis, it is more suitable to store data in column storage in order to greatly reduce the time consumed by the analysis process. If it is intended for historical data range queries such as querying historical time series data for a certain day or month, both storage methods are acceptable. In the future, we will also consider the index structure to provide a more comprehensive basis for storage choices for time series databases.

Acknowledgement. The paper is sponsored by CCF-Huawei Populus euphratica Innovation Research Funding.

References

1. Chaalal, H., Hamdani, M., Belbachir, H.: Finding the best between the column store and row store Databases. In: Proceedings of the 10th International Conference on Information Systems and Technologies, pp. 1–4 (2020)
2. Ordonez, C., Bellatreche, L.: A survey on parallel database systems from a storage perspective: rows versus columns. In: Elloumi, M., et al. (eds.) DEXA 2018. CCIS, vol. 903, pp. 5–20. Springer, Cham (2018). https://doi.org/10.1007/978-3-319-99133-7_1
3. Bhagat, V., Gopal, A.: Comparative study of row and column oriented database. In: Fifth International Conference on Emerging Trends in Engineering & Technology. IEEE (2013)
4. Abadi, D.J., Madden, S.R., Hachem, N.: Column-stores vs. row-stores: how different are they really? In: Proceedings of the 2008 ACM SIGMOD International Conference on Management of Data, pp. 967–980 (2008)
5. Halverson, A., Beckmann, J.L., Naughton, J.F., et al.: A comparison of c-store and row-store in a common framework. University of Wisconsin-Madison Department of Computer Sciences (2006)
6. Ramamurthy, R., DeWitt, D.J., Su, Q.: A case for fractured mirrors. VLDB J. **12**, 89–101 (2003)
7. Stonebraker, M., et al.: C-store: a column-oriented DBMS. In: VLDB, pp. 553–564 (2005)
8. Harizopoulos, S., Liang, V., Abadi, D.J., Madden, S.: Performance tradeoffs in read-optimized databases. In: VLDB, pp. 487–498 (2006)
9. Abadi, D., Madden, S., Ferreira, M.: Integrating compression and execution in column-oriented database systems. In: Proceedings of the ACM SIGMOD International Conference on Management of Data, Chicago, USA. ACM (2006)

10. Plattner, H.: A common database approach for OLTP and OLAP using an in-memory column database. In: Proceedings of the ACM SIGMOD International Conference on Management of Data. ACM, USA (2009)
11. Rösch, P., Dannecker, L., Hackenbroich, G., et al.: A storage advisor for hybrid-store databases. Proc. VLDB Endow. **5**(12) (2012)
12. Tahmassebpour, M.: A new method for time-series big data effective storage. IEEE Access **5**, 10694–10699 (2017)
13. Wang, C., Huang, X., Qiao, J., et al.: Apache IoTDB: time-series database for internet of things. Proc. VLDB Endow. **13**(12), 2901–2904 (2020)
14. Waddington, D.G., Lin, C.: A fast lightweight time-series store for IoT data. arXiv preprint arXiv:1605.01435 (2016)
15. Fouad, T., Mohamed, B.: Model transformation from object relational database to NoSQL column based database. In: Proceedings of the 3rd International Conference on Networking, Information Systems & Security, pp. 1–5 (2020)
16. Rhea, S., Wang, E., Wong, E., et al.: LittleTable: a time-series database and its uses. In: ACM International Conference, pp.125–138. ACM (2017)
17. Tsubouchi, Y., Wakisaka, A., Hamada, K., et al.: HeteroTSDB: an extensible time series database for automatically tiering on heterogeneous key-value stores. In: 2019 IEEE 43rd Annual Computer Software and Applications Conference (COMPSAC), pp. 264–269. IEEE (2019)

LOACR: A Cache Replacement Method Based on Loop Assist

Tian Li[1], Zhiming Ding[2(✉)], Jian Miao[3], Xinjie Lv[3], Xueyu Gao[3], Fulin Wang[3], and Xiangbin Wan[3]

[1] Beijing University of Technology, Beijing 100124, China
litian@emails.bjut.edu.cn
[2] Institute of Software, Chinese Academy of Sciences, Beijing 100190, China
zhiming@iscas.ac.cn
[3] Highgo Infrastructure Software Co., Ltd., Jinan 250000, China
{miaojian,lvxinjie,gaoxueyu,wangfulin,wanxiangbin}@highgo.com

Abstract. Cache is used to reduce performance differences between storage layers. It is widely used in databases, operating systems, network systems, and applications. Loop reference pattern where blocks are referenced repeatedly with regular intervals is a common phenomenon during data referencing. Good management of looping reference blocks can effectively help improve the performance of cache management. In this work, we propose a loop assistant cache replacement (LOACR) policy. We divide the cache into two parts, one part is used to store looping reference data, and the rest of the cache uses an ML-based algorithm to manage. We regularly identify the looping reference pattern and the specific information of the loop at the end of every window. At the same time, we will place the looping reference data that may appear in the next window into the cache in advance to improve the hit rate of the cache. The remaining space in the cache drives the LRU and LFU specialists to cache replacement through a parameter-free machine learning approach. Finally, we evaluated LOACR across a broad range of experiments using multiple sets of cache configurations across multiple data sets.

Keywords: Cache Replacement · Cache Policy · Reuse Distance

1 Introduction

Cache is a widely used and indispensable component of computer science. The cache was used to solve the problem of the memory wall [22] in von Neumann computers: calculations are orders of magnitude faster than memory access. As the gap widens, the problem of the memory wall becomes the bottleneck of the

This work is supported by the Key R&D Program of Shandong Province under Grant 2021CXGC010104.

system performance. A quick and small cache is placed between storage levels for commonly used content to solve this bottleneck. This allows data to be accessed directly from the faster cache rather than from slower memory, improving system performance. In addition, caching is also widely used in Web servers, which tend to cache frequently accessed items to alleviate the problem due to network latency. 1% increase in the cache hit rate reduces latency by 35% [5]. Meanwhile, content delivery networks (CDNS) deliver content to users through a network of cache servers to improve latency, broadband, and availability. However, due to the limitation of cache size, data cannot be stored indefinitely. Therefore, the management of cache space must be effective.

Most cache accesses show regularity, either because of the underlying program access loop or because of the correlation between accesses. Cache replacement strategy is built based on regular data access, if the data access is completely disorderly, any cache replacement strategy will be ineffective. Therefore, the capture of some regular access data is useful to improve the cache hit ratio. Many cache replacement algorithms [6,8,13,16,17] are effective in some datasets but not others. In past studies, we found that few cache replacement strategies specifically manage cyclic data separately. This paper attempts to propose a loop-assisted cache replacement strategy by identifying and managing loop reference data separately.

To summarize, our contributions are listed as follows:

- We have designed a loop detection method in the interval. Through this method, the specific information of the cycle can be identified such as the loop period and the loop length.
- We proposed a cache replacement strategy based on loop assistant, which we call LOACR(LOop Assistant Cache Replacement). It is inspired by frequent regular access to the loop data, LOACR identifying the loop data and screening data in the detection interval. Put these data into the cache at a fixed period to improve the cache hit rate.
- We conducted simulation experiments on the 10 different cache configurations on the 8 workloads to evaluate the LOACR. The experiment has proved that the LOACR has increased the LRU method by 10%, and the ARC algorithm has increased by 4%, it is slightly better than the current most advanced cache strategy.

2   Background

2.1   Reuse Distance

Reuse distance is the reference number of other blocks between two consecutive accesses to the same block. Reuse distance measures the frequency of the data reference currently, and a larger reuse distance indicates that the data is less hot in a certain time interval. Reuse distance is divided into forward reuse distance and backward reuse distance. Generally in cache replacement, we can get the backward reuse distance of the data. Also, some studies [2,9] predict the forward reuse distance based on the backward reuse distance to perform cache replacement. Here we only use the backward reuse distance, and all reuse distance in this paper refers to the backward reuse distance.

2.2 Reference Pattern

Reference patterns are classified into four patterns [3]: sequential, looping, temporally clustered, and probabilistic reference pattern.

Sequential Pattern: All blocks are referenced one after another and never referenced again, similar to scanning.

Looping Pattern: All blocks are accessed repeatedly at a fixed interval (period).

Temporally Clustered Pattern: Recently accessed blocks are more likely to be accessed in the near future.

Probabilistic Pattern: Each block has a fixed reference probability, and all blocks are accessed independently.

From the reuse distance graph, we can identify the data's reference pattern. The reference trajectory of the reuse distance figure should be straight at this period since all the data are referenced at the same interval when the data are referring to the loop data, as illustrated in Fig. 1. The block reference is depicted on the left side of the graph, with the virtual address of the referenced data block on the y-axis and the logical time, starting at 0 and increasing by 1 for each reference, on the x-axis. Five repeated 0–100 loop accesses are simulated to create the load.

The reuse distance for load references is depicted on the right side of the figure, with the logical time on the x-axis and the reuse distance on the y-axis. The reuse distance for the first reference of any data is ∞. For presentation purposes, we denote ∞ by 0 in the figure. Thus, the bottom line (y-axis equals 0) shows the first visit of the data. It can be seen that the reuse distance values remain constant during the loop references and appear as straight lines in the image. The same can be used to detect the loop reference pattern by the reuse distance figure.

When the data presents a sequential pattern, each referenced data is referenced for the first time, and the reuse distance is ∞ at the time of reference, which is expressed in the reuse distance image as a straight line with a y value of 0. When the data is referenced in a temporally clustered pattern, it means that the referenced data will be referenced again in the near future, so the value of y in the reuse distance image should be generally distributed at a smaller value.

2.3 Understanding Workloads

In reality, storage workloads frequently result in complicated combinations of many reference patterns rather than just one. A workload may have several

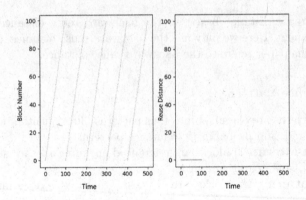

Fig. 1. An example of the looping pattern.

looping references with different loop periods as well as sequentially and temporally clustered pattern references. It's essential to recognize that whenever a loop is referenced, the linear mode to the memory address space is not always used. A loop may be accessing a data structure such as a linked list or a binary tree, in which case the access is regular and repetitive, but the space address accessed may not follow a linear pattern. Therefore some loop patterns are difficult to detect in the original image by the naked eye alone. By mapping the spatial addresses to an increasing virtual space it can be easier to discover more features of the accesses. As seen in Fig. 2, this mapping approach can aid in a better understanding of the access patterns of the workload.

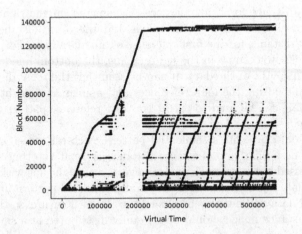

Fig. 2. Access pattern from the FIU trace collection.

2.4   Related Work

Low Inter-reference Recency Set (LIRS): [19] LIRS inherits the feature of LRU to predict hot and cold data in memory based on temporal locality, and introduces Inter-Reference Recency(IRR) and Recency to increase the prediction accuracy of hot and cold data, thus reducing erroneous data elimination and improve the cache hit rate. The core assumption is that data with a perceived large IRR will then have a larger IRR next time, that is to say, the next access will be more distant. Thus it is the preferred choice for memory culling. LIRS filters one-time accesses by its smaller list Q and thus can handle scanning workloads. The LIRS algorithm has better adaptability to global data access patterns, while it performs poorly for certain access patterns with time-local characteristics.

Adaptive Replacement Cache (ARC): [13] ARC algorithm is an adaptive algorithm that achieves cache space management by dynamically maintaining two lists, LRU as well as LFU. The ARC algorithm divides the cache space into LRU and LFU lists, while each of the two lists has ghost lists to keep the evicted data blocks. The space size of the two partitions is dynamically adjusted by hitting the ghost list, and when the ghost list of LRU is hit, it indicates that the LRU space needs to be expanded to achieve an optimal cache management state. The ARC algorithm takes into account both the access frequency and the recency [14], but as the cache capacity increases, the ARC algorithm faces the problem of the rapid increase in the chance of conflict invalidation, and after reaching a critical point, the hit rate of the algorithm cannot increase further, similar to the case of increasing the capacity of a single data block.

Learning Cache Replacement (LeCaR): [20] LeCaR is a machine learning-based cache replacement algorithm that maintains LRU and LFU weights by regret minimization [10,11] online learning. LeCaR assumes that at each moment the workload can be best solved by a combination of two basic but mutually orthogonal policies LRU and LFU. Whenever cache replacement is performed, one of the LRU and LFU policies is selected for cache replacement based on the learned weights. While the weights are adjusted by the history of hits, if the requested block is found in the history then the decision will be considered bad, so regrets will cause. However, LeCaR needs to set the initial learning rate, and different workloads often have different learning rates [15], so the selection of the learning rate has a certain degree of influence on the effectiveness of the algorithm.

3   LOACR

Considering the large number of loop access patterns in workloads, we believe that the cache algorithm needs to improve the cache hit rate by taking loop references into account in the cache space during the design process. However, there is no regularity in the occurrence of loops, and the number and frequency of loop references can vary greatly from workload to workload, which is very uncertain. Therefore, we consider using a loop assistant approach to periodically add the detected loop content to the cache. The remaining cache space we consider using a machine learning approach to manage, and here we draw on the idea of LeCaR to manage the remaining areas of the cache.

3.1 Loop Cache Space

As mentioned earlier, the cache space is divided into two parts, one for storing detected loops, and the rest of the cache space is managed using the method proposed in Sect. 3.2. We choose the window size as the size of the cache, trigger a loop detection operation at the end of each window period (Algorithm 2), and selectively put some contents into the cache according to the detected loops (Algorithm 1), so as to achieve the goal of improving the cache hit rate.

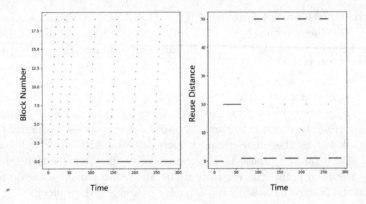

Fig. 3. An example of multiple group loop pattern.

The main feature of the loop mode is that the loop data is always accessed at the same reuse distance in the image presenting a straight line. Here we want to relax the bounds of loops and our aim is to detect some data of the class loop. The reuse distance of the data fluctuates within a certain degree or the loop is interrupted within a certain limit we consider that it is making a loop reference. Under loose conditions, we are more likely to capture some loop patterns. So the core idea of loop detection becomes finding a set of data where the reuse distance and the number of interruptions remain within a certain range, and these data are the set of loops we find. By analyzing the reuse distance figure we can also get some relevant information about the loops. Figure 3 on the left shows the artificially set loop workload which sets the loops with different loop intervals, and Fig. 3 on the right shows a reuse distance image corresponding to the workload on the left. Different straight lines can be observed in the reuse distance image. The reuse distance can be understood as the access interval from the last access, when the loop interval is 0 which means the loop is in continuous access the reuse distance value is the size of the loop and the length of the captured straight line is larger than the loop length. When the loop is not continuously accessed but there is an access interval, the reuse distance at this time includes both the loop length and the loop interval, and the length of the loop at this time can be judged by the continuous length of the line. At the end of the detection, we can get all the loops in the window, meanwhile, we can get the basic information of the loop including the loop length, loop interval, and other information.

Algorithm 2 gives the loop detection algorithm, which captures loops that occur within a window mainly at the end of that window by the reuse distance of the data accessed within the window. The loop we capture is not a loop in the strict sense, but a more loosely defined class of loops. We allow loop breaks to be generated, and we also give an allowed error for the access interval so that we can detect more useful information. The output of Algorithm 1 is a collection of loops that contains all the loops detected within the window. Each loop is a structure that stores some basic data information about the loop. With the existing information and the direct information we get from detecting the loops, we can obtain two key pieces of information, the loop interval and the address of the loop data block. We control whether the loop data block is placed in the cache based on the loop interval. If the loop interval is larger than the window length, the next window interval must not access the loop data, so we will do a general filtering of the detected loop intervals.

The filtering of loops to decide what to place into the cache is given by Algorithm 1. The core filtering factor is the detected loop interval, and only loops with a loop interval smaller than the window size are selected for placement. A loop size limit is also set, and Fig. 5 give the impact of different size loop limit intervals on the cache hit rate.

Algorithm 1: SetLoopToCache

Data: Detected loops loops; Space for storage loops LS; Cache size C;Size of loop space L; Limit of loop size LL

1 LS.clear
2 $L = 0$
3 loops.SortbyLoopInterval
4 **for** *loop in loops* **do**
5   **if** *loop.interval* $> C$ **then**
6 | break
7   **else**
8   **if** $L + loop.length < LL$ **then**
9 | LS.putin(loop)
10   **end**
11   **end**
12 **end**

Algorithm 2: DetectLoop

Input: Reuse distances RD; Length of window L;Float threshold
       FT;Maximum number of interruptions MI;Minimum continuous
       length MC

Output: a collection of loop

1 **while** *not at end of L* **do**
2   **if** *RD[i] in (RD[i-1]-FT,RD[i-1]+FT)* **then**
3   TempRD.ADD(RD[i])
4   ContinuousCount = ContinuousCount + 1
5   InterruptCount = 0
6   **else**
7   **if** *InterruptCount <MI* **then**
8   ContinuousCount = ContinuousCount + 1
9   InterruptCount = InterruptCount + 1
10   **else**
11   ContinuousCount = 0
12   InterruptCount = 0
13   **end**
14   **end**
15   **if** *ContinuousCount >MC* **then**
16   RDavg = GetMajority(TempRD)
17   **while** *not at end of L* **do**
18   **if** *RD[i] in(RDavg-FT,RDavg+FT)* **then**
19   ContinuousCount = ContinuousCount + 1
20   InterruptCount = 0
21   **else**
22   **if** *InterruptCount <MI* **then**
23   ContinuousCount = ContinuousCount + 1
24   InterruptCount = InterruptCount + 1
25   **else**
26   ContinuousCount = 0
27   InterruptCount = 0
28   **end**
29   **end**
30   **end**
31   Construct(loop)
32   loops.ADD(loop)
33   **end**
34 **end**
35 **return** loops

We intercepted part of the cpp workload to show the detected loop as shown
in Fig. 4, where (a) the image represents the original content of the intercepted
part of the workload to visualize the access pattern, and (b) is the image of
the reuse distance calculated based on the original image (a), the data in the

image showing a straight line means that the data is accessed at the same reuse distance, that is, in a loop.This is the part of the data that we are detecting. (c) is the reuse distance image of the detected loop content from (b), which is the class loop content detected by Algorithm 1. Figure (d) shows the position of the detected loop content in the original image, and the loop detection effect can be observed by comparing with figure (a).

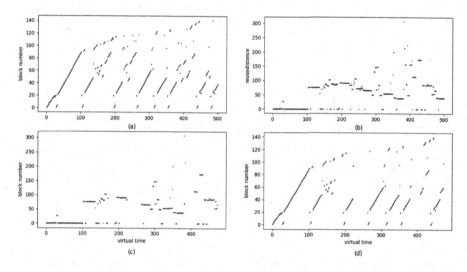

Fig. 4. Part of cpp workload

As mentioned above, we divide the cache space into two parts, one part for storing the contents of the detected loops and the other part for storing the general contents. Since the occurrence of loops is very random, not every detection window has a looping pattern. If we fix the ratio of the two parts in the cache, the loop space will be a waste when no loop pattern is detected. Therefore, we set a maximum loop rate here and dynamically set the size of the two contents at the end of each detection window based on the loop content detected this time. First, we clear the loop reference data block obtained in the last detect interval. When the detected number of loop reference quantity is less than the maximum limit of the loop space, put all loop reference data blocks in the loop storage space. Calculate the remaining space size as the maximum remaining space storage in the next interval.

Figure 5 show the cache hit rate images obtained by verifying different maximum occupancy rates of loop content in different workloads respectively. The x-axis represents the artificially fixed maximum limit percentage of loop space in the cache space, and the maximum capacity of the loop space is determined by the maximum limit percentage on the one hand and the cache size on the other. Here we set three different cache sizes for each workload, 0.1%, 0.5%, and 1% of the workload, and Fig. 5 show the average of the cache hit rate for the three cache sizes at the loop rates. After several experiments, we choose the rate of 0.6, which gives the best average result in the multiple cache comparison experiments.

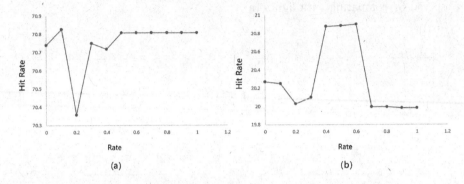

Fig. 5. Average cache hit rate in sprite(a) and multi3(b) workload X-axis represents the maximum rate of loop space to cache space

3.2 Remaining Cache Space

Our proposed method mainly divides the cache space into two parts, one part is used to store the detected loop contents and the other part is managed using a LeCaR-based approach, here we call it LeCaRp.

LeCaR performs well in the field of cache replacement and is an algorithm that has successfully applied machine learning in the field of cache replacement and achieved better results. However, as mentioned earlier, LeCaR requires two parameters to be set manually during use. Although the original authors provide the recommended parameter settings, experiments have shown that there are different optimal learning rate values for different workloads, which means that the learning rate settings have a certain degree of impact on the cache hit rate. Gradient-based stochastic hill climbing approach [18] is considered a better learning method in CACHEUS [15], which can eliminate the learning parameters and enhance the algorithm the adaptability as well as simplicity. Here we use an improved learning algorithm based on LeCaR which is also the gradient-based stochastic hill climbing method.

The learning rate of LeCaR is fixed, and the weights are adjusted at a fixed learning rate each time. The gradient-based stochastic hill-climbing method automatically adjusts the size of the learning rate according to the change of the local cache hit rate, and the adjustment step of the learning rate is also adjusted according to the change of the cache hit rate. This machine learning method is highly adaptive, and the algorithm does not negatively affect the final hit rate due to the artificially set parameters. Figure 6 show the comparison of the cache hit rate effect between the original LeCaR algorithm and the improved learning algorithm LeCaRp. Improved cache hit rate can be seen on the two real workloads multi3 and sprite [12].

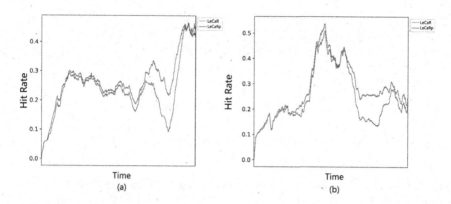

Fig. 6. Cache hit-rate difference distributions using LeCaR algorithm and LeCaRp on multi3(a) and sprite(b) workload

Above we compared LeCaR with his improved algorithm, here tentatively called LeCaRp. From the images as well as the data it can be seen that the improvement in the machine learning algorithm has helped in the improvement of the cache hit rate. We have added loop storage space on top of this and split the original cache space. Figure 7 shows the cache hit rate images of LOACR and LeCaRp on the actual workload multi3. The average cache hit rate for LOACR is 29.28%, with an average improvement of 0.92%. It can be seen that dividing the area in the cache for separate storage of the detected loop content is helpful for the improvement of the cache hit rate.

4   Experiments

This section evaluates several advanced cache replacement algorithms using public storage I/O workloads.

4.1   Cache Policies

LOACR is compared with three cache replacement policies using LRU, ARC, and LeCaR. LRU and ARC are classical cache replacement algorithms that are widely used in production systems [21]. LeCaR is a successful example of using machine learning for cache replacement algorithms, and our proposed algorithm is inspired by LeCaR.

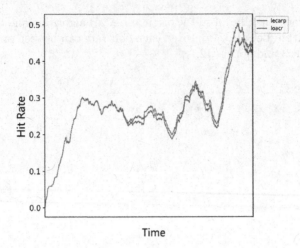

Fig. 7. Cache hit-rate difference distributions using LeCaRp algorithm and LOACR on multi3 workload

4.2 Workloads

We test cache replacement algorithms on a number of public available datasets [1,12]. These traces collect real working production environments with fast disk accesses, and a large number of cache replacement studies have recently been evaluated by these traces [4,7]. Table 1 summarizes the specific characteristics of these workloads.

Table 1. Descriptions for the 8 datasets used.

Dataset	Requests	Details
cscope	6781	An interactive C source program examination tool
postgres	10448	Joins queries among four relations in a relational database system
cpp	9047	Cpp is the GNU C-compatible compiler preprocessor
sprite	133996	The Sprite network file system
multi1	15858	cscope,cpp
multi2	26311	cscope,cpp,postgres
multi3	30241	cpp,gnuplot,glimpse,postgres
FIU	559556	End user home directories; Webpage and web-based email servers

4.3 Result

In this section, we evaluate the experiments on our proposed method. The cscope and postgres datasets are purely loop pattern data, and the miti1, multi2, and multi3 datasets are mixed models, which are artificially blended from multiple datasets. The remaining datasets are traces of real production environments, of which the FIU dataset we test on its day 16 data, which is widely used in the field of cache replacement.

Looping Pattern. Cscope Fig. 8 (a), postgres Fig. 8 (b) have different loop access patterns. Loop in postgres is a little more complex. Since LRU always replaces the data that has not been accessed for the longest time, when the loop size is larger than the cache size, LRU always keeps what has just been accessed and discards the earliest content, and LRU gets poorer results. In this experiment, LOACR improves the cache hit rate of LRU by 19%, improves ARC by 19%, and improves LeCaR by 5% on the cscope dataset. On the postgres dataset LOACR improved LRU by 6%, ARC by 3%, and LeCaR by 0.4%. The cache hit rate for LRU and ARC remained at 1.83% in the cscope dataset regardless of the cache size change. The hit rate for LeCaR only improved from cache sizes greater than 500. In contrast, LOACR reaches 4.73% at a cache size of 100. Because LOACR is able to periodically identify loop and place them in the cache, this approach helps to improve the cache hit rate.

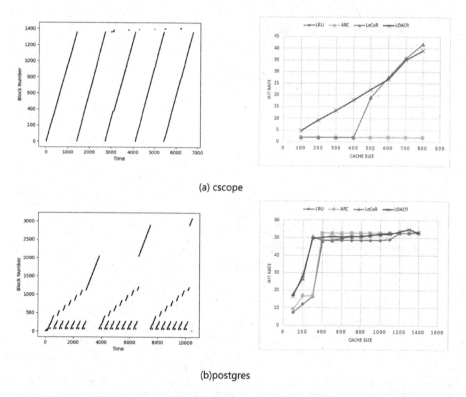

(a) cscope

(b)postgres

Fig. 8. Block reference and hit rate of the looping pattern workload.

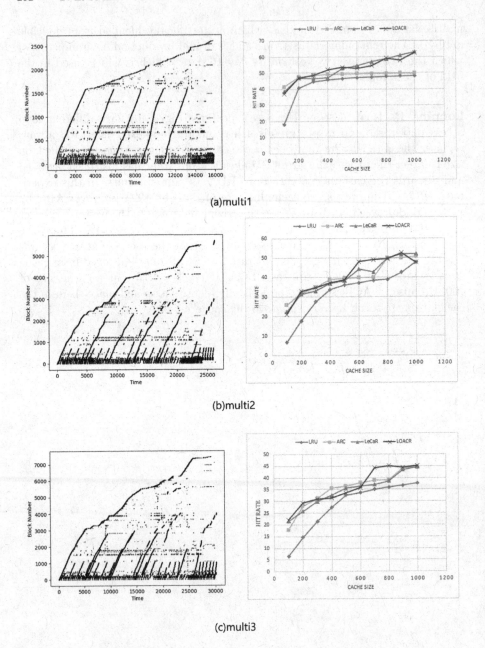

(a)multi1

(b)multi2

(c)multi3

Fig. 9. Block reference and hit rate of the mixed workload.

Mixed Workload. Multi1 Fig. 9 (a), multi2 Fig. 9(b), multi3 Fig. 9 (c) these three datasets mix multiple datasets, although not real environment-generated datasets, with a mix of access patterns. LOACR performs well overall on the

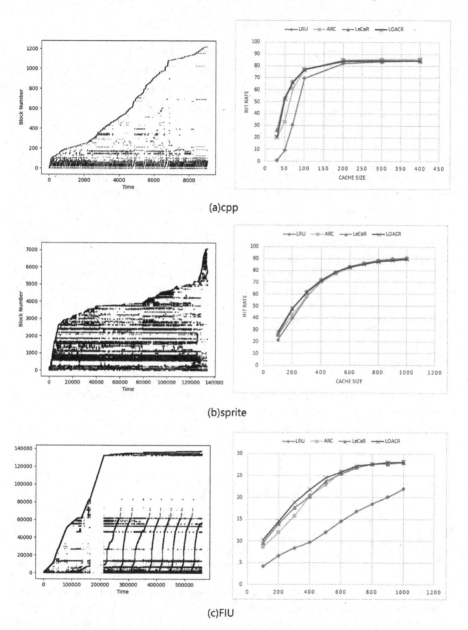

(a)cpp

(b)sprite

(c)FIU

Fig. 10. Block reference and hit rate of the real environment workload.

three datasets. Table 2 shows the performance of each algorithm on the three datasets. On average LOACR had a cache hit rate 9% higher than LRU, 2% higher than ARC, and 0.8% higher than LeCaR on the three datasets.

Table 2. Hit rate of four algorithms.

	LRU	ARC	LeCaR	**LOACR**
multi1	43.424	48.426	52.619	**52.515**
multi2	32.648	40.132	40.296	**41.159**
multi3	28.174	35.345	34.565	**36.201**

Real Environment Workloads. Cpp Fig. 10(a), sprite Fig. 10(b), FIU (Day 16) Fig. 10(c) shows the tracking of the system data in a real environment. On the sprite dataset, there is little difference in hit rate between the algorithms. LRU performs significantly worse on the FIU dataset, with LOACR's cache hit rate being 9% higher than LRU, 1% higher than ARC, and 0.6% higher than LeCaR. These three sets of experiments show that LOACR performs well on datasets generated by real environments.

On average, LOACR has a cache hit rate 10% higher than LRU, 4% higher than ARC, and 0.8% higher than LeCaR across all datasets. Our proposed approach of periodically putting loop content into the cache is effective, especially when loop patterns occur frequently in the dataset.

5   Conclusion

In this paper, we propose a cache replacement method, LOACR, where we put loop pattern data into cache space that other cache replacement algorithms ignore. The core idea of this approach is to periodically detect loops and store the valid part of the loop content in the cache. Due to the prevalence of loop accesses, the algorithm performs well in real environment workloads. LOACR has an average cache hit rate of 10% higher than LRU, 4% higher than ARC, and 0.8% higher than LeCaR over all datasets.

References

1. Association, S.N.I., et al.: The snia's i/o traces, tools, and analysis (iotta) repository (2021)
2. Choi, H., Park, S.: Learning future reference patterns for efficient cache replacement decisions. IEEE Access **10**, 25922–25934 (2022)
3. Choi, J., Noh, S.H., Sang, L.M., Cho, Y.: An adaptive block management scheme using on-line detection of block reference patterns. In: International Workshop on Multi-media Database Management Systems (1998)
4. Choi, J., Noh, S.H., Min, S.L., Cho, Y.: An implementation study of a detection-based adaptive block replacement scheme. In: USENIX Annual Technical Conference, General Track, pp. 239–252 (1999)
5. Cidon, A., Eisenman, A., Katti, S., Attar, M.A.: Cliffhanger: Scaling performance cliffs in web memory caches. In: Networked Systems Design and Implementation (2016)

6. Huang, S., Wei, Q., Feng, D., Chen, J., Chen, C.: Improving flash-based disk cache with lazy adaptive replacement. ACM Trans. Storage (TOS) **12**(2), 1–24 (2016)

7. Kim, J.M., et al.: A low-overhead high-performance unified buffer management scheme that exploits sequential and looping references. In: Proceedings of the 4th Conference on Symposium on Operating System Design & Implementation-Volume 4 (2000)

8. Li, C.: Dlirs: Improving low inter-reference recency set cache replacement policy with dynamics. In: Proceedings of the 11th ACM International Systems and Storage Conference, pp. 59–64 (2018)

9. Li, P., Gu, Y.: Learning forward reuse distance (2020)

10. Littlestone, N., Warmuth, M.K.: The weighted majority algorithm. Inf. Comput. **108**(2), 212–261 (1994)

11. Loomes, G., Sugden, R.: Regret theory: an alternative theory of rational choice under uncertainty. Econ. J. **92**(368), 805–824 (1982)

12. Manes, B.: Caffeine: A high performance caching library for java 8. https://github.com/ben-manes/caffeine (2016)

13. Megiddo, N.: Arc : A self-tuning, low overhead replacement cache. In: USENIX File and Storaqe Technologies Conference (FAST'03), San Francisco, CA (2003)

14. Robinson, J.T., Devarakonda, M.V.: Data cache management using frequency-based replacement. In: Proceedings of the 1990 ACM SIGMETRICS Conference on Measurement and Modeling of Computer Systems, pp. 134–142 (1990)

15. Rodriguez, L.V., et al.: Learning cache replacement with cacheus. In: File and Storage Technologies (2021)

16. Santana, R., Lyons, S., Koller, R., Rangaswami, R., Liu, J.: To arc or not to arc. In: Proceedings of the 7th USENIX Conference on Hot Topics in Storage and File Systems, pp. 14–14 (2015)

17. Shi, Z., Huang, X., Jain, A., Lin, C.: Applying deep learning to the cache replacement problem. In: Proceedings of the 52nd Annual IEEE/ACM International Symposium on Microarchitecture, pp. 413–425 (2019)

18. Smith, W.L.: Regenerative stochastic processes. Proc. Royal Society of London. Series A. Math. Phys. Sci. **232**(1188), 6–31 (1955)

19. Song, J., Zhang, X.: Lirs: An efficient low inter-reference recency set replacement to improve buffer cache performance. In: Proceedings of the International Conference on Measurements and Modeling of Computer Systems, SIGMETRICS 2002, June 15–19, 2002, Marina Del Rey, California, USA (2002)

20. Vietri, G., et al.: Driving cache replacement with ml-based lecar. In: USENIX Annual Technical Conference (2018)

21. Waldspurger, C.A., Saemundsson, T., Ahmad, I., Park, N.: Cache modeling and optimization using miniature simulations. In: USENIX Annual Technical Conference, pp. 487–498 (2017)

22. Wulf, W.A., Mckee, S.A.: Hitting the memory wall: Implications of the obvious. Acm Sigarch Computer Architecture News (1995)

Metaverse

Unifying Reality and Virtuality: Constructing a Cohesive Metaverse Using Complex Numbers

Haibo Li[✉]

Department of Media Technology and Interaction Design, School of Computer
Science, KTH Royal Institute of Technology, Stockholm 100 44, Sweden
haiboli@kth.se
http://www.kth.se

Abstract. In this position paper we present a novel mathematical
framework for building metaverses, which is a potential way to unify
reality and virtuality to create a cohesive whole universe. We argue that
the nature of metaverses is inherently mathematical, and propose that
the system of complex numbers could play a key role in constructing
them. Specifically, we provide context for our argument and offer a supporting example, *the analytic signal*, to demonstrate how to construct its
imaginary counterpart with the Hilbert transform to a given real signal
and how to unify them to form a cohesive complex signal that facilitates
the analysis of local dynamic behaviors of the signal. This framework has
significant potential for building a metaverse. By leveraging the power
of complex numbers, one can create a unified mathematical system that
merges the physical and virtual worlds. We believe that this proposal will
inspire further research and development of metaverses in this field and
that our framework will contribute to the construction of a metaverse
that offers unprecedented levels of interactivity and immersion.

Keywords: metaverse · complex numbers · analytic signal · Hilbert
transform · phenomenology

1 Introduction

The concept of a metaverse has been popularized in science fiction and is often
associated with the virtual world depicted in Neal Stephenson's novel Snow
Crash, as well as the movie The Matrix. However, in recent years, the concept
has gained momentum as advancements in VR and AR technologies have made
it possible to create increasingly realistic and immersive virtual environments.

The potential applications of metaverses are vast and varied. They range
from entertainment and gaming to education, healthcare, and even commerce.
A metaverse could enable people from different parts of the world to interact in
real-time, attend virtual events, and collaborate in the virtual space. It could

X. Meng et al. (Eds.): SpatialDI 2023, LNCS 13887, pp. 259–269, 2023.
https://doi.org/10.1007/978-3-031-32910-4_18

also provide new opportunities for remote work and learning, and offer new ways for businesses to connect with customers.

As the concept of metaverses gains traction, it becomes increasingly clear that constructing one is a daunting technical challenge. To succeed in this endeavor, we must first answer several fundamental questions such as *What is a metaverse? What is the nature of a metaverse? How should a metaverse be constructed?*

With respect to the first question, there have been numerous discussions on the meaning of the term "metaverse." One way of discussing it is from the meaning of the word "metaverse" itself. The term is derived from two words: "-verse," meaning universe, and "meta-," meaning "after", "beside" [7]. While "meta-" has multiple meanings, the interpretation of "after" or "beside" is often adopted to describe a metaverse as a virtual world that exists *parallel* to the real world.

This is the most common understanding of a metaverse today and its realization accordingly is a virtual-reality (VR) type where a person's body is in the real world while his head is immersed in the virtual world. This separation of the body and mind can be seen an empirical evidence for the philosophical notion of Cartesian dualism, famously captured in Descartes' dictum, "cogito ergo sum" - I think, therefore I am [2]. This doctrine posits that mind and body are fundamentally distinct and that thinking and being are separate sets of phenomena. The mind is the seat of reason and meaning, and through observation, it assigns meaning to the world by relating it to abstract understandings of an idealized reality, which in turn informs a plan of action.

Heidegger rejected the doctrine and turned it around [2]. From his perspective, the meaningfulness of everyday experience lies not in the head, but in the world. It is a consequence of our mode of being, of the way in which we exist in the world. This is the new doctrine from phenomenology. To perceive and experience the world thinking and being must be fundamentally intertwined.

Hence, any virtual reality-type implementation may not be the most suitable approach to constructing a metaverse. Rather, the term "meta" carries a more profound connotation, denoting a system's capability to augment the comprehension of another system through explanatory enhancements. The objective of a metaverse, therefore, should be to unify the physical and virtual realms and further enhance the collective understanding of the world. By enabling people to coexist simultaneously in both worlds, we can unify them to create a harmonious whole where the virtual world complements and elevates the real world. While individuals can still opt to indulge in distinct experiences in each realm, the metaverse provides a pathway to merge the two worlds and generates a novel, integrated experience that transcends what either domain can offer in isolation. Such a realization is shown in Fig. 1. Thus, one can expect that such a metaverse opens up fresh avenues for unparalleled experiences.

Because we ask how to build a metaverse, we have to answer the question of what the nature of the metaverse is. As a concept that enhances our experience

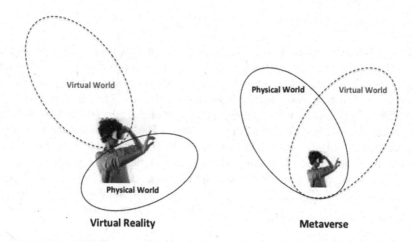

Virtual Reality   **Metaverse**

Fig. 1. Two different ways of implementing a metaverse. In the realization like virtual reality, the virtual world is isolated from the real world. The realization right illustrates how people coexist simultaneously in both worlds.

of the real world, a metaverse is not a new technology rather is a complex amalgam of various technologies, such as sensory technology, the internet, blockchain, big data, artificial intelligence, quantum technology, and more. Notably, these technologies rely heavily on mathematics, as seen in blockchain's use of digital numbers to establish trust (proof of trust). In the virtual world, physical laws can be ignored, as illustrated in the movie "Avatar," where floating mountains abound in Pandora. In this paper, we argue that the nature of a metaverse is inherently mathematical, that is, a metaverse is fundamentally rooted in mathematics. To build a metaverse we need to lay down a mathematical framework.

In this paper, we suggest using the system of complex numbers, more specifically, using the imaginary unit "i" to unify the real and world worlds into a cohesive whole:

Metaverse World(M) = Real World(S) + i Virtual World(V)
or

$$M = S + i\,V$$

Here i is a mathematical operation of "unification". It will bring together or merge two worlds into a single cohesive whole and achieve harmony and consistency between the two worlds. In the following sections, we will discuss how to use i to unify two parts and particularly illustrate how to construct an imaginary part to complement a given real part.

2   Complex Numbers

What if -1 had a square root? We cannot find a real number whose square is negative, so we need to introduce a totally new type of number. The new quantity is called i, which is defined as the square root of -1. This gives rise to the expression of imaginary numbers in the form of $a + i\,b$, where a and b are real numbers. i is known as the imaginary unit, first introduced by Descartes [2].

A complex number of the form $a + i\,b$ consists of a real part a and an imaginary part b. A real number a can be regarded as a complex number $a + i0$, with an imaginary part of 0. Similarly, a purely imaginary number ib can be regarded as a complex number $0 + ib$, with a real part of 0. Here, we no longer treat a, b, as a pair of numbers, but rather as a single number, denoted by the symbol $z = a + ib$. It can be verified that complex numbers satisfy all algebraic rules [6].

The discovery of complex numbers in mathematics sparked skepticism and confusion initially due to their abstract nature. However, as scientific knowledge advanced, it became evident that complex numbers possess unique properties that make them essential in describing physical phenomena. In particular, in the latter half of the 20th century, the behavior of the subatomic world was found to be fundamentally governed by the laws of complex numbers. Furthermore, modern particle physics relies also on complex numbers as quantum numbers [6].

In the field of electrical engineering, understanding the dynamic relationship between current I and voltage V in AC circuits is of utmost importance. Although current and voltage can be represented by trigonometric functions such as $V = \sin \omega t$ and $I = \cos \omega t$, their relationship is not explored in depth. In fact, like two sides of a coin, these two quantities represent the same electrical phenomenon but just from different perspectives. Therefore, we can combine them with a complex number, $z = \cos \omega t + i \sin \omega t = e^{i\omega t}$, which provides a unified representation of the electrical phenomenon of AC circuits. Current and voltage are unified into a circle on the complex plane. At first glance, it appears that the time component has disappeared as only the circle is observed. However, what vanishes is not time but the time axis. The complex number $z = e^{i\omega t}$ represents the combination of current and voltage on the circle, creating a three-dimensional spiral signal varying over time.

As we observe the circle along the time axis, a point moving around the circle is seen, forming a spiral that advances with time. This spiral represents the combined current and voltage signals that vary over time, which cannot be observed without their unification into a three-dimensional spatial signal. The resulting three-dimensional spiral is an exciting and informative visualization that highlights the interplay between current and voltage in AC circuits.

By viewing current as analogous to the real world and voltage as the virtual world, the complex number z can be considered a realization of a metaverse. Furthermore, complex numbers could support the possibility of having multiple virtual environments, notwithstanding the existence of a singular real world. For example, a promising solution is to use generalized complex numbers, such as quaternions, for combining several virtual worlds. The form of Quaternions, a

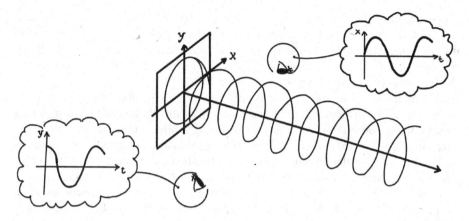

Fig. 2. AC is a three-dimensional spiral signal that changes over time. One can see its two components, current and voltage signals if one watches it from two different viewing angles (after [4]).

type of mathematical object, was invented by the Irish mathematician William Rowan Hamilton (1805–1865) [6], who discarded the commutativity of multiplication to form a four-dimensional vector space over the field of real numbers, expressed as $z = a + i\,b + j\,c + k\,d$. Quaternions have four independent "basis" elements, namely 1, i, j, and k, that span the entire space. One can envision a representing the real space, while b, c, and d represent three virtual spaces. The algebraic structure of quaternions offers an elegant and powerful tool for performing calculations in the metaverse and multiple virtual spaces, especially for geometric construction problems.

Complex numbers offer a viable mathematical tool for constructing a metaverse. However, the crux is not about a simple combination of the real and imaginary rather lies in the synergy between the two parts to create a cohesive entity. An exquisite illustration of this synergy is the electromagnetic field F, which is described as $F = E + iB$ - where $\mathbf{E}$ and $\mathbf{B}$ are the electric and magnetic fields, respectively, and together they form a perfectly unified entity. The interaction between these two fields is demonstrated clearly in the famous Maxwell's equations [6], which describe their behaviors in space and time:

$$
\begin{aligned}
\nabla \cdot \mathbf{E} &= \frac{\rho}{\epsilon_0} \\
\nabla \cdot \mathbf{B} &= 0 \\
\nabla \times \mathbf{E} &= -\frac{\partial \mathbf{B}}{\partial t} \\
\nabla \times \mathbf{B} &= \mu_0 \mathbf{J} + \mu_0 \epsilon_0 \frac{\partial \mathbf{E}}{\partial t}
\end{aligned}
\tag{1}
$$

where ρ is the charge density, $\mathbf{J}$ is the current density, ϵ_0 is the electric constant (also known as the vacuum permittivity), and μ_0 is the magnetic constant (also known as the vacuum permeability).

The interaction between the electric field $\mathbf{E}$ and the magnitude field $\mathbf{B}$ can be seen in Gauss's law, which states that the divergence of the electric field is proportional to the charge density at a point in space. This means that the electric field at a point in space is influenced by the distribution of charges around it. The magnitude field, on the other hand, is determined by the charge distribution itself. In this way, the electric and magnitude fields interact to produce the behavior of electric charges in space and time.

When it comes to metaverse applications, one can also expect E and B to be deeply intertwined. One of the most daunting challenges is constructing an imaginary counterpart to a given real part. While combining any two parts with the imaginary unit i can yield a complex number, generating a meaningful unification can be demanding. The question then arises as to whether there exists a *systematic* approach for creating an imaginary part to match a given real part. The answer to this question is affirmative, and in the following section, we provide an example from the field of signal processing to demonstrate how such a systematic approach is designed.

3   Construction of Analytic Functions

In this section, we present an illustrative example from the field of signal processing that showcases the potential of utilizing complex numbers to achieve meaningful unification. Our hope is that this example could inspire and inform efforts towards building a metaverse.

Real-world signals can often be complex and pose significant challenges for analysis. Fortunately, the development of Fourier Transform by the brilliant mathematician Josef Fourier revolutionized spectral analysis [1]. This powerful tool enables us to represent any infinite periodic function as a linear combination of sine and cosine functions, providing us with the ability to decompose continuous signals into a set of spectral components. By analyzing and processing individual sine or cosine functions, we can gain insights into the underlying patterns and structure of complex signals.

Suppose here we have a physical signal from the real world, denoted by $f(x)$ with a known frequency:

$$f(x) = A cos(\omega x), \quad A > 0. \tag{2}$$

The function $f(x)$ is a cosine function with amplitude A and angular frequency ω. Even though the function is very simple, there is no *direct* way to obtain information about the signal, for example, the amplitude A, from the signal [3]. This is simply because the instantaneous measurement of the function at any point, such as $x = x_0$, will result in any value between $-A$ and A, depending on x_0. The value of the function f at $x = x_0$ gives no information regarding whether the signal is at a local maximum or minimum, or whether f is increasing or decreasing in a neighborhood around x_0. This signal representation greatly restricts its usage in signal analysis.

Additionally, in the case of real physical signals, the negative frequencies they produce are physically meaningless. As a result, it is imperative to eliminate negative frequencies from real-world signals. In the field of communication and signal processing, a technique has been developed and implemented to suppress negative frequencies. This approach involves constructing an imaginary function, denoted as b, for a given real function a, and then combining them using the imaginary number i to form a complex number $a + ib$. The selection of b is not arbitrary and one practical way to determine it is to use the Hilbert transform of a.

The function created using this method is referred to as an **analytic function**. In the subsequent discussion, we shall introduce the Hilbert transform (HT) and demonstrate its application in constructing an analytic function. Our aim is to inspire the use of imaginary numbers in constructing a metaverse that comprises both real and imaginary worlds.

3.1 The Hilbert Transform

Different from the Fourier transform, the Hilbert transform is a mapping between two sets of functions.

The Hilbert transform H_i is defined as [3]

$$f_{H_i}(x) = \frac{1}{\pi} \int_{-\infty}^{\infty} \frac{f(\tau)}{\tau - x} d\tau. \tag{3}$$

This is usually written as

$$f_{H_i}(x) = H_i\{f\} \tag{4}$$

Since the Hilbert transform simply maps one spatial function to another, we can calculate the Hilbert transform in the Fourier domain:

$$f_{H_i}(x) = f * \frac{-1}{\pi x} \tag{5}$$

It can be seen that the Hilbert transform of a function f can be obtained by convolving f with the function $\frac{-1}{\pi x}$. Therefore, the Hilbert transform is a just linear mapping.

Let F_{H_i} denote the Fourier transform of f_{H_i}. According to Eq. (4) we have:

$$F_{H_i}(u) = F(u) \cdot i \, sign(u) \tag{6}$$

Given that convolution in the spatial domain is equivalent to multiplication in the Fourier domain, the Fourier transform of f_{H_i} can be obtained by multiplying the Fourier transform F by the imaginary unit i, and then changing the sign of the resulting product for frequencies that are negative. Another way to explain this procedure is to rotate the argument of the frequency components by an angle of $\frac{\pi}{2}$ in the positive direction for positive frequencies and in the negative direction for negative frequencies [3]. It can be observed that applying the Hilbert transform twice simply changes the sign of a function.

Here are some typical functions and their corresponding Hilbert transforms [1,3]:

$$\textbf{Function Hilbert transform}$$

$$\begin{aligned} cos(x) \qquad &-sin(x) \\ sin(x) \qquad &cos(x) \\ \delta(x) \qquad &\frac{-1}{\pi x} \end{aligned} \qquad (7)$$

With the Hilbert transform of a function f, we can define its analytic function f_A.

3.2 Analytic Signal

The analytic function f_A corresponding to the function f is defined as

$$f_A = f - if_{H_i} \qquad (8)$$

From this definition, it is clear that the construction of an analytic function is a linear mapping. From the Hilbert transform table in the previous section, we can obtain the following correspondences: The analytic signal corresponding to the function $cosx$ is e^{ix}. The analytic signal corresponding to the function $sinx$ is $-ie^{ix}$. Since both $cosx$ and $i\,sinx$ correspond to the same analytic signal e^{ix}, the construction of an analytic function is obviously not a one-to-one mapping.

The definition of the analytic function f_A can be rewritten using convolution as

$$f_A = f * [\delta(x) + \frac{i}{\pi x}] \qquad (9)$$

In the Fourier domain, this has the form

$$F_A = F \cdot [1 + sign(u)] = 2F \cdot step(u) \qquad (10)$$

Hence, the analytic signal related to the function f can be obtained by eliminating all of its negative frequencies and multiplying by a factor of 2. It is important to note that this implies that an analytic function cannot be both real and non-zero. This is because the Fourier transform of a real function is always Hermitian, but F_A is not. Consequently, the Hilbert transform of a real function f is a one-to-one mapping, as the values of F for $u < 0$ can be derived from F for $u > 0$ [3].

In conclusion, we can observe that the analytic signal is only relevant for real signals. For such signals, the corresponding analytic signal is complex, with the real part being the original signal and the imaginary part being its Hilbert transform. An example of how to construct an analytic signal is presented in the following section.

3.3 Analytic Signals in Signal Analysis

Let us reconsider how to analyze a real-world signal $f(x)$ addressed in the beginning of Sect. 3.

$$f(x) = A\cos(\omega x), \quad A > 0. \qquad (11)$$

To help signal analysis, we construct an analytic signal f_A for function f which could provide us with information on the local behavior of the signal. We define its Hilbert transform

$$f_{H_i}(x) = -A\sin(\omega x),\qquad(12)$$

and put them together

$$f_A(x) = A[\cos(\omega x) + i\sin(\omega x)] = Ae^{i\omega x}.\qquad(13)$$

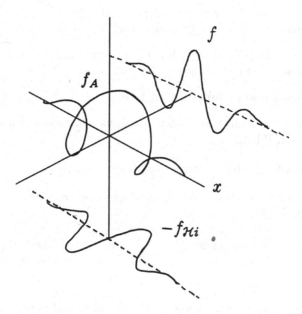

Fig. 3. The analytic signal f_A corresponding to a real function f. The Hilbert transform f_{H_i} of function f is shown in the imaginary domain with the reversed sign [3].

This means that the amplitude A can be directly obtained by

$$A = |f_A(x)| = \sqrt{[f(x)]^2 + [f_{H_i}(x)]^2}.\qquad(14)$$

Note that this is a big advantage over function f whose amplitude A cannot be obtained directly.

Therefore, an analytic signal can provide a direct measure of the local behavior of the signal. For example, this information can be given by $\arg[f_A]$ when the signal is a linear function of x. This is commonly referred to as the *phase* of f.

Here shows how to use the phase to infer the local behavior of the signal in some typical cases [3].

- If $arg[f_A] = 2\pi k$, the function f reaches its maximal value A at $x = x_0$
- If $arg[f_A] = \pi + 2\pi k$, the function f reaches its minimal value $-A$ at $x = x_0$
- If $arg[f_A] = \frac{\pi}{2} + 2\pi k$ then function f is just passing the zero going from negative to positive at $x = x_0$
- If $arg[f_A] = -\frac{\pi}{2} + 2\pi k$, the function f is just passing the zero going from positive to negative at $x = x_0$

For a real signal, its analytic signal is well-defined. It means for a given real signal, we can consider the absolute value, argument, and the arguments derivative of the corresponding analytic signal. Thus, we can make the following definitions:

Instantaneous amplitude of function $f(x) = |f_A(x)|$.

For a real signal in general, its instantaneous amplitude may not be a constant function. Similarly, the instantaneous phase of function f(x) is

Instantaneous phase of function $f(x) = arg[f_A(x)]$.

Finally, for any real function, such that its phase has a well-defined derivative with respect to x. We define

Instantaneous frequency of function $f(x) = \frac{d}{dx} arg[f_A(x)]$.

As with instantaneous amplitude, instantaneous frequency is usually not a constant function of x.

One may notice that for the example we discussed if we change x to t, the generated analytic signal is nothing but the AC signal. The Hilbert transform of the voltage signal is the current signal. The information of the local behavior and spatial frequency of a signal can be directly obtained from its counterpart analytic signal. Notice that local behavior and spatial frequency have always been considered important properties for signal processing and image processing.

4   Final Remarks

This position paper presents a mathematical framework for constructing a metaverse, which unifies reality and virtuality to create a cohesive whole universe. We argue that the nature of a metaverse is inherently mathematical, and propose that complex numbers could play a key role in constructing a metaverse. In the paper we offer a supporting example, the construction of analytic signals, to demonstrate how the power of complex numbers can be leveraged to create a unified mathematical system that merges the physical and virtual worlds. We believe that the proposed mathematical framework has significant potential for building a metaverse. We hope that this paper inspires further research and development in the field of metaverse construction and serves as a catalyst for the creation of new and innovative digital experiences that blur the line between reality and virtuality.

References

1. Bracewell, R.: The Fourier Transform and its Application. McGraw-Hill (1986)
2. Dourish, P.: Where the Action Is. The MIT Press (2004)
3. Granlund, G.H., Knutsson, H.: Signal Processing for Computer Vision (2008)
4. Yotaro, H: Graphical Method of Learning Mathematics, Nankai Press House (2008)
5. Heidegger, M.: Being and Time. Harper & Row (1962)
6. Penrose, R.: The Road to Reality. VINTAGE BOOKS (2004)
7. Meta Wikipedia Homepage .www.en.wikipedia.org/wiki/Meta. Accessed 3 Mar 2023

Author Index

X. Meng et al. (Eds.): SpatialDI 2023, LNCS 13887, pp. 271–272, 2023.
https://doi.org/10.1007/978-3-031-32910-4

Printed in the United States
by Baker & Taylor Publisher Services